Hiking California's Wine Country

A Guide to the Area's Greatest Hikes

Bubba Suess

FALCONGUIDES

GUILFORD, CONNECTICUT
HELENA, MONTANA

FALCONGUIDES®

An imprint of Rowman & Littlefield
Falcon, FalconGuides, and Outfit Your Mind are registered trademarks of Rowman & Littlefield.

Distributed by NATIONAL BOOK NETWORK

Copyright © 2016 by Rowman & Littlefield
All photos by the author.
Maps: Melissa Baker and Alena Joy Pearce © Rowman & Littlefield

British Library Cataloguing-in-Publication Information available

Library of Congress Cataloging-in-Publication Data available

ISBN 978-1-4930-0985-5 (paperback)
ISBN 978-1-4930-1510-8 (e-book)

∞™ The paper used in this publication meets the minimum requirements of American National Standard for Information Sciences—Permanence of Paper for Printed Library Materials, ANSI/NISO Z39.48-1992.

The author and Rowman & Littlefield assume no liability for accidents happening to, or injuries sustained by, readers who engage in the activities described in this book.

To my incredible parents, Ron and Jane Suess:
Without their love and sacrifice, nothing I have
accomplished would have been possible.

Contents

Section I. Sonoma County

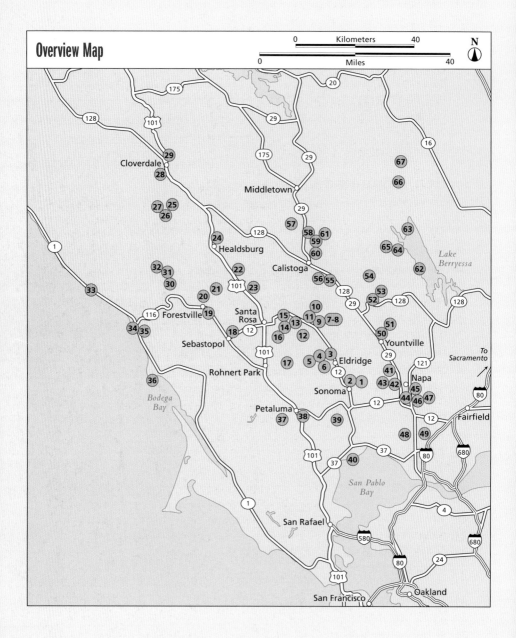

Overview Map

Section II. Napa County

Acknowledgments

It is to my wife, Harmony, that I am most grateful. Her encouragement, wisdom, and patience enabled me to complete this project. More importantly, she shares my vision of life, and I am honored to travel that road with her.

It is not possible for me to express how grateful I am for my parents, Ron and Jane. I had the great fortune of being their son, and from them I learned integrity, hard work, and selflessness. Through them, I received the blessing of growing up in Sonoma County. The genesis of this book lies in the many hikes, Boy Scout outings, and other adventures in this corner of the world that they made possible. Their giving does not end there. Their logistical support was the linchpin of the entire project. More importantly, they happily invested in my children while I was on the trail. Their selfless giving is an outward expression of their love for me and my family.

I am thankful for the input that others have put into this book. John Phillips was instrumental in helping me understand the geomorphology and geology of the Wine Country. His thoughts on the area's geography were essential to my understanding of what was where. Equally important, he encouraged me to be bold in writing about places where there is a paucity of information.

Steve Moore, of Teac Mor Vineyards, has been one of my best friends since high school. His conversations about grape growing have been entertaining and informative, and they shaped the way I think about earth and agriculture.

Longtime friends Steve and Cathi Fowler of the Honor Mansion in Healdsburg are the fount of Wine Country insights. Their taste is excellent, and I trust their recommendations without question. More importantly, they have always been supportive of me even when I did not deserve it. I am humbled and grateful.

I was joined on the trail by a few people, and I appreciated their company immensely. In addition to my wife, my children, Carson and Laramie, joined me on a few hikes. I had a great day with my father-in-law, Bill McPherson, in Sonoma. It was a blast hiking, talking, and exploring with him. My brother, Matt Suess, joined me for a great day hiking the Palisades shuttle. I never get enough time with my hero. My nephew, Conor Lawlor, was brave enough to spend a very long day on the trail with me. I had an excellent time with him and hope that we are able to do it again soon.

Introduction

"I firmly believe, from what I have seen, that this is the chosen spot of all the earth as far as Nature is concerned."

Luther Burbank, the preeminent botanist and horticulturalist, wrote this sentiment in a letter to his sister describing the land around Santa Rosa. Burbank, a man of deep and abiding understanding about the natural world, had hit upon the magic that permeates California's Wine Country.

Even beyond being an ideal place for the production of grapes, the Wine Country is a land blessed by nature's gentlest and kindest hand. It has an optimal climate, rarely enduring extreme heat or extreme cold, but remaining comfortably temperate throughout most of the year. Yet, the climate is only the beginning of the wonderful environment of the Wine Country. It is a beautiful land, with rolling hills, rugged mountains, large rivers, towering redwoods, a stunning coastline, and a remarkable amount of remote backcountry beckoning to be explored. Even though Luther Burbank is not associated with the area's wine-making history, it is not surprising that the land he saw as the choicest place on Earth for the raising of plants would be given over to the production of grapes and the making of some of the finest wines in the world.

While the Wine Country is justly famous as a destination for viticulture tourism, it is often overlooked as a fantastic place for hitting the trail and exploring some fantastically beautiful landscapes. Many of the qualities that help produce world-class wines also make the Wine Country an incredible hiking experience. The temperate climate means that all of the trails can be hiked year-round. Whether it is the heart of winter or the peak of summer, you can still get out and hike spectacular trails. The land itself demands to be enjoyed and presents itself to the hiker with amazing diversity. Hikes in the Wine Country travel through large, lovely valleys filled with vast vineyards as well as to rugged mountaintops with sweeping views. The windswept coastline and tall redwoods seem far removed from the volcanic cliffs and serpentine deserts that are only a short distance away.

As beautiful and diverse as the land may be, it is embellished by human works, both past and present. The vineyards and wineries add a peaceful, bucolic quality to many of the trails. They cover the ground with their ordered rows, a giant, productive quilt yielding some of the finest wine grapes in the world. Where many human endeavors detract from the beauty of the land, viticulture only seems to increase it. Vineyards are not the only man-made works that can be appreciated from the trails in the Wine Country. Many of the hikes are filled with history, including the birth of California statehood, colonial forts, and rugged pioneers. The Wine Country is one of the most historic parts of California, and hikers have a fantastic opportunity to explore these landmarks while enjoying the wonderful natural setting.

Geography

The heart of the Wine Country consists of Napa and Sonoma Counties, the north-ernmost and most rural of the nine San Francisco Bay Area counties. Their inclusion with the large urban area is based on, among other things, their presence along the northern edge of San Francisco Bay and their historic orientation toward the events and economics of the bay. Geographically, however, Napa and Sonoma Counties both lie at the southern end of the North Coast Range. This means that many of the factors that go into the production of wine are brought about by a geography that is northward looking, away from the bay.

California's North Coast Range hugs the coastline, extending north from San Francisco Bay until it pushes up against the vast Klamath Mountains. From there, it continues north along the coast as a narrow strip of mountains until it merges into Oregon's Coast Range. This mountainous region can be divided into the three general regions. The first is the long string of rugged, low hills and ridges that extend north from San Francisco Bay all the way to Oregon. The second region lies to the east and consists of an extensive high-elevation alpine area with vast stands of conifer forests; a few small, alpine lakes; and tall, rugged peaks over 7,000 feet high. The highest point is Mount Linn, sometimes known as South Yolla Bolly Mountain, which climbs to a lofty 8,092 feet. This part of the North Coast Range begins north of Lake County's Clear Lake and continues north until it runs into the geologically distinct Klamath Mountains. The third and final area is in the south, between Clear Lake and San Francisco Bay. This area is also very mountainous, but the elevation is much lower and the mountains are punctuated by several large valleys.

The Wine Country covers most of the third area—the lower mountains and valleys—as well as a section of the coastal hills and ridges. The spine of this entire area is the long Mayacamas Mountains, a significant subrange of the North Coast Range. The Mayacamas extend from the Cow Mountain area, on the west side of Clear Lake, nearly 75 miles to the south, where the mountains finally fade away into the tidal marshes at San Francisco Bay. These are the highest and most rugged mountains in Wine Country and are at the heart of the wine-producing areas.

In the north, the Mayacamas are composed of sedimentary rock. The southern half of the range is, somewhat surprisingly, composed of volcanic rock, deposited from large lava flows. Even though the northern part is not volcanic, active forces lie close to the surface. The most dramatic manifestation of these forces is the presence of the Geysers, an extensive geothermal field where naturally occurring steam fumaroles have been harnessed to produce enough electricity to supply the needs of 60 percent of northern coastal California.

In addition to the Mayacamas and the coastal hills and ridges, the Sonoma Mountains form a significant upland in the center of Sonoma County. Though these mountains are heavily weathered and not very rugged, they, too, are composed of lava flows and other volcanic matter. On the east side of Napa County, things get much more

Fog swirls in Pope Creek Canyon, below the Cedar Roughs Trail.

complex. Although the hills at the southeastern end of the Napa Valley are volcanic, most of the eastern side of the county consists of sedimentary rock that has been uplifted and folded through extensive faulting. The geomorphology of this area is incomplete, and many names have been used to label the area, or some sections of the area, which include the Howell Mountains and the Vaca Mountains. Of the two names, the former seems the more appropriate, because Howell Mountain is located on the east side of Napa Valley. The heart of the Vaca Mountains lies farther to the east, along the edge of the great Central Valley. The valleys of the Wine Country are where most of the population and agriculturally productive land is found. The largest of the valleys are the Santa Rosa Plain and the Napa Valley. The former is a large floodplain lying between the Mayacamas and Sonoma Mountains in the east and the coastal hills on the west. The Napa Valley is a long valley that runs between the Mayacamas Mountains and the vast complex of mountains of the eastern side of the county. In Sonoma County, other significant valleys include Sonoma Valley, Alexander Valley, the Dry Creek Valley, Knights Valley, and the Russian River Valley. In Napa County, Pope Valley is the largest and most significant but the smaller Chiles Valley is still an important grape-growing area. The coast, usually referred to as the Sonoma Coast, is one of the most important physical features in the Wine Country. It is dramatic coastline, full of sea stacks, tall cliffs rising out of the surf, long beaches, and grassy hills. The coast is also one of the most dramatic examples of the San Andreas Fault's influence on the land. The Bodega Head is a small cluster of hills connected to the coast by a narrow strip of land that barely rises above sea level. The San Andreas Fault, infamous for causing the great 1906 earthquake that destroyed San Francisco, runs right through the narrow finger of land that lies between the Bodega Head and the coastline. Interestingly, the rock that constitutes the Bodega Head is granite, which is located nowhere else in the Wine Country.

Granite also appears just to the south, on the Point Reyes Peninsula. In both cases this rock was transported here from areas far to the south by the San Andreas Fault. The coast's influence is felt in parts of the Wine Country far removed from the sea because of the copious amounts of marine fog that is sent inland. The fog plays a significant role in moderating the Wine Country's temperature, often keeping things much cooler than nearby areas that receive no fog.

Inland water plays an important role in shaping the geography of the Wine Country. Of first importance is the Russian River, which flows through Sonoma County. The river begins far to the north in Mendocino County and flows 110 miles to the sea at Jenner. The Napa River and Petaluma River are also important but are shorter, and much of their length is estuarine, where they are mixed with the brackish bay water and are heavily influenced by the tide. Other major creeks, including Santa Rosa Creek, Sonoma Creek, Dry Creek, Austin Creek, Conn Creek, Moore Creek, Pope Creek, and Putah Creek, are all important water resources for the Wine Country. Some of these have been impounded to form reservoirs, the largest of which are Lake Berryessa, Lake Sonoma, and Lake Hennessey.

History

The land that now makes up the Wine Country was initially occupied by the Pomo, Miwok, and Wappo tribes. The Miwok lived near the coast, the Wappo in the north part of Sonoma County and in Lake and Napa Counties. The Pomo lived in western Sonoma County, far into Mendocino County to the north, and in small pockets of Napa County. They all survived on fishing, hunting, and gathering. They were also prodigious basket weavers.

The first Europeans to establish a permanent presence here were the Russians. In 1812 they established Fort Ross on the Sonoma Coast, north of the Russian River estuary. The colony was built to ply the fur trade and to supply food for Russia's colonies farther north in Alaska. The fort consisted of a wooden stockade, several large buildings including an Orthodox church, and numerous dwellings outside the stockade. Fort Ross was also the site of the first windmills and shipyard in California. The Russians dispatched scientific expeditions into the interior of Sonoma County. Botanists studied native plants, made other scientific observations, and went so far as to climb Mount Saint Helena, one of the tallest and most spectacular mountains in the Wine Country.

The establishment of Fort Ross was followed eleven years later by Mexico's founding of Mission San Francisco Solano in modern Sonoma, the twenty-first and final of the missions built along the California coast. It was the only mission established by the Mexican government after that nation achieved independence from

Spain. Initially intended to be an outpost of the mission in San Rafael, it was eventually developed into its own autonomous mission. The Mexican government was eager to project its presence north of San Francisco Bay, in part to prevent the Russians from pushing too far into the interior. The two outposts managed to maintain friendly relations, and there was no conflict between the two groups. For eleven years the mission thrived. It was connected to the other twenty missions by the famous El Camino Real, the Royal Road, which led all the way down to San Diego, the first mission in Alta California when entering from Mexico. The town of Sonoma grew up around the mission and proved to outlast its founding institution.

In 1834 the Mexican government decided to secularize all of the missions in California. Mariano Vallejo, the commanding officer of the Presidio in San Francisco, was sent north to oversee the secularization. Vallejo decided to stay in the area and built a large adobe house at the center of a huge rancho. The rancho employed over 2,000 workers. The ending of the mission period was followed seven years later by the closing of Fort Ross. Economics caused the Russians to pull back and abandon their most far-flung outpost. Though it was unlikely recognized at the time, this ended a unique moment in the colonization of the New World. The mission at Sonoma and the Russian fort on the coast was the only meeting of European powers in the Western Hemisphere where one power traveled west across the Atlantic Ocean and the other journeyed east across Asia and the Pacific Ocean.

By the time Fort Ross was shuttered, Americans had begun migrating into California. At first the Mexican government either expelled them or they became Mexican citizens. The most prominent of the new wave of settlers was John Sutter, who established his outpost, known as Sutter's Fort, in the wilderness along the Sacramento River. Sutter accrued significant land grants and became a major power broker in California. When Fort Ross was abandoned, Sutter purchased its munitions from the Russians.

Many of the new American settlers in California began agitating for a rebellion against the Mexican government, similar to the war of independence that Texas had successfully prosecuted in 1836. Events came to a head on June 14, 1846, when a group of Americans took Vallejo hostage in Sonoma and raised the flag of the California Republic over the city. The flag was emblazoned with a grizzly bear, which led to the event being called the Bear Flag Revolt. Vallejo, who was sympathetic to the American cause and favored American annexation of California, was taken to Sutter's Fort, where a small contingent of American troops under the command of John C. Fremont awaited. After bloodshed in Sonoma between Mexicans and members of the revolt, Fremont traveled to Sonoma with a group of men that included famed mountain man Kit Carson. Fremont's contingent joined forces with the revolt and together they celebrated Independence Day. The following day they issued a proclamation affirming their rebellion against Mexico and the formation of the California Battalion.

While these events were transpiring, the United States and Mexico were waging a wider war that included a full invasion of Mexico by the United States that culminated in the capture of Mexico City. Part of this war included a campaign to wrest California from Mexican control. On July 9, just twenty-five days after the Bear Flag Revolt, American naval ships arrived in Monterey Bay and captured the city of Monterey, the capital of Alta California. This ended the brief effort to establish California as an independent republic and ensured its full incorporation into the United States. Although the Bear Flag Revolt was short-lived, it was still regarded as a significant event and the birth of American California.

Most of the land in the Wine Country had been divided up into large grants. After the annexation of California, many of these grants were voided or were sold off in smaller parcels to the influx of Americans that followed both annexation and the discovery of gold in 1849 at Sutter's Mill. In Napa, grant holders included George C. Yount, who owned the Rancho Caymus Grant, and Edward Bale, who owned the Rancho Humana Carne Grant. Both men lived well into the American period and saw the Napa Valley prosper. Yount planted the first grapevines in Napa Valley. The city of Yountville was named in his honor. Bale built a large gristmill at the north end of the Napa Valley, which is still a popular attraction.

Grapes were first planted in the Wine Country at the mission in Sonoma to supply wine for communion. In 1856 Hungarian entrepreneur and adventurer Agoston Haraszthy moved to Sonoma and bought a small vineyard northeast of the city. Over time he built up his holdings to more than 5,000 acres. He named the operation Buena Vista. He hired Charles Krug to be his winemaker, and they introduced many European wine-making practices to California. In the midst of the growing winemaking empire, Haraszthy's two sons married two of Mariano Vallejo's daughters in a double wedding, cementing the old California to the new. In 1860 Charles Krug left Sonoma and moved to the Napa Valley. He married one of the daughters of Edward Bale and received over 500 acres of land north of the town of Saint Helena, not far from his father-in-law's gristmill. In 1861 Krug planted his first vineyard on the land and established the first winery in the Napa Valley. Though a phylloxera (an insect that devastates grapevines) outbreak severely damaged the vineyards and resulted in Haraszthy's departure from California, both the Buena Vista Winery and the Charles Krug Winery continue to operate to the present day. The former is the oldest California winery still in operation; the latter is the oldest winery in the Napa Valley.

Viticulture

Growing grapes for wine is a very challenging endeavor. Grapevines can be very delicate and demanding and must be attended with a degree of care, not unlike a parent caring for their child. The quality of care given to the vines is manifested in the quality of the fruit. However, as important as the husbandry of the vines is, there is an equally important component to raising good wine grapes. Environmental factors are essential to growing grapes and making great wine. Everything must be taken

Hood Mountain dominates the northern end of the Sonoma Valley.

into account: soil composition, elevation, temperature, hours of sunshine, rainfall, fog, wind, and many other factors. Together these combine to form a *terroir*, which is the term used to identify a distinct sum of an area's attributes that are salient to wine making.

In this way viticulture is not unlike hiking. The quality of a trail often depends on similar factors. What makes a good hiking experience may also result in an excellent wine. The distinct terroirs that are found in the Wine Country are what make the area so conducive to making wine. The volcanic soils of the Mayacamas and Sonoma Mountains, the temperate climate, the fog pushing inland off of the coast are only a few of the elements that combine to make the Wine Country both a wine-making region and a hiking destination.

In recognition of distinct environmental factors that contribute to making wine, the federal government has recognized American viticulture areas (AVAs). These are more popularly referred to as *appellations* and are used to identify areas that produce wine. Some of the early appellations were based more on man-made boundaries, such as drawing a distinction between wines made around Rutherford and those produced around Oakville in the Napa Valley. These two communities are less than 2 miles apart, and although there may some differences in their environmental factors, those differences are minor. After these early AVAs were established, there was a move to determine appellations more on the basis of terroir rather than on man-made distinctions. Newer AVAs reflected this shift in emphasis, which led to the division of larger AVAs into smaller units that reflect a particular area's microclimate. This is the case

Mount Saint Helena, the monarch of Wine Country mountains.

with the Moon Mountain appellation, the newest AVA in Sonoma County. Once a part of the prestigious Sonoma Valley appellation, the vineyards in Moon Mountain (the name is derived from the Sonoma Valley's nickname, the Valley of the Moon) are located high in the mountains at elevations ranging from 1,000 feet to over 2,000 feet. The elevation and intensely volcanic soil are different from the terroir of the valley floor, which results in different properties in the grapes and wine.

Some of the early appellations were large areas that have since been broken down into more distinct areas. For example, there is a Napa Valley appellation, but most of that is now covered in a dozen smaller appellations. The same is true in Sonoma County, where large AVAs like the Sonoma Coast and Northern Sonoma are overlapped by numerous smaller areas. Excluding the older, larger areas that have since been refined into smaller areas, Napa County has sixteen distinct AVAs and Sonoma County has fourteen. The amazing diversity of these different wine-making areas is reflected in the incredibly varied trails that wind through California's Wine Country.

Public Land

Most of the hiking destinations in California are found in national forests and national parks, where there are expansive blocks of public land to explore. The Sierra Nevada, the Cascades, and even California's vast deserts are all administered by federal agencies with a few scattered state parks thrown in for good measure. Unlike these

Views of Hood Mountain standing guard above the Sonoma Valley are great on the Bald Mountain Loop.

well-known areas, the Wine Country does not have much land administered by the federal government.

A few state parks are scattered around Sonoma and Napa Counties, and many of the trails in this guide travel through these parks. The rest of the trails in this book are found on county parks and a handful of privately owned areas that are open to the public. Sonoma County in particular has an incredibly well-developed county park system. In many ways it is like a miniature national park system, with units both large and small scattered throughout all corners of the county, offering the public the opportunities to enjoy unique environments and spectacular landscapes. The foresight and effort to bring the Sonoma County Regional Park system into being is to be commended. The public in general and hikers in particular owe heartfelt thanks to those who have been and continue to be involved with building this incredible system. Napa and Lake Counties are slowly building their own impressive network of public lands. Napa County's addition of the large Moore Creek Park is an enormous step in developing a set of spectacular parks.

Weather

The Wine Country has a temperate, Mediterranean climate, with warm, dry summers and cool, wet winters. There is minimal humidity, and the temperatures rarely veer into extremes. Consequently, hiking the trails in the Wine Country is a viable option throughout the year, though spring is undoubtedly the best season. The hills are brilliant green and explode with great wildflower displays, the creeks run full, and the days are the perfect temperature for being outdoors. Summers are drier and warmer, but even on the hottest days, the mornings are cool and comfortable for hiking. Fall is also a dry season, but the Wine Country has a surprising amount of fall color, highlighted by the vineyards' changing from green to bright yellow, orange, and red. While winter can sometimes be cold and many of the trees have lost their leaves, much of the forests are still full of evergreens, the days are generally cool and crisp, and the rains have recharged the creeks. It is only on the rainy days or the handful of hottest days in summer that hiking is not a desirable option in the Wine Country.

Hazards

The Wine Country does have some dangers that hikers must be aware of. The three most common are poison oak, mountain lions, and rattlesnakes.

Poison oak: If there is a drawback to hiking the trails in the Wine Country, it is poison oak. This miserable plant is present along a large number of trails in this guide. Contact with the plant usually produces an irritating rash. The plant is identifiable by its green or reddish leaves that always appear in clusters of three. The leaves do have a resemblance to oak leaves. Be aware that this plant can have a varied appearance, growing in bushes and vines, and the leafless stems in winter are still full of the rash-producing oils. Although poison oak is seen frequently along trails, the trails are usually wide enough to make avoiding the plant easy. It is important to watch children in areas with poison oak and make sure that they stay on the trail. Even though dogs do not get poison oak, they are able to transfer the plant's oils through contact.

Mountain lions: Mountain lions live throughout the mountains in the area but are rarely seen, and it is unlikely that you will encounter one on the trail. As always, hiking in groups is safer than hiking alone. If you do encounter a mountain lion, pick up any small children. The cats consider smaller animals easier to catch. Do not run. Mountain lions expect their prey to flee, and running will cause them to pursue. Try to look as large as you can and do not crouch, kneel, or sit. People do not resemble the normal prey when they are standing. Lastly, if you are attacked, fight back. They can be made to flee.

Rattlesnakes: Rattlesnakes are found throughout the Wine Country. These snakes are venomous and should be avoided at all costs. Be alert to what is on the trail. If you see one, do not try to handle it. Stay at least 6 feet away—the farther, the better. Be especially careful when climbing up rock piles and similar places where snakes may hide. Also be careful to keep dogs away from the snakes.

Trail Finder

Sonoma County

	1. Batholomew Park	2. Sonoma Overlook Trail	3. Sonoma Valley Regional Park	4. Wolf House Ruins	5. Sonoma Mountain	6. Old Orchard Loop	7. Sonoma Creek Falls	8. Bald Mountain Loop	9. Goodspeed-Nattkemper Trail	10. Hood Mountain Summit Trail	11. Johnson Ridge Trail	12. Lawndale Trail	13. Central Annadel Loop
Kids			•	•			•						
Backpackers										•	•		
History Buffs	•	•		•	•	•			•		•		
Interesting Geology										•	•		
Redwood Trees	•				•	•	•					•	
Canyons							•						•
Waterfalls							•						
Rivers and Creeks	•									•			
Lakes					•	•					•		•
Peak Baggers					•			•	•	•	•		
Wildflowers						•						•	•
Vineyard Views	•				•			•					
Great Views		•			•			•	•	•	•		•

	14. Lake Ilsanjo–Spring Canyon Loop	15. Spring Lake	16. Taylor Mountain	17. Crane Creek Regional Park	18. Laguna de Santa Rosa Trail	19. West County Trail	20. Steelhead Beach Loop	21. Riverfront Regional Park	22. Shiloh Ranch Regional Park	23. Foothill Regional Park	24. Healdsburg Ridge Open Space Preserve	25. Woodland Ridge Loop	26. South Lake Trail	27. Half-a-Canoe Loop	28. Clover Springs Preserve
Kids	•	•		•	•	•	•	•			•	•			
Backpackers													•	•	
History Buffs			•			•	•								
Interesting Geology					•										
Redwood Trees								•				•			
Canyons	•														•
Waterfalls															
Rivers and Creeks	•						•	•	•						•
Lakes	•	•						•	•	•	•			•	
Peak Baggers			•								•				
Wildflowers			•	•										•	
Vineyard Views				•	•	•			•		•				
Great Views			•						•		•		•	•	•

	29. Cloverdale River Park	30. Armstrong Redwoods	31. Armstrong Ridges Loop	32. Austin Creek	33. Fort Ross	34. Kortum Trail	35. Pomo Canyon–Red Hill Loop	36. Bodega Head	37. Helen Putnam Regional Park	38. Petaluma River	39. Tolay Lake Regional Park	40. Lower Tubbs Island Trail	Napa County	41. Alston Park	42. Westwood Hills Park
Kids	•	•			•	•		•	•	•				•	•
Backpackers				•											
History Buffs					•			•		•	•	•			
Interesting Geology					•	•	•	•				•			
Redwood Trees		•	•	•			•								
Canyons				•			•								
Waterfalls			•												
Rivers and Creeks	•			•						•					
Lakes									•		•				
Peak Baggers							•				•				•
Wildflowers	•					•	•			•	•				
Vineyard Views											•			•	•
Great Views			•	•	•	•	•	•	•		•	•			

	43. Timberhills Park	44. Napa River Trail: John F. Kennedy Memorial Park	45. River to Ridge Trail	46. Lower Skyline Loop	47. Rim Rock Loop	48. Napa River and Bay Trail	49. Newell Open Space Preserve	50. Napa River Ecological Preserve	51. Rector Reservoir Wildlife Area	52. Lake Hennessy	53. Moore Creek Park	54. Las Posadas State Forest	55. Bale Grist Mill History Trail	56. Bothe–Napa Valley State Park	57. Mount Saint Helena
Kids	•	•	•			•		•			•		•		
Backpackers														•	
History Buffs			•			•					•	•	•		
Interesting Geology				•	•	•			•		•	•			•
Redwood Trees												•		•	
Canyons					•						•			•	
Waterfalls															
Rivers and Creeks		•			•			•			•			•	
Lakes					•					•					
Peak Baggers					•									•	•
Wildflowers	•			•			•		•						
Vineyard Views					•				•						•
Great Views	•			•	•		•		•		•				•

	58. Table Rock Trail	59. Palisades Trail	60. Oat Hill Mine Road	61. Oat Hill Mine Road: Aetna Springs Trailhead	62. Smittle Creek Trail	63. Barton Hill	64. Pope Creek Canyon	65. Cedar Roughs Trail	66. Zim Zim Falls	67. Long Canyon
Kids					•	•	•			
Backpackers										
History Buffs		•	•	•						•
Interesting Geology	•	•	•	•			•	•	•	
Redwood Trees										
Canyons	•						•		•	•
Waterfalls									•	
Rivers and Creeks							•	•	•	
Lakes					•					
Peak Baggers	•									
Wildflowers									•	•
Vineyard Views	•	•	•					•		
Great Views	•	•	•	•		•		•		•

Map Legend

80	Interstate Highway	✕	Airport
101	US Highway	▬	Bench
1	State Highway	◥	Boat Ramp
515	County Road	⌣	Bridge
	Local Road	▪	Building/Point of Interest
	Unpaved Road	⚠	Campground
	Railroad	▲	Campsite
	Utility/Power Line	†	Cemetery
	Featured Trail	○	City/Town
	Trail	—	Dam
	Paved Trail	⚲	Gate
	Boardwalk	▭	Inn/Lodging
	State Line	▲	Mountain/Peak
	Small River/Creek	P	Parking
	Intermittent Stream	🛆	Picnic Area
	Body of Water	🏠	Ranger Station
	Marsh/Swamp	◩	Scenic View/Viewpoint
	National/State Forest	×	Spot Elevation
	National Wilderness Area	10	Trailhead
	State/County Park	❓	Visitor/Information Center
	Miscellaneous Park	≋	Waterfall
	Miscellaneous Area		

SECTION I.

Sonoma County

Sonoma County is the largest and most diverse of the Wine Country counties. It consists of the rugged coastline and the North Coast Range in the west, the high Mayacamas Mountains and the lower but still notable Sonoma Mountains in the east, and San Francisco Bay at its southern end. In between the North Coast Range and the Mayacamas are a collection of valleys, where both the majority of the population and the vineyards are located. Many of these valleys are well-known appellations that include Sonoma Valley, Alexander Valley, Dry Creek Valley, and the Russian River Valley. Not only does Sonoma County have the highest population of any of the Wine Country counties but it also produces the most grapes.

The hiking trails in Sonoma County are also the most diverse in the Wine Country. Coastal trails, towering redwoods, vast wetlands, tall mountaintops, rugged rock formations, large rivers, rolling hills, historic buildings, and remote, isolated backcountry are all features of the trails in Sonoma County. These trails are part of the largest and most well-developed network of public lands in the Wine County. The core of this network is a number of large state parks that include several thousand acres of land crisscrossed by trails. On top of this is the remarkable Sonoma County Regional Park system, which has done an incredible job of making beautiful landscapes and prominent landmarks available for the general public to enjoy and explore. Amazingly, this process is far from over, and several large and beautiful parks are now in development, with many more planned. This is a world-class park system. Other private groups have contributed lands to the panoply of parks that make up Sonoma County's open space. The sum of all of these different pieces is a beautiful county loaded with beautiful trails waiting for hikers to experience.

1 Bartholomew Park

A few blocks east of downtown Sonoma is Bartholomew Park, a privately owned historic park that is open to the public. Home to the eponymously named winery, the loop through the park's backcountry is a great primer to a lot of the best of Wine Country hiking: vineyards, redwoods, creeks, beautiful views, and access to wineries right off of the trail.

Total Distance: 2.4-mile loop
Hiking Time: About 1.5 hours
Difficulty: Moderate
Elevation Gain: 770 feet
Season: All year

Canine Compatibility: Dogs must be leashed
Fees: None
Trail Contact: Bartholomew Park Foundation; (707) 938-2244; www.bartholomewpark.org
Other: The hike passes two wineries.

Finding the trailhead: From CA 12 / West Napa at the downtown plaza, stay straight, continuing onto East Napa Street. Drive 1.0 mile, then turn left onto 7th Street and continue for 0.3 mile. Turn right on Castle Road and immediately stay left at a fork. Drive straight on Castle Road for 0.9 mile to Bartholomew Park. The parking area is on the left side of the large mansion. GPS: N38°18.04433' / W122°25.59417'

The Hike

The trail through Bartholomew Park is a perfect slice of many of the best features hiking in the Wine Country has to offer. The trail passes through vineyards, chaparral-covered slope, and a mixed forest of madrone, oak, bay, and fir, as well as a surprising redwood grove. The trail also has fine views of Sonoma. In addition to the natural setting, the park itself is historic, being part of the estate of Agoston Haraszthy, the Hungarian pioneer who settled here and established the Buena Vista Winery, California's oldest active winery, which can be accessed via the trail. Bartholomew Park encompasses much of the original Haraszthy estate, which is now a park that is owned by a private foundation that maintains public access to the property. In addition to connecting to Buena Vista Winery, the Bartholomew Park Winery is located at the beginning and end of the loop. It makes a fantastic place to enjoy a picnic overlooking vineyards.

Beginning at the parking area next to the park's large mansion, follow the trail north into the vineyards. On the right are some grassy bluffs next to the Bartholomew Park Winery, which are a great spot for having picnics. After a short distance through the vineyards, the trail turns to the right and skirts the edge of a small pond while still being flanked by a vineyard on the right side of the trail. Pass through a small gate that marks the official beginning of the Grape Stomp Trail. The path enters the forest and climbs easily before crossing a small stream. On the other side of the stream, the

Vineyards highlight the beginning of the hike.

climbing gets a little harder but is aided by log steps built into the trail. The forest recedes a bit and is replaced by more chaparral-like conditions and more sun exposure. The climb levels off a bit near a bench with some views before reentering the forest. The trail then descends a bit before arriving at another creek flowing through a small redwood grove, about 0.8 mile from the trailhead. It is a scenic and peaceful place and a cool break from the climb up to this point.

Cross the creek and a private road and then regain the trail, which now climbs through forest to the east. Soon the sound of water may be audible as the trail passes a dam and small pond, called Benicia's Lake, on Arroyo Seco Creek. The path then descends down to the creek itself, just upstream from the pond. The creek flows through a wonderful redwood grove. The tall trees nearly block out the sun, and on hot days especially, the running water is incredibly refreshing. Cross the creek and begin climbing a series of switchbacks, then climb out of the canyon passing a short trail that leads down to the lake. As the trail climbs up the switchbacks, it comes to a junction. To the right is the Angels Flight Trail, which is a shorter and less scenic route back to the trailhead. Stay to the left on the You–Walk Miwok Trail, which continues to climb out of the canyon.

The trail finally crests 0.25 mile after crossing Arroyo Seco Creek, having climbed 125 feet. The path continues through the forest, maintaining a fairly level but undulating course for another 0.25 mile. The path then begins to descend, eventually coming to another junction. Stay to the left again at the junction with the Short Cut Trail and quickly arrive at Szeptaj Point. The name, which means "beautiful" in Hungarian,

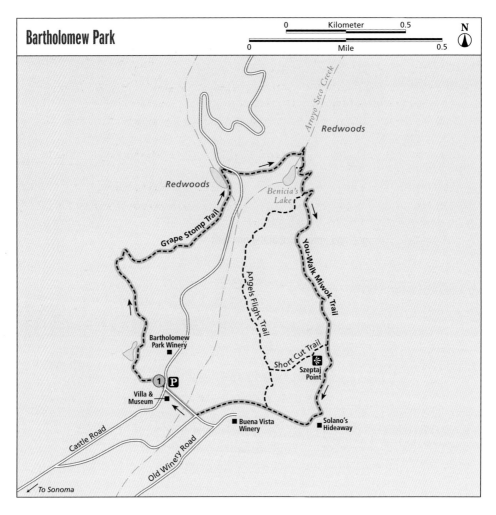

reflects the legacy of Agoston Haraszthy, who founded the vineyards and winery here. Situated on a series of boulders, the point has some good views of the city of Sonoma hundreds of feet below and a large hilltop winery to the south.

From this point the trail begins to descend in earnest, and the forest cover gets thicker. It finally levels off when it arrives at yet another junction near the south fork of Arroyo Seco Creek. Bear left and follow the trail a short distance to a large rock formation called "Solano's Hideaway." Return back to the junction and continue along the creek, staying left at another junction with the Angels Flight Trail. Across the creek, the buildings of Buena Vista Winery, California's oldest active winery, come into view. A fence prevents crossing the creek and arriving at the winery from this direction. Proceed a short distance farther, passing through two gates and arriving at a road. Going right will lead across the creek and into Buena Vista Winery. Going left leads through vineyards and back to the trailhead and the Bartholomew Park Winery.

Miles and Directions

0.0 Begin hike by walking west through vineyards adjacent to the parking area.

0.8 Cross a creek and a private paved road.

1.0 Arrive at Arroyo Seco Creek in a beautiful redwood grove. A small reservoir lies just downstream. Cross the creek and climb out of the canyon.

1.25 Stay left and continue on the You-Walk Miwok Trail, climbing past the junction with the Angels Flight Trail.

1.65 Stay left at the junction with the Short Cut Trail. Just after the fork, a spur leads to a bench and rocky vista at Szeptaj Point.

1.9 At the bottom of the canyon, a spur to the left leads to Solano's Hideaway.

2.2 Arrive at the south trailhead. Turning right here will lead to Buena Vista Winery. Turn left and walk on paved roads back to the trailhead.

2.4 Complete the loop and arrive back at the trailhead.

2 Sonoma Overlook Trail

This is a short, easy, and scenic hike to a high bluff overlooking the city of Sonoma, much of southern Sonoma County, and parts of Marin County. San Pablo Bay, the northern part of San Francisco Bay, is also visible.

Total Distance: 2.7-mile lollipop
Hiking Time: About 1.5 hours
Difficulty: Easy
Elevation Gain: 425 feet
Season: All year

Canine Compatibility: Dogs are permitted
Fees: None
Trail Contact: Sonoma Ecology Center; (707) 996-0712; www.sonomaecologycenter.org

Finding the trailhead: From CA 12 / West Napa Street by the downtown Plaza in Sonoma, drive north on 1st Street West. Stay straight for 0.5 mile. Just before the road climbs into the hills, turn right into the signed parking lot for the Mountain Cemetery. Park in the trailhead parking lot. GPS: N38°17.97650'/W122°27.43100'

The Hike

The town of Sonoma began as the northernmost of twenty-one Spanish missions founded in California during the eighteenth and nineteenth centuries. The missions were established to colonize the Pacific Coast and to convert the native populations to Roman Catholicism. The Sonoma mission, named Mission San Francisco Solano, was also established as a buffer against Russian expansion coming from Fort Ross on the coast. Sonoma grew up around the mission and was the site of the Bear Flag Revolt, which led to California breaking away from Mexico in 1846. The Sonoma Overlook Trail begins just blocks from the historic town square and climbs up the southernmost tip of the Mayacamas Mountains to a fantastic vista above the city. From there hikers can get a sense of how strategic Sonoma's location was and appreciate Spain's northernmost reach into California.

The trail begins at the Mountain Cemetery, one of the oldest cemeteries in California that is still in use. Among the notable people interred here are Mariano Vallejo and his wife, Benicia. Vallejo was a military leader of the old Mexican province of Alta California and, following the territories annexation to the United States, a civic leader in early California politics. From the trailhead the path heads north through trees. After 0.25 mile the trail crosses a small creek and continues a little farther before making a switchback to the south. Hike across a small grassy field to another switchback and continue climbing moderately to the north. A large stone bench offers a chance to rest during the climb. Another switchback turns the trail to the south.

Emerging from the woods again, the trail now crosses a larger grassy area. The views of the surrounding hills begin to improve as the trail continues up the hill.

A view of the hills behind the Sonoma Overlook.

At 0.75 mile from the trailhead, a path branching off to the right leads to the Toyon trailhead, the Sonoma Overlook Trail's alternate starting point. Stay to the left and proceed a little farther to another switchback, which turns the trail back to the north. Follow the path for another 0.3 mile, staying on the main trail and avoiding the increasingly frequent use trails splitting off to the right. Dark volcanic rocks protrude from the slopes above the trail, indicating the fiery past that formed these mountains.

The trail eventually arrives at the top of the hill and begins a short 0.3-mile loop around its level plateau. Stay to the right and head south a short distance with increasingly excellent views. A stone bench marks the best vantage point. At the time of the Bear Flag Revolt, the hill was known as Battery Hill, because artillery could be placed at its summit and the battery would have a commanding position over the entire region. The view extends far to the south and includes San Pablo Bay, the Sonoma Mountains, and the vast tidal marshes to the south of Sonoma. The city itself spreads out immediately below the hill.

After enjoying the view, continue on the trail, climbing slightly to the east and then turning to the north. Cross grassy, rock-dotted fields while completing the loop. The area to the east was the site of quarries operated by nineteenth-century merchant Solomon Schocken, who supplied stone for the construction of buildings in San Francisco as well as cobbles for streets throughout the Bay Area. Today what was once Battery Hill is named Schocken Hill, after the man who supplied some of the materials that helped rebuild San Francisco after the 1906 earthquake. When the short loop arrives at the junction with the main trail, retrace your steps back to the trailhead.

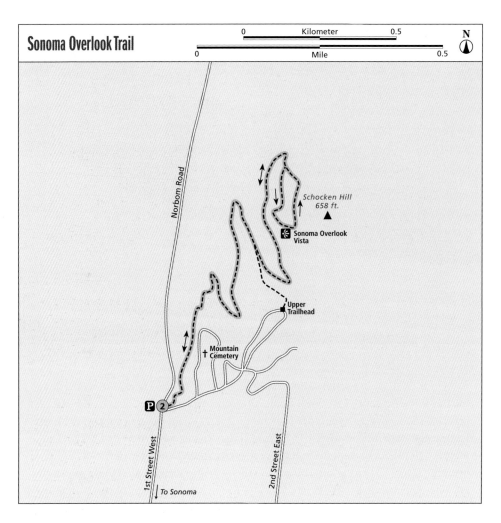

Sonoma Overlook Trail

Schocken Hill
658 ft.

Sonoma Overlook
Vista

Norbom Road

Upper
Trailhead

Mountain
Cemetery

1st Street West

2nd Street East

To Sonoma

Miles and Directions

0.0 The hike begins in the small Mountain Cemetery parking lot.

0.3 The trail begins the first of a series of switchbacks that end at the summit loop.

0.75 Stay left at the Toyon Trail junction. This path leads from an upper trailhead.

1.2 Begin the summit loop.

1.3 Arrive at Sonoma Overlook.

1.5 Complete summit loop and begin descending the trail.

2.7 Arrive back at the trailhead.

3 Sonoma Valley Regional Park

Exploring hills in the lowlands in the Sonoma Valley, this hike is a gentle trip through dense forest and a pleasant canyon. A few good views and a chance to connect to quaint, downtown Glen Ellen are bonuses.

Total Distance: 2.4-mile loop
Hiking Time: About 1.5 hours
Difficulty: Easy
Elevation Gain: 250 feet
Season: All year
Canine Compatibility: Dogs are permitted on leash
Fees: $7 parking fee at the trailhead

Trail Contact: Sonoma Valley Regional Park, 13630 Highway 12, Glen Ellen CA 95442; (707) 539-8092; http://parks.sonomacounty .ca.gov/Get_Outdoors/Parks/Sonoma_Valley_ Regional_Park.aspx
Other: The west end of the loop has an easy connection to downtown Glen Ellen.

Finding the trailhead: *From Kenwood:* Drive south on CA 12 for 4.0 miles. Turn right into the signed parking lot for Sonoma Valley Regional Park. GPS: N38°21.84233'/W122°30.73650'
   From the downtown plaza in Sonoma: Drive west for 0.9 mile. Turn right onto CA 12 and continue north for 5.5 miles. Turn left into the signed parking lot for Sonoma Valley Regional Park.

The Hike

Home to large, spectacular parks like Hood Mountain, Sugarloaf Ridge, Annadel, and Jack London, the Sonoma Valley has the highest concentration of public land anywhere in the Wine Country. The parks all line the high walls of the valley, looking down on the beautiful valley floor and all of its thriving activity. The only place to hike in the lower section of the valley is diminutive Sonoma Valley Regional Park. This small slice of the historic, beautiful valley is found near the lovely little town of Glen Ellen. With rolling hills, winding canyons, and walking access to Glen Ellen, the park also has great views of the Sonoma Valley. The small park's main trail consists of a loop, first traversing the top of the hills and then looping past the edge of Glen Ellen before returning to the trailhead through the canyon. It is not a long hike, but it is an easy outing in the beating heart of the Wine Country.

The trail begins in the large parking lot at the east end of the park. Just beyond the trailhead the path splits. Stay to the left and hike toward the large water tanks. Stay right at a fork. Going left leads to Lake Suttonfield, which is on the Sonoma Developmental Hospital's property but has been incorporated into the park's trail system. This is a great option for a side trip. Past the fork, climb up an open hillside punctuated by a few oak trees. There are good views to the east, where the high towers of Sugarloaf Ridge rise alongside the dark rock of Gunsight Rock's tall cliff. From here the trail weaves along the top of a series of hills for a mile. Much of the hilltop is

High peaks rise above Sonoma Valley Regional Park.

covered in oak woodlands. Here are occasional and sometimes filtered views through the trees of the Sonoma Valley. Even though this spot is close to Glen Ellen and busy CA 12, it feels surprisingly remote. A few side trails branch off to the right and drop down into the canyon below. Stay on the main path on top of the hills. Eventually the trail will arc to the south and begin to descend. It deposits hikers at a trailhead at the west end of town right on the edge of Glen Ellen's little downtown area, which is an easy walk from there.

To continue the loop, hang a right on the paved trail and follow it back to the east. The trail parallels Sonoma Creek, the main creek that drains the Sonoma Valley, although dense vegetation prevents any view of the water. Restaurants and tasting rooms are visible on the opposite side of the creek.

Leaving the development behind, the trail enters a long canyon that skirts the edge of the hills traversed by the first half of the loop. A small seasonal creek flows through the valley, though it is usually dry by summer. Several side trails cross the trail. Stay on the main path. About 1 mile from the west trailhead, the canyon narrows as the trail turns to the south and climbs out of the canyon onto a flat, grass–covered area. From here it is only 0.2 mile back to the parking lot.

Miles and Directions

0.0 Begin the hike at the west end of the trailhead parking lot. Immediately past the trailhead, stay right at a fork with a paved road leading to water tanks. Then stay left at the next fork in the trail.

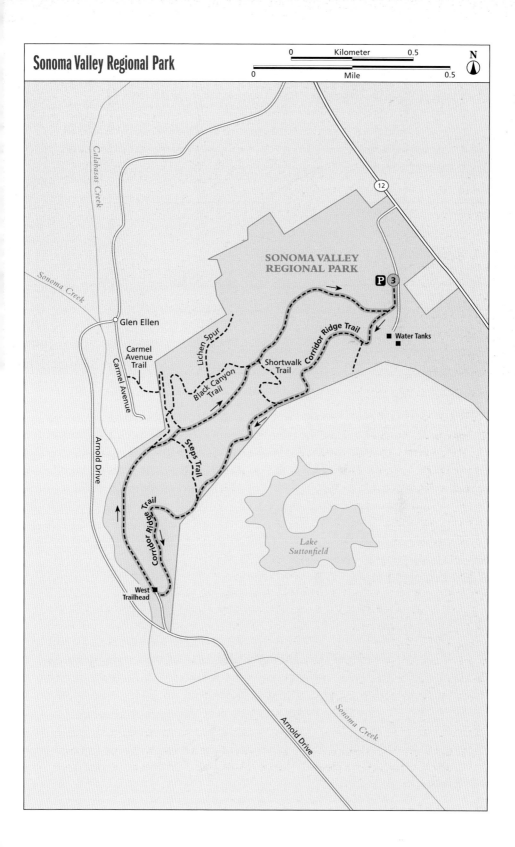

Sonoma Valley Regional Park

0.4 Signs mark the left turn to Lake Suttonfield. Stay right to continue on the main park loop.

0.55 Continue straight at the junction where a trail branches off to the left. A few more side trails pop up as you continue west. Stay on the main trail on top of the hill.

0.9 Begin the descent down to the west trailhead.

1.2 At the trailhead, turn right onto a paved walkway and begin the hike back to the trailhead.

2.4 After rejoining the trail at the beginning of the loop, arrive back at the trailhead and finish the hike.

4 Wolf House Ruins

The hike to the Wolf House is an easy introduction to Jack London State Historic Park. The trail leads to the ruins of London's sprawling Wolf House, which burned down shortly after its construction was completed.

Total Distance: 1.4 miles out and back
Hiking Time: About 1 hour
Difficulty: Easy
Elevation Gain: 250 feet
Season: All year
Canine Compatibility: Dogs are not permitted outside of the park's historic areas

Fees: $10 entrance fee
Trail Contact: Jack London State Historic Park, 2400 London Ranch Rd., Glen Ellen, CA 95442; (707) 938-5216; www.jacklondonpark .com
Other: The trail passes the park's museum, which is worth a stop.

Finding the trailhead: On CA 12, either 3.6 miles south of Kenwood or 6.9 miles from Sonoma's downtown plaza, turn west onto Arnold Drive. Continue for 0.9 mile, entering the small town of Glen Ellen. Turn right onto London Ranch Road and proceed 1.3 miles to the entrance station. Pass the station and turn left into the visitor center parking lot. GPS: N38°21.37883'/W122°32.51600'

The Hike

Famed early twentieth-century author Jack London, who wrote *Call of the Wild*, *Sea Wolf*, and *White Fang* among other books, was a long-time resident of the Sonoma Valley. He established a large ranch on the slopes of Sonoma Mountain, just west of the town of Glen Ellen. He lived at the ranch, where he continued to write while managing the ranch's operations. The centerpiece of the property was to be the epic Wolf House, an enormous, magnificent mansion. Made of native materials and boasting many modern innovations, the house was an epic testimony to London's tremendous success as an author. Unfortunately the home burned down in 1913, just weeks before Jack London and his wife, Charmian, were due to move into it. Broken by the loss of Wolf House, London's health began to decline. He died three years later and was buried in a small cemetery near the house. Today the ruins of Wolf House are part of Jack London State Historic Park, which encompasses much of London's old ranch. The hike from the park's visitor center to Wolf House is a classic Sonoma County outing.

The hike to Wolf House ruins begins at the visitor center parking lot. The wide, paved path climbs a short hill to a large stone structure known as the House of Happy Walls. Now serving as the visitor center, the house was originally built by Charmian London after the death of Jack London. Though it is a smaller version of Wolf House, it is still a large and impressive house. Walk past the visitor center and turn right onto

Wolf House Ruins; Sonoma Mountain

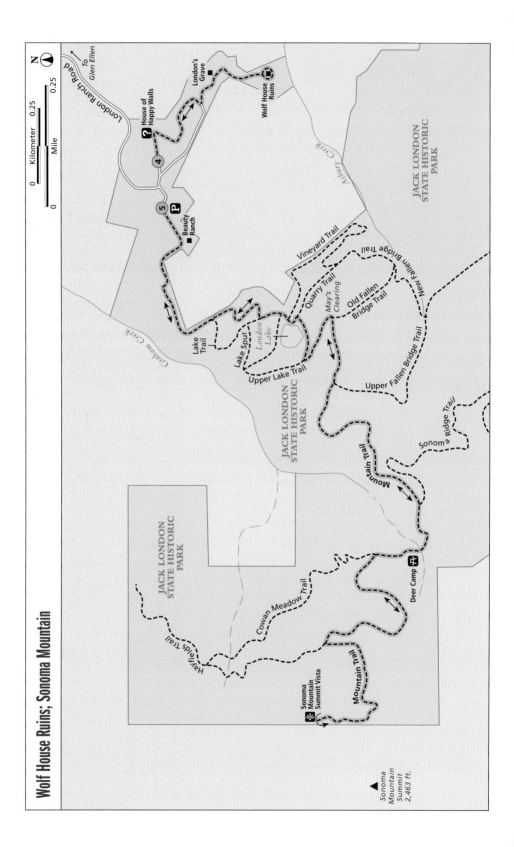

the dirt trail that goes down through the woods. The path descends through the mixed forest of fir, madrone, oak, and laurel, dead-ending at a paved road 0.35 mile from the parking area.

Turn left onto the paved road. It continues through the woods, running alongside a small, seasonal creek for a short time. The road climbs slightly toward some service buildings before dropping back downhill to a small clearing. A dirt path branches off to the left and leads to Jack and Charmian London's grave, located next to the graves of some pioneer children. Returning to the paved road, it climbs briefly through the clearing before making the final, short descent down to the ruins.

Built with large stones, the ruins of Wolf House are a silent and haunting place. Large window openings and towering chimney towers give silent testimony to the lost glory of this home. It is possible to walk all the way around the ruins and peer in through the windows, though little remains in the interior of the structure. The west side is flanked by a small grove of redwood trees, which add to the site's appeal. Following the trail around to the south side of the house leads to an observation deck that has good views of the central part of the house. Loop back up the east side of the house, passing the dilapidated entrance. After pondering the splendor and futility of Jack London's dream, retrace your steps back to the parking lot.

Miles and Directions

0.0 Start hiking from the large visitor center parking lot. The trail climbs a paved walkway to the large, stone visitor center. To the right a dirt path is the beginning of the trail.

0.35 The trail ends at a paved road. Turn left and hike on the service road.

0.5 A spur trail leads to Jack and Charmian London's grave.

0.65 Arrive at the Wolf House ruins. A short loop circles the house and accesses a viewing platform. Return to the trailhead.

5 Sonoma Mountain

Sonoma Mountain is one of the most significant landmarks in southern Sonoma County. The hike to the top explores preserved portions of Jack London's ranch, remote forests, and a redwood grove and delivers a magnificent view of the Sonoma Valley for hikers who make it to the end of the trail.

See map for Hike 4.
Total Distance: 7.5 miles out and back
Hiking Time: About 4 hours
Difficulty: Strenuous
Elevation Gain: 1,700 feet
Season: All year
Canine Compatibility: Dogs are not permitted outside of the park's historic areas

Fees: $10 entrance fee
Trail Contact: Jack London State Historic Park, 2400 London Ranch Rd., Glen Ellen, CA 95442; (707) 938-5216; www.jacklondonpark .com
Other: The trail passes through Jack London's Beauty Ranch.

Finding the trailhead: On CA 12, either 3.6 miles south of Kenwood or 6.9 miles from Sonoma's downtown plaza, turn west onto Arnold Drive. Continue for 0.9 mile, entering the small town of Glen Ellen. Turn right onto London Ranch Road and proceed 1.3 miles to the entrance station. Pass the station and turn right into the trailhead parking lot. GPS: N38°21.38017'/W122°32.69683'

The Hike

Jack London is one of the Wine Country's most colorful characters. The famed author loved the beautiful landscape of Sonoma County and used many locales as inspiration for his books. He lived on a large ranch at the southern end of the Sonoma Valley, near the town of Glen Ellen. Today, the ranch is known as Jack London State Historic Park, a 1,400-acre paradise in the heart of the Wine Country. London himself referred to the homestead as the Beauty Ranch, and many of the original buildings are still maintained today.

Beauty Ranch was not limited to the agricultural operation. A substantial part of the property climbed high up the wild slopes of Sonoma Mountain. Towering over the surrounding landscape, the large, broad-topped mountain is an imposing presence throughout southern Sonoma County. It forms the divide between the Santa Rosa Plain, the Petaluma Valley, and the Sonoma Valley. The peak is the highest point of the Sonoma Mountains, a small volcanic mountain range just west of the Mayacamas Mountains.

An extensive trail network spreads throughout Jack London State Historic Park, but the most scenic is the route that leads to a high vista just below the summit of Sonoma Mountain. The trail combines all the best features of the park. It passes

Open vineyards along the trail present an early opportunity to observe the summit of Sonoma Mountain.

through the grounds of the Beauty Ranch, past vineyards, and then climbs into beautiful redwood forests and tall hillsides covered in oak trees. From the top there is a fantastic view of the irresistible Valley of the Moon, the heart of the Wine Country.

The hike begins at the Beauty Ranch trailhead at the west end of the large parking lot. The wide path climbs up to the preserved buildings of the Beauty Ranch. In addition to the cottage where Jack London lived and wrote, several large stone barns and other buildings still stand. The trail makes a right-hand turn between a large grove of eucalyptus trees and a vineyard. Before London bought the ranch, it had been a vineyard operated by Frohling & Kohler, the pioneer of Southern California wine making. The ruins of its winery are located just off the trail next to the cottage. The eucalyptus trees were planted to produce fast-growing timber that could be used for lumber.

The path soon turns left, rounding the corner of the vineyard. It follows the rows of grapevines to yet another turn to the left, where the trail now runs between the edge of the vineyard and the vast, native forest that blankets the flanks of Sonoma Mountain. Finally, at 0.6 mile from the trailhead, the path veers away from the vineyard and begins to climb. After a few lazy switchbacks, the trail—an old fire road— reaches the edge of London Lake. Walk along the large hewn boulders that form the lake's dam.

Just past the dam are a number of trails heading out into the state park's backcountry. Stay to the right on the Mountain Trail. Hike up a moderate grade on the old

Beautiful Sonoma Valley, 2,000 feet below the end of the Sonoma Mountain Trail.

road, rounding a hairpin turn and then breaking out into a meadow known as May's Clearing. Find memorable views to the south toward Mount Diablo, one of the Bay Area's iconic mountains. Stay to the right at a junction in the clearing and continue climbing the Mountain Trail. The left-hand route is Old Fallen Bridge Trail, which loops back down toward the vineyards and Beauty Ranch. Stay right again a little later at the junction with the Upper Fallen Bridge Trail. After the Mountain Trail rounds a shoulder, the path is slung on the gentle slopes of Graham Creek's canyon. The sound of water crashing through the creek is audible below the trail. Nearly 0.8 mile past May's Clearing is another fork. The trail to the left is the Sonoma Ridge Trail, which heads south along the side of Sonoma Mountain. Proceeding on the Mountain Trail, the path crosses a few small streams fed by springs. Large redwoods begin to appear along the trail. After listening to the sounds of Graham Creek for over a mile, the trail finally crosses the creek where it emerges from a cliff-lined gorge. Just past the crossing is a beautiful picnic area set amid springs, ferns, and towering redwood trees. A few picnic tables make great places to take a break. This was the site of Jack London's Deer Camp, which he used when hunting in the remote corners of his ranch.

When leaving Deer Camp behind, the Mountain Trail also leaves the redwoods and the cool, shady forest. It crosses a large meadow and then resumes the climb toward the summit. Oak trees offer some shade, but this part of the trail is drier and hotter than the lower sections. Long, almost unnoticeable switchbacks ease the grade as the trail nears the top of the mountain. Stay left on the Mountain Trail when both the Cowan Meadow and Hayfields Trails branch off to the right.

Finally the old fire road arrives at a gate. A narrow single-track path splits off to the right and climbs the grassy slope for 0.2 mile to the state park's high point, which is just east of the summit. The view is magnificent. The Sonoma Valley, Jack London's beloved Valley of the Moon, is a gaping chasm 2,000 feet below. Vineyards cling to the high peaks on the other side of the valley, climbing ever higher toward the tall peaks of the southern Mayacamas Mountains. It is a magical spot, and there is no difficulty imagining the roguish author spending an idle afternoon here, soaking up inspiration to write his next tale.

Miles and Directions

0.0 Start the hike by climbing up the wide trail to the historic Beauty Ranch.

0.15 At Beauty Ranch, turn right and hike parallel to a vineyard. At the junction for the Pig Palace, stay left, following the vineyard.

0.55 Stay left when the Upper Lake Trail splits off to the right. The trail then begins to switchback up a hill.

0.9 The trail passes London Lake. Stay straight and hike alongside the dam, then stay right, continuing on the Mountain Trail.

1.25 Pass through May's Clearing, with great views of Mount Diablo and the southern Sonoma Valley. In the clearing, stay right at the junction and keep climbing up the Mountain Trail.

1.5 Stay right again at the junction with the Upper Fallen Bridge Trail.

2.1 At the fork with the Sonoma Ridge Trail, stay to the right.

2.4 Cross over Graham Creek and arrive at the Deer Camp picnic area.

2.55 Stay left at the junction with the Cowan Meadow Trail.

3.25 Stay left at the Hayfields Trail.

3.55 The main trail dead-ends at the property line. Turn right onto a steep trail climbing up the hill.

3.75 Arrive at the Sonoma Mountain summit vista and enjoy the view. Return to the trailhead.

6 Old Orchard Loop

This hike is a back door into Jack London State Historic Park. It climbs through grassy hills with great views and passes beautiful Fern Lake. In a large redwood grove, a spur connects to the Ancient Redwood, a fantastically gnarled and weathered old tree. Past the redwoods, the trail loops through an old orchard where the forest is slowly reclaiming many of the fruit trees.

Total Distance: 4.1-mile lollipop
Hiking Time: About 2.5 hours
Difficulty: Moderate
Elevation Gain: 700 feet
Season: All year
Canine Compatibility: Dogs are not permitted outside of the park's historic areas

Fees: None
Trail Contact: Jack London State Historic Park, 2400 London Ranch Rd., Glen Ellen, CA 95442; (707) 938-5216; www.jacklondonpark .com
Other: The trail begins at the Sonoma Developmental Center; please be respectful.

Finding the trailhead: On CA 12, either 3.6 miles south of Kenwood or 6.9 miles from Sonoma's downtown plaza, turn west onto Arnold Drive. Drive for 2.2 miles, passing through the town of Glen Ellen. At the Sonoma Developmental Center, turn right onto Holt Road and continue for 0.25 mile. Turn right onto Manzanita Road and drive for another 0.15 mile. There is a small parking area backed by a concrete retaining wall. GPS: N38°20.90567'/W122°31.37383'

The Hike

Hidden on the eastern flank of tall Sonoma Mountain, the Sonoma Developmental Center is a state-run hospital for people with developmental needs. The sprawling campus is on the edge of the community of Eldridge and extends westward onto Sonoma Mountain. The hospital once maintained extensive properties above the hospital that were essentially undeveloped and retained their natural character. In 1991 a significant portion of this property was transferred over to neighboring Jack London State Historic Park. The hospital property and the state park shared a common border in their upper reaches, and today trails connect the two sections. However, a great trail begins at the Sonoma Developmental Center and travels through scenic country not usually accessed via the state park.

The trail has three distinct parts. The lower section is composed of open hills and forests. The second section is a large redwood grove highlighted by a spectacularly massive, ancient, and grizzled redwood. The final area is an old orchard planted on the slopes of Sonoma Mountain. Portions of the orchard, an experiment from the early twentieth century that was intended to give patients at the Developmental Center an opportunity for work, are now being reclaimed by nature. Though there are a couple steep stretches, most of the trail is moderately graded and makes a scenic

The incredibly gnarled ancient redwood.

and diverse outing that sees fewer hikers than other trails in Jack London State Historic Park.

Beginning at the humble, unsigned little parking area across the street from the Developmental Center, go around the chain gate on an old road and hike uphill through the woods. Cross over two gullies, one of which may have water running through it late into the summer. The trail soon breaks out onto grass-covered slopes as it climbs where views of the mountains on the Sugarloaf area on the east side of the Sonoma Valley open up. The trail passes through another band of trees before crossing another clearing with even better views to the north.

In addition to clear views of the peaks at Sugarloaf, the massive, rugged face of Gunsight Rock on Hood Mountain looms across the valley. It is one of the most impressive mountains in the entire Wine Country. About 0.35 mile from the beginning of the hike, the trail splits. There are no signs, and both paths are distinct. The official trail goes to the right and makes a switchback as it climbs. The left-hand trail climbs steeply and then quickly rejoins the main trail. Both lead to the same place in short order. Continuing to the west, the route soon levels off and crosses an open area with fantastic views. To the right rises the high summit of Sonoma Mountain. To the south, the lower end of the Sonoma Valley broadens as it meets San Francisco Bay. The two peaks of distant Mount Diablo pierce the horizon. Past this great spot, the trail makes a brief climb before topping out on a knoll above Fern Lake.

The small lake is nestled between two low hills. The trail surmounts the small knoll on the east side of the lake and runs parallel to the short knoll down below. Near the east end of the lake a trail branches off to the right. Stay left and round the short, north end of the lake before encountering another fork. Stay left again and cross over a narrow diversion channel that connects to nearby Asbury Creek and funnels water over to Fern Lake.

Past the lake the trail enters the land officially administered by Jack London State Historic Park. As if marking the transition in ownership, a deep, dark forest closes in on the trail as it begins a steep ascent up an old, rocky road. Note a side trail branching off to the left. This narrow path is a little longer than the old road, but it has a milder grade, making it easier for those not looking to climb the steep slope. The two trails rejoin right when large redwoods begin to appear along the trail. The redwoods get increasingly dense as the trail levels off and arrives at a picnic area.

A number of trails converge at the picnic area. To the right, the Vineyard Trail connects to the lower section of the trail network in the heart of Jack London State Historic Park. The trail to the historic orchard lies straight ahead. When approaching it, take the narrow trail on the left with signs indicating the ancient redwood down the path. The trail quickly arrives at an observation point looking out on the gargantuan, gnarled trunk of an obviously ancient tree. Branches the size of normal tree trunks grow off branches larger than normal tree trunks in a convoluted knot of burls and branches. It is clear from its twisted shape that the tree is very old. Despite

Old Orchard Loop

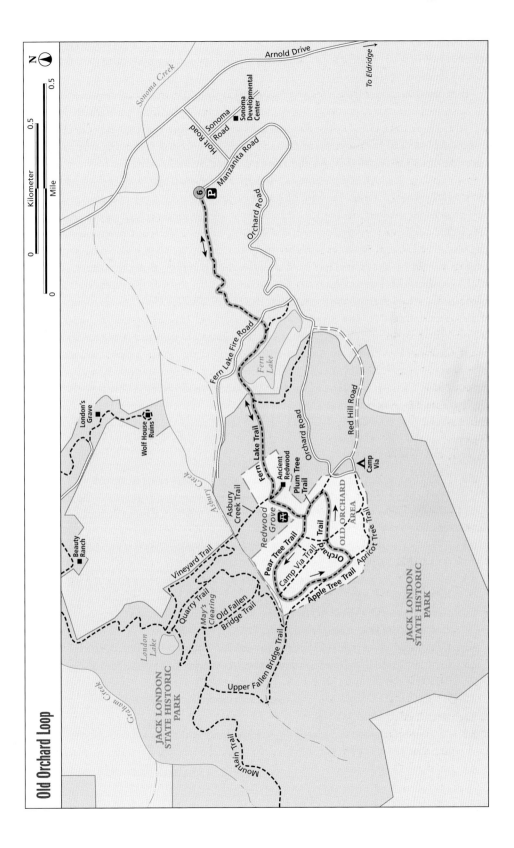

its great size, it is not a particularly tall redwood. Its top was toppled sometime in the past by unknown causes.

Returning to the picnic area, continue hiking on the trail leading up to the orchard. It soon ends at a fork. This is the beginning of the loop through the old orchard. There are several trails that encircle and crisscross the orchard. The best option is to stick to the outer perimeter and circle the orchard. To do this, turn right onto the Pear Tree Trail. Stay on the main path and avoid veering onto side trails. Initially passing through natural forests, the native trees soon give way, and untended fruit trees spring up along the trail. This part of the orchard is very overgrown. The trail narrows as it swings to the left and climbs along the outer fringe of the cleared area. After 0.35 mile the trail arrives at a signed junction. The path disappearing in the woods to the right connects to the upper section of the state park's trail system. Stay to the left on the Apple Tree Trail and continue climbing along the upper edge of the orchard. This area is a little less overgrown, and the rows of fruit trees are more obvious. There are limited views out over the Sonoma Valley from points along the trail. After another 0.3 mile turn left onto the Orchard Trail and gradually descend through the heart of the clearing. Cross over the Camp Via Trail and continue down-hill. Views out over the lower orchard area soon open up on the right. This area is not overgrown, and the rows of old fruit trees are still present. The path soon reaches another fork. Turn left onto the Plum Tree Trail and quickly arrive at the trail climbing up from the redwoods and Fern Lake. Turn right and retrace your steps back to the trailhead.

Miles and Directions

0.0   At the small parking area, walk around the chain gate and begin hiking on the trail.

0.3   After crossing two little gullies and climbing through two clearings with great views, the trail splits. The official trail goes to the right, but both are well-established routes. The paths reconvene soon.

0.6   Following a short climb, arrive at beautiful Fern Lake. Turn right and follow the east shore, staying left at the junction at the lake's northeast corner.

0.9   A side trail splits off the main route. It rejoins the trail at the top of a long grade. It is less steep but a little longer.

1.3   Take a break in the midst of a large redwood grove. A spur trail goes a short distance to the south where there is an amazing view of the ancient redwood.

1.55 Climb a short hill and turn right onto the Pear Tree Trail to begin the Old Orchard Loop.

1.9   The loop is joined by the main trail coming from Jack London State Historic Park. Stay left, continuing onto the Apple Tree Trail.

2.2   Turn left onto the Orchard Trail, which cuts through the center of the orchard.

2.5   Turn left onto the Plum Tree Trail.

2.6   Complete the loop and turn right on the main trail, heading back down to the redwoods, Fern Lake, and the trailhead.

4.1   Arrive back at the trailhead.

7 Sonoma Creek Falls

The short hike to Sonoma Creek Falls packs a lot of scenery into its short mileage. The loop first climbs high, crosses a beautiful fern-laden area along a small creek, and then drops down to Sonoma Creek. The trail then follows the creek, weaving through redwoods and large boulders before arriving at a beautiful seasonal waterfall on Sonoma Creek. When the water is flowing strongly, the waterfall can be very impressive. From the falls it is a steady climb through rock gardens back to the trailhead.

Total Distance: 1.65-mile loop
Hiking Time: About 1 hour
Difficulty: Easy
Elevation Gain: 450 feet
Season: All year

Canine Compatibility: Dogs are not permitted
Fees: $8 entrance fee
Trail Contact: Sugarloaf Ridge State Park, 2605 Adobe Canyon Rd., Kenwood, CA 95452; 707-833-5712; www.sugarloafpark.org

Finding the trailhead: From Kenwood, drive north on CA 12 for 0.3 mile. Turn right onto Adobe Canyon Road and drive 3.3 miles through Sonoma Creek Canyon. Look for the pullout parking area on the left. GPS: N38°26.29383'/W122°31.12433'

The Hike

Sonoma Creek flows 33 miles from its headwaters in Sugarloaf Ridge State Park to San Pablo Bay. It is the primary waterway through the beautiful Sonoma Valley, one of the loveliest regions in the Wine Country. While its entire course is extremely scenic, perhaps the most attractive is the creek's descent down a rocky canyon below its large headwaters basin. Flowing through a rocky channel and flanked by rugged cliffs, the creek's path is lined by large redwoods. The highlight is a beautiful waterfall pouring through a notch in a tall band of rock and then tumbling over large, car-size boulders. It is an inspiring sight, especially during the rainy season when the creek is swollen with runoff. While it is possible to hike to the waterfall, it is also possible to reach the falls on a scenic little loop. The loop is a combination of the Pony Gate Trail and the Canyon Trail and enables hikers to enjoy reaching the falls without traveling the same stretch of trail twice.

The Pony Gate Trail begins at the east end of the parking area. It climbs gently through areas that alternate between oak forests and open areas. In about 0.3 mile the trail reaches the top of the climb and begins to descend into the canyon. The forest grows thicker as you head downhill. The pleasant trail loses elevation gradually. About 0.75 mile from the trailhead, the path crosses a small creek. In the spring, when the water is full, it is a very pretty stream, tumbling through a narrow gulch filled with boulders and bedrock chutes. The trail continues downhill for another 0.2 mile

Sonoma Creek Falls.

before it arrives at Adobe Canyon Road. Cross over the road and find the Canyon Trail on the opposite side.

The Canyon Trail makes a quick descent to the edge of Sonoma Creek, which, in the spring, may resemble a large river. Lined with steep, rocky walls and scattered

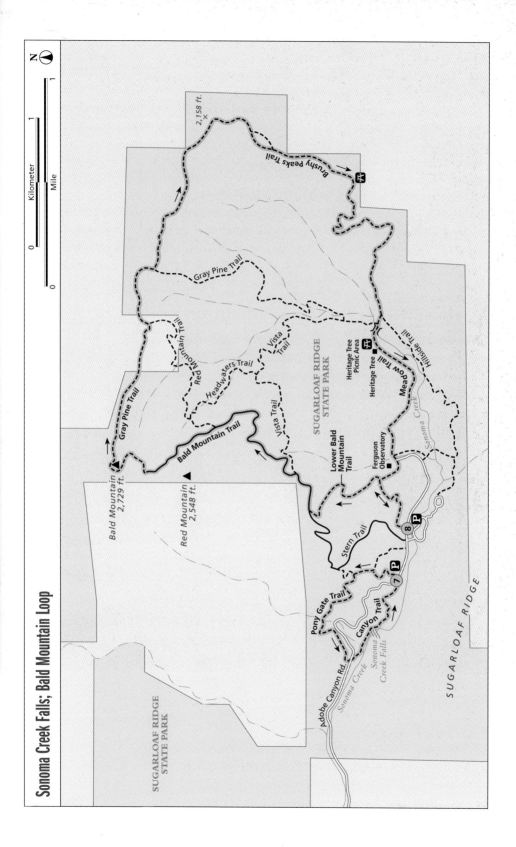

Sonoma Creek Falls; Bald Mountain Loop

SUGARLOAF RIDGE STATE PARK

SUGARLOAF RIDGE STATE PARK

SUGARLOAF RIDGE

Bald Mountain
2,729 ft.

Red Mountain
2,548 ft.

2,158 ft.

Gray Pine Trail

Gray Pine Trail

Red Mountain Trail

Headwaters Trail

Vista Trail

Vista Trail

Bald Mountain Trail

Lower Bald Mountain Trail

Ferguson Observatory

Stern Trail

Brushy Peaks Trail

Heritage Tree Picnic Area

Heritage Tree

Meadow Trail

Hillside Trail

Sonoma Creek

Pony Gate Trail

Canyon Trail

Adobe Canyon Rd.

Sonoma Creek

Sonoma Creek Falls

N

Kilometer

Mile

0   1   1

redwood trees, the canyon is a magical place. The trail follows the creek as it races over large rocks. The tall redwoods form a nearly impenetrable canopy over the canyon.

When the trail crosses a bridge over a small, seasonal creek, watch for a short spur turning to the right. This leads to the edge of the creek amid a huge pile of large boulders. The canyon narrows to a tight gap in the cliffs. Sonoma Creek pours through the gap and drops 10 feet before crashing into a large rock and cascading another 19 feet through a narrow chute. In spring it is an awesome sight and one of the finest waterfalls on public land in the Wine Country.

When it is time to depart from the spectacle, return to the main trail and begin climbing steeply out of the canyon. The trail passes through moss-covered rock out-croppings and piles of boulders. Though the grade is steep, the rocks add enough interest to make the climb a little easier. Finally, after climbing for 0.4 mile, the trail reaches the edge of Adobe Road Canyon. Cross the road back to the trailhead.

Miles and Directions

0.0 Depart from the trailhead on the Pony Gate Trail as it climbs gently up a hill.

0.3 Reach the top of the climb and begin heading downhill.

0.75 Pass a small, swift-moving seasonal creek.

0.85 Cross over Adobe Canyon Road and drop down alongside Sonoma Creek.

1.25 Arrive at Sonoma Creek Falls.

1.65 After climbing up from the falls, the trail reaches Adobe Canyon Road. Cross the road to the trailhead.

8 Bald Mountain Loop

The loop to the summit of Sugarloaf Ridge State Park's Bald Mountain is one of the epic Wine Country hikes. The hike climbs the remote headwaters of Sonoma Creek while reaching the summit of Bald Mountain. From the top of the peak, hikers enjoy the most spectacular vista of the entire region.

See map for Hike 7.
Total Distance: 8.1-mile loop
Hiking Time: About 5 hours
Difficulty: Strenuous
Elevation Gain: 1,500 feet
Season: All year

Canine Compatibility: Dogs are not permitted
Fees: $8 entrance fee
Trail Contact: Sugarloaf Ridge State Park, 2605 Adobe Canyon Rd., Kenwood, CA 95452; 707-833-5712; www.sugarloafpark.org

Finding the trailhead: From Kenwood, drive north on CA 12 for 0.3 mile. Turn right onto Adobe Canyon Road and drive 3.4 miles up Sonoma Creek Canyon. Continue past the entrance station for 100 yards before turning left into the trailhead parking lot. GPS: N38°26.28133'/W122°30.84400'

The Hike

The southern half of the Mayacamas Mountains forms the divide between the Napa Valley in Napa County and the Sonoma Valley and Santa Rosa Plain in Sonoma County. This part of the range's highest point is awesome Hood Mountain, which is 2,730 feet high. Only 1 foot lower, Bald Mountain may have just missed being the highest point in the southern Mayacamas, but it has the distinction of being the highest point in Sugarloaf Ridge State Park and the highest point along the Sonoma-Napa County line. The unassuming peak sits atop the large basin that constitutes the headwaters of Sonoma Creek, one of the longest and most significant waterways in Sonoma County. Although there are several trails in the state park, the undeniable highlight is the ascent to the summit of Bald Mountain.

The hike up may not inspire much confidence, since it climbs relentlessly up a paved road without many views to make the climb more enjoyable. But once on the summit of Bald Mountain, the climb will seem insignificant compared to the astounding panorama that unfolds in all directions. The stunning view stretches from San Francisco and Mount Diablo in the south to Snow Mountain far to the north. Both the Sonoma and Napa Valleys are visible from the summit, and most of the major peaks of the Wine Country are prominent on the horizon.

The view from the top of Bald Mountain is not the only highlight of the trail either. The hike down follows the Sonoma County line for 2 miles through isolated, seldom-traveled country. On the hike down, the Planet Walk adds an unusual wrinkle

Memorable views of the Napa Valley are found along the Brushy Peaks Trail.

to the hike. A series of displays along the path identify the planets of the solar system and are placed along the trail at distances that are scaled to the actual miles between each of the planets. It imparts a sense of vastness that far exceeds that already immense emptiness of the Sugarloaf backcountry.

To start the hike, head east from the trailhead on the Lower Bald Mountain Trail. Soon after leaving the trailhead, the path makes a series of easily graded switchbacks up a hillside and then levels off in a large field. On the far side of the field, stay left at a fork. The path to the right is the final part on the return leg of the loop. Past the junction, the trail continues across the field before entering an oak forest. Climb through the trees, passing a few switchbacks, before the trail ends at the edge of a paved road, about 0.9 mile from the trailhead. Turn right on the road and begin the long climb to the top of Bald Mountain.

The uphill grade is consistent almost the entire time. Soon after reaching the road, the Vista Trail departs to the right. Continue the climb up the road. While the route travels through some forested areas initially, it soon breaks out into dry chaparral-covered slopes that offer little shade. Around 0.8 mile after passing the Vista Trail, the Red Mountain Trail also splits off to the right. Red Mountain is actually above the road on the left. A large microwave tower sits on its summit. Continue hiking a little farther, passing a picnic table. This is one of the few places to sit and rest during the ascent.

Finally, after hiking for 2.3 miles, the road arrives at a fork. The pavement follows the route to the left, which leads to Red Mountain. Turn to the right and follow the dirt road. Views to the west are fantastic. The Sonoma Valley and Santa Rosa are visible far below. Hood Mountain looms just a short distance away from the trail. Follow the path as it rounds a knoll and finally reaches a junction. Stay right and follow the spur the last few feet to the summit of Bald Mountain, about 2.85 miles from the trailhead. At the summit are large displays that identify many of the landmarks visible from the top of Bald Mountain. This is one of the few 360-degree views in the Wine Country, and it is, without doubt, the finest. Both Sonoma and Napa Counties are visible from here, as well as many places in the Bay Area and to the north and beyond.

When it is time to continue, hike off the summit and stay straight through the junction, beginning the return to the trailhead on the Gray Pine Trail. This path follows the ridge that forms the boundary between Sonoma and Napa Counties. Though the namesake gray pines and a large amount of chaparral line the pathway, there are occasional views along the top of the ridge. After following the ridge for 0.75 mile, you arrive at a junction with the Red Mountain Trail. This connects back over to the paved road that leads to the summit of Bald Mountain. Stay left and continue hiking on the county line for another 0.35 mile to the junction with the Brushy Peaks Trail. Most hikers choose to go right and descend the Gray Pine Trail. This is a fair option, especially if you need to get back right away. However, the much more scenic and interesting trip is on the Brushy Peaks Trail. To take this route, turn left.

Once you are on the Brushy Peaks Trail, you will hike some of the most forsaken trail in the Wine Country. This area is about as remote and forgotten as it feels. Powerful winds sweep over the ridge, and the gray pines and brush sound as lonely as the trail. If there is a drawback to this part of the hike, it is the constant undulation of the trail. It climbs steeply up small hills and drops back down just as steeply. Though the climbs are never long, they each inflict a little punishment on wearying hikers. Fortunately, there are occasional views through the thickets of brush that line the trail. In particular are some spectacular vantages above the Yountville area in the Napa Valley. The rows of vineyards blanket the valley floor from one side to the other. Keen eyes will notice the dam that forms the Rector Reservoir and the ridge climbed in Hike 54.

After hiking along the ridge in an easterly direction for 0.9 mile, the ridge turns south. The trail follows suit, and soon Mount Saint John, one of the tallest peaks in this part of the Mayacamas Mountains, comes into view. The trail finally comes off the crest of the range and traverses the east side of the ridge. Nearly 0.35 mile after turning south, the trail encounters the Pluto display, the first of the Planet Walk markers. In some ways this is encouraging because it means you have begun the journey back to the trailhead. Unfortunately, the scale of the distance between Earth and Pluto is now going to be made very clear. Continue hiking for another 0.45 mile before arriving at a nice, shaded picnic area with views into a secluded valley just south of the park's boundary.

After leaving the picnic area, the trail passes the Neptune marker, followed quickly by a series of switchbacks that descend down into a thick, heavily shaded forest. The cool temperatures are a welcome respite after so many shadeless trails. A little more than 0.8 mile after leaving the picnic area, the trail reaches the headwaters of a seasonal creek. Follow the often-dry channel for about 0.3 mile before it is joined by the Malm Fork of Sonoma Creek. Though flows may be small late in the season, it is not unusual to see at least a little trickle of water here.

From here it is only a short distance along the creek before the trail arrives at a junction, passing the Uranus marker just before meeting the other trails. At the junction, stay right and then almost immediately stay left. Cross Sonoma Creek by the Heritage Tree picnic area, which has nice views of the creek and the massive namesake tree. Proceed along the creek before entering a large meadow.

After passing the Saturn, Jupiter, and Mars markers, the trail arrives at Ferguson Observatory. The other planetary markers are nearby to the left, near a group camp. To continue the hike, stay straight, passing the entrance to the observatory. Climb the little slope and cross a field before reaching a junction and turning left, back onto the Lower Bald Mountain Trail. Follow it briefly back to the trailhead.

Miles and Directions

0.0 Depart from the trailhead on the Lower Bald Mountain Trail.

0.25 Stay left to continue on the Lower Bald Mountain Trail.

0.9 Turn right onto the paved road and begin climbing steadily. Avoid the trails splitting off to the right and stay on the paved road.

2.3 When the pavement bends around to the left, turn right onto a dirt road and keep climbing.

2.85 Arrive at the top of Bald Mountain and the best view in the Wine Country.

3.55 Stay left on the Gray Pine Trail.

2.95 At the Gray Pine Trail's junction with the Brushy Peaks Trail, turn left and begin hiking on the latter.

5.3 Begin the Planet Walk at the Pluto marker.

5.65 The path reaches the picnic area at the park's boundary.

6.9 Turn right when the trail arrives at a junction. Stay to the left at a second junction immediately following the first, then cross over Sonoma Creek on a bridge.

7.75 Hike past the front entrance of the observatory.

7.9 Turn left back onto the Lower Bald Mountain Trail.

8.1 Arrive back at the trailhead.

9 Goodspeed-Nattkemper Trail

The steep climb to the summit of Hood Mountain from Sonoma Creek is one of the most difficult trails in the Wine Country, and yet it is one of the most rewarding. Beginning in redwood forests, the trail climbs through chaparral, forests, and open hillsides on the way to a stunning vista atop Gunsight Rock.

Total Distance: 6.7 miles out and back
Hiking Time: About 4.5 hours
Difficulty: Strenuous
Elevation Gain: 1,900 feet
Season: All year
Canine Compatibility: Dogs are not permitted

Fees: $8 fee at the trailhead
Trail Contact: Sugarloaf Ridge State Park, 2605 Adobe Canyon Rd., Kenwood, CA 95452; 707-833-5712; www.sugarloafpark.org
Other: This trail can be combined with either Hike 10 or Hike 11 for a great shuttle hike.

Finding the trailhead: From Kenwood, drive north on CA 12 for 0.3 mile. Turn right onto Adobe Canyon Road and drive 2.3 miles up Sonoma Creek Canyon. Park in the large pullout on the left side of the road, near a grove of redwood trees. GPS: N38°26.55250' / W122°31.85133'

The Hike

The climb to Gunsight Rock via the Goodspeed-Nattkemper Trail is possibly the most strenuous hike in the Wine Country. In less than 3.5 miles, the trail gains nearly 2,000 feet of elevation. With hardly a single flat spot on the trail, it is a relentless ascent. Yet, for all that it demands of those who make the journey, the rewards are equally great. Varied landscapes, wonderful views, and great solitude are constant companions during the climb. The final payoff comes at Gunsight Rock, one of the great vistas of the Wine Country. The Goodspeed-Nattkemper Trail is one of three routes to the top of Hood Mountain. If a shuttle is available, this hike can be combined with either the Johnson Ridge Trail (Hike 11) or the Summit Trail (Hike 10) for a long but spectacular shuttle hike. The ideal shuttle hike begins at the Goodspeed-Nattkemper Trailhead, climbs up to Gunsight Rock and the summit of Hood Mountain, and then descends the Summit Trail to a waiting shuttle car at the park's northern trailhead. This gets all the climbing done in the first part of the hike and preserves the great views of the Goodspeed-Nattkemper Trail while allowing hikers to make a northward descent, facing the great northern vistas of the Summit Trail.

The hike begins in Sugarloaf Ridge State Park amid a beautiful redwood grove along Sonoma Creek. Follow the trail down to the edge of the creek and cross over the large footbridge. The area is a small slice of paradise, where the trees, creek, and bridge combine to form a perfectly arranged outdoor wonderland. The bridge is just upstream from the confluence of Sonoma and Bear Creeks.

The Goodspeed-Nattkemper Trail climbs open slopes on Hood Mountain.

The trail quickly leaves the former behind and follows Bear Creek for a short distance before crossing it on a second footbridge. On the far side of Bear Creek, the trail begins to climb. It first makes a long traverse across a steep hillside and then begins a series of long, increasingly tight switchbacks. The lush redwood forest at the beginning of the trail has now given way to hot, exposed chaparral. After 0.65 mile the trail tops out on a ridge and then cuts down to a dirt road. Once you pick up the trail on the far side of the road, it discouragingly loses almost 150 feet of elevation before arriving at a creek in a narrow, rocky gully. Large boulders and a fallen tree aid in the crossing.

Across the creek, the trail continues to climb to the west through dense, over-grown woods. About 0.25 mile past the creek, the trail makes a hairpin turn and heads back to the east. More overgrown forest lines the route as the path merges onto an old roadbed as it continues to climb. After another set of switchbacks, the grade eases a little bit. A spur trail to the left leads to a cluster of large boulders where you get your first good view on the hike. As nice as it is, it is nothing compared to what lies just a short distance ahead.

Continue on the trail and round the top of a small drainage. When the path turns back to the west, the forest cover fades away, and the narrow track traverses steep, grass-covered hillsides. The view increasingly improves as the trail rounds a broad shoulder and continues climbing across the open slopes to the north. A sign along the trail marks the transition from Sugarloaf Ridge State Park to Hood Mountain

Looking across the Sonoma Valley toward Sonoma Mountain and the Glen Ellen area.

Regional Park. A short distance away, a bench along the path allows a chance to sit, rest weary feet, and enjoy a spectacular view. The mountain falls away steeply to the west in a sea of fir trees as the Sonoma Valley extends far to the south toward San Francisco Bay. Vineyards and small oak-covered hills line the valley floor. Broad, flat-topped Sonoma Mountain rises dramatically on the far side of the valley.

After enjoying the awesome view, proceed up the trail, entering the woods briefly before crossing along the bottom of a large patch of chaparral. Beyond the dry brush, keep climbing along the border between the forest that falls away below the trail and grass-covered slopes overhead. A pair of switchbacks climbs onto the open slopes, crossing some rocky outcroppings along the way. Continuing to the north, the path crosses some chaparral-covered slopes. Even though the trail is not in the forest cover, tall trees on either side of you block the views.

After a little more climbing, the trail finally levels off, and the path crosses an exposed ridge with a nice view to the west. All too soon the trail dives back into the forest and begins climbing again. However, this marks the final ascent of the hike. Make the push up the last 0.15 mile to a trail junction. To the right, the Goodspeed-Nattkemper Trail completes the final, short leg to the top of Hood Mountain. However, there are no views from the summit, which is generally only of interest to peak baggers. Instead, turn left at the fork and hike 0.1 mile to Gunsight Rock, where you can enjoy one of the finest views in the Wine Country. Vineyard-covered Sonoma Valley lies 2,000 feet below you. Almost the entire Sonoma Mountains range is visible

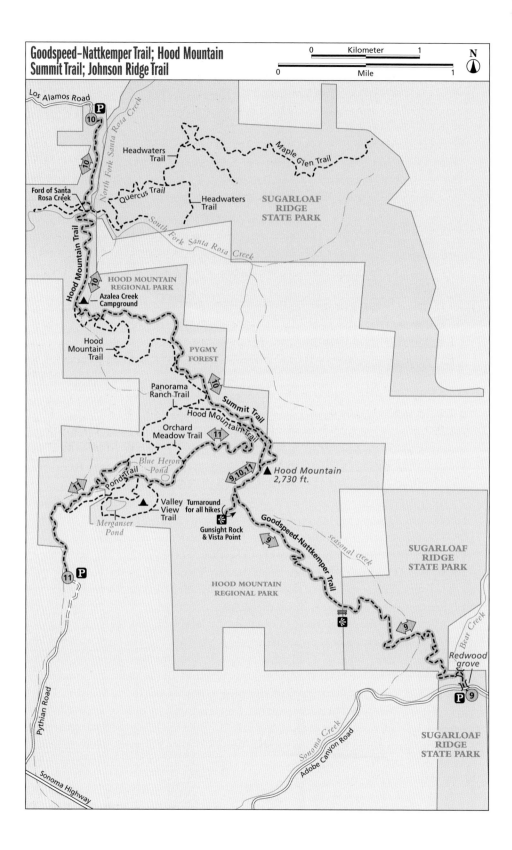

Goodspeed–Nattkemper Trail; Hood Mountain Summit Trail; Johnson Ridge Trail

0   Kilometer   1

0   Mile   1

N

Los Alamos Road

P

10

10

North Fork Santa Rosa Creek

Headwaters Trail

Maple Glen Trail

Ford of Santa Rosa Creek

Quercus Trail

Headwaters Trail

South Fork Santa Rosa Creek

SUGARLOAF RIDGE STATE PARK

Hood Mountain Trail

10

HOOD MOUNTAIN REGIONAL PARK

Azalea Creek Campground

Hood Mountain Trail

PYGMY FOREST

Panorama Ranch Trail

10

Summit Trail

Hood Mountain Trail

Orchard Meadow Trail

11

Blue Heron Pond

Pond Trail

9,10,11

Hood Mountain 2,730 ft.

11

Valley View Trail

Turnaround for all hikes

Gunsight Rock & Vista Point

Goodspeed–Nattkemper Trail

seasonal creek

SUGARLOAF RIDGE STATE PARK

Merganser Pond

9

11

P

HOOD MOUNTAIN REGIONAL PARK

9

Bear Creek

Pythian Road

Redwood grove

P

9

Sonoma Creek

Adobe Canyon Road

SUGARLOAF RIDGE STATE PARK

Sonoma Highway

across the valley. Large Sonoma Mountain looms to the south, while Bennett Mountain and the expansive uplands of Annadel State Park lies just to the north of Sonoma Mountain. The city of Santa Rosa spreads out far to the west. The northern Mayacamas Mountains, crowned by Cobb Mountain and Mount Saint Helena, form the horizon to the north.

From here retrace your steps back to the trailhead or, if you are able to arrange a shuttle, return to the fork and proceed up to the summit of Hood Mountain. From there take either the Summit Trail or the Johnson Ridge Trail to where you have left a second vehicle, or turn around and retrace your steps back to the trailhead.

Miles and Directions

0.0 From the trailhead, walk down into the redwoods and cross the bridge over Sonoma Creek.

0.2 Hike across the bridge over Bear Creek and begin the long ascent to the summit of Hood Mountain.

0.85 The trail crosses a dirt road.

1.1 Using a downed tree and boulders, cross a seasonal creek.

1.65 A cluster of boulders reveals the first view of the Sonoma Valley.

1.9 The trail emerges from the forest and traverses a grass-covered hillside with incredible views.

2.0 Depart Sugarloaf Ridge State Park and enter Hood Mountain Regional Park.

2.9 The trail finally levels off and crosses a ridge overlooking the Sonoma Valley.

3.25 Arrive at the junction with the spur trail leading to Gunsight Rock. Turn right here to reach the summit of Hood Mountain in 0.2 mile. The more scenic option is to turn left and hike to the end of the trail at Gunsight Rock.

3.35 Arrive at Gunsight Rock and enjoy the awesome spectacle.

10 Hood Mountain Summit Trail

The hike up the Hood Mountain Summit Trail is a journey through remote, rugged country. The lush Santa Rosa Creek headwaters are a stark contrast to the harsh climate found at the pygmy forest, an area where poor soils cause the trees to be stunted. The trail ends at Gunsight Rock and a magnificent view high above the Sonoma Valley.

See map for Hike 9.
Total Distance: 8.4 miles out and back (shuttle is possible)
Hiking Time: About 5 hours
Difficulty: Strenuous
Elevation Gain: 1,950 feet
Season: All year
Canine Compatibility: Dogs are permitted on leash

Fees: $7 parking fee at the trailhead
Trail Contact: Hood Mountain Regional Park, 3000 Los Alamos Rd., Santa Rosa, CA 95409; (707) 565-2041; http://parks.sonomacounty .ca.gov/Get_Outdoors/Parks/Hood_Mountain_ Regional_Park_Open_Space_Preserve.aspx
Other: Requires crossing a stream that may be impassable after storms and in the spring

Finding the trailhead: *From Santa Rosa:* Starting at the intersection of CA 12 and US 101 in Santa Rosa, drive east on CA 12 for 1.4 miles. At the freeway's end, turn left onto Farmers Lane and continue for 1 mile. Turn right onto 4th Street / CA 12 and drive east for 3.5 miles. Turn right onto Los Alamos Road and drive 2.3 miles. Veer left to stay on Los Alamos Road and proceed for 2.9 miles to the end of the road at the park's trailhead. GPS: N38°29.29683' / W122°34.33083'
   From Kenwood: Drive north on CA 12 for 5.1 miles. Turn right onto Los Alamos Road and drive 2.3 miles. Veer left to stay on Los Alamos Road and proceed for 2.9 miles to the end of the road at the park's trailhead.

The Hike

Hood Mountain, the highlight of Hood Mountain Regional Park, is one of the most rugged and spectacular peaks in the Wine Country. Gunsight Rock, which forms the mountain's craggy west face, is an impressive and scenic landmark that dominates the northern end of the Sonoma Valley. Rather than the high but rounded peaks that characterize much of the Mayacamas Mountains, Hood Mountain has the appearance of a *real* mountain: rocky, vertical, and towering high above everything in its area. Indeed, the mountain looms more than 2,000 feet above the valley floor.

Such a lofty summit demands the attention of nature lovers, and the hikes to the top of Hood Mountain do not disappoint. There are three routes to the top, and the Hood Mountain Summit Trail is possibly the most diverse and interesting of the three. The trail first passes through typical Wine Country terrain: grass-covered hills and mixed forests of oak, bay, fir, and madrone. After crossing Santa Rosa Creek, the trail climbs through the strange pygmy forest before making the final push to the

The trail crosses Santa Rosa Creek near its headwaters.

summit through more rock-strewn hillsides. The interesting geology and trees are complemented by quality views to the north. It is worth noting that the Summit Trail is distinct from the Hood Mountain Trail. The latter is an old road that runs roughly parallel to the narrow Summit Trail. It is not as scenic, but the two can be combined to make an interesting loop.

There are two options to begin the hike at the trailhead. On the east side of the parking lot, the Santa Rosa Creek Trail begins on the wide, main path. The other option is to the south, near the parking lot entrance. There the narrow Alder Glen Trail begins a switchbacking descent down the steep slopes. Both trails lead to the same place, but the Alder Glen route is a little more scenic. Once the two routes have joined, the main trail continues along the side of a steep canyon until it emerges from the trees and crosses a grass-covered hillside. The path makes a broad turn to the east and drops down to a level area, where there is a picnic space and a map of the Hood Mountain Regional Park.

Continue past the picnic area and arrive at the edge of Santa Rosa Creek. A narrow path splits off to the right and follows the creek downstream for almost 0.5 mile. To reach Hood Mountain, it is necessary to cross Santa Rosa Creek. Even though it is close to its headwaters, the creek is already large and has a steady flow throughout the year. No bridge crosses the water so it is necessary to hop on rocks. If the creek is full after a large storm, it may be impassable; it's best not to attempt a crossing in this case.

If conditions are safe and you are on the other side, turn right when the trail splits. To the left the path quickly enters the new McCormick addition to Sugarloaf Ridge

State Park, one of the more remote backcountry corners of the Wine Country that hikers can explore. Bearing right is the beginning of the Hood Mountain Trail. It starts the long, steady climb that does not let up until the summit of Hood Mountain. To get out of Santa Rosa Creek's deep canyon, the trail, which is an old fire road, makes a series of sweeping switchbacks. The grade makes you work, but it is never unreasonable. When the trail finally straightens out, it continues to climb through dense forest cover. About 1 mile beyond the crossing of Santa Rosa Creek, the trail finally arrives at Azalea Creek Campground, one of two backcountry campsites in Hood Mountain Regional Park. Here are outhouses, tables, fire pits, and even some benchwork to use as a counter. It is amazing to think that you could go backpacking so close to Santa Rosa and all of the wineries of the Sonoma Valley.

The trail splits at Azalea Creek Campground. The Hood Mountain Trail—the old fire road—is the main path leading to the top of the mountain. The alternate route is the Summit Trail. The latter is a narrow footpath that climbs through the famed pygmy forest that covers the north side of Hood Mountain. The main trail continues up through similar terrain but is much wider. The Summit Trail is the prettier of the two options and feels more remote and wild. It also gets you deeper into the pygmy forest. To find the trail, follow the spur through the campsites and cross a short bridge over Azalea Creek. This is the last water on the trail.

Once you have crossed the creek and begun climbing up the Summit Trail, be sure to stay left at a pair of junctions a little farther up the path. These lead back down to the Hood Mountain Trail. The route climbs through typical forest for about 0.5 mile before it begins to change. The firs, oaks, and laurels gradually begin to recede and are replaced by short and scrubby Sargent cypress. Though these trees are not endemic to the Wine Country, the majority of their habitat is within Sonoma and Napa Counties. These trees often grow to be 30 to 40 feet high, but here on Mount Hood, they have proliferated along a band of serpentine rock, which produces very harsh, inhospitable soils. Consequently, the trees here only grow to be 10 to 15 feet high. It has the appearance of being a glorified bonsai forest. The russet-colored rock that populates this area is weathered serpentine. The trail continues to climb through the pygmy forest for almost 1.75 miles. Along the way are clearings in the cypress that reveal great views of the Mayacamas Mountains to the north. The great bulk of Mount Saint Helena is prominently visible from the trail. The route crosses a road about 1.35 miles past Azalea Creek Campground. On the far side of the road, the trail plunges back into the cypress trees and continues climbing.

Finally, about 1.65 miles past the campground, the Summit Trail comes to within a few feet of the Hood Mountain Trail. A short path connects the two routes. Stay to the left and continue climbing on the Summit Trail. The cypress trees have begun to fade away and are replaced once again by firs, bays, and oaks. The trail climbs for another 0.3 mile through the forest before finally arriving at the top of Hood Mountain. Unfortunately, the summit amounts to a large clearing surrounded by brush and trees, and there is no view.

To find a vista worthy of a mountain as awesome as Hood, continue hiking to the west. The trail descends steeply, crossing over rocky outcroppings before reaching a junction. Stay to the right and hike just a little farther before arriving at the precipice of Gunsight Rock. From here the cliffs fall away steeply, and the Sonoma Valley spreads out below. It is an inspiring sight. When it is time to go, head back to the summit, where you can either return the way you came or hike down on the Hood Mountain Trail. This will return you to Azalea Creek Campground where you then retrace your steps back to the trailhead.

Miles and Directions

0.0 From the parking lot, descend the Alder Glen Trail down to the junction with the Hood Mountain Trail.

0.15 Turn right on the Hood Mountain Trail.

0.75 Cross over Santa Rosa Creek and begin a series of switchbacks that climb up the side of the canyon.

1.75 At the Azalea Creek Campground, turn left, cross over Azalea Creek, and begin the long climb up to the summit of Hood Mountain.

2.6 Enter the pygmy forest.

3.1 The trail crosses over a service road.

3.5 The pygmy forest comes to an end as the trail nears the summit of Hood Mountain.

3.9 Arrive at the summit of Hood Mountain. To reach Gunsight Rock, stay straight and continue on the trail, proceeding to the west.

4.2 The trail ends at Gunsight Rock, where there are amazing views. Retrace your steps back to the trailhead.

11 Johnson Ridge Trail

This hike is one of three difficult trails that climb to the summit of Hood Mountain, one of the most impressive and scenic mountains in the Wine Country. The trail climbs past creeks in deep gullies, scenic ponds and historic ranches on the way to the summit. The view from nearby Gunsight Rock is one of the best in the area.

See map for Hike 9.
Total Distance: 6.2 miles out and back
Hiking Time: About 4 hours
Difficulty: Strenuous
Elevation Gain: 1,900 feet
Season: All year
Canine Compatibility: Dogs are permitted on leash
Fees: $7 parking fee at the trailhead

Trail Contact: Hood Mountain Regional Park, 3000 Los Alamos Rd., Santa Rosa, CA 95409; (707) 565-2041; http://parks.sonomacounty .ca.gov/Get_Outdoors/Parks/Hood_Mountain_ Regional_Park_Open_Space_Preserve.aspx
Other: There is a backcountry campsite near Merganser Pond, making this a good option for backpackers.

Finding the trailhead: From Kenwood, drive north on CA 12 for 1.7 miles. Turn right onto Pythian Road and continue for 1.1 miles to the trailhead parking lot at the end of the road. GPS: N38°27.12150' / W122°34.44750'

The Hike

Gunsight Rock is the craggy west face of Hood Mountain, one of the most stunning mountains in the Wine Country. It rises over 2,000 feet above the vineyard-covered floor of the Sonoma Valley, creating one of the region's memorable and breathtaking skylines. Hikers standing on the top of Gunsight Rock enjoy a commanding view of the Sonoma Valley and much of the rest of Sonoma County.

There are three ways to reach the summit of Hood Mountain and nearby Gunsight Rock. Of the three, the Johnson Ridge Trail is the most direct. While the other trails approach the mountain from the north and south, the Johnson Ridge Trail climbs from the west. The Johnson Ridge Trail is composed of lower and upper sections that are connected by the Pond Trail. The hike climbs alongside a creek before passing ponds and a historic ranch on the way to the summit. It also has one of the few backcountry campsites in the Wine Country, making this a good option for backpackers.

To begin the hike, walk east along the Lower Johnson Ridge Trail, which skirts the edge of some private property. A pair of homes is just few feet from the route; please respect the privacy of the residents. The route soon intersects a paved service road just beyond the homes. Though a narrow footpath exists immediately adjacent to the road, it is easier to simply walk on the pavement because the road here climbs

The Johnson Ridge Trail winds along Blue Heron Pond.

steeply. During winter and spring, the creek can be heard crashing through the canyon below the road.

A little over 0.5 mile from the trailhead, the road passes a final private residence, perched on a hillside above the Valley of the Moon. The pavement ends here, and signs indicate that the route continues along a dirt service road. Shortly after passing through a gate, a trail splits off from the road and goes to the left. Though it parallels the service road, it is distinct enough that it is more pleasant to follow the path rather than the road. Eventually, however, the trail rejoins the road in time to cross the seasonal creek. When the creek is full, a thick plank is laid over the creek so hikers can cross with dry feet.

Once across the creek, the road curves around a bend, the trail veers off to the right into another single track. The trail climbs a second series of switchbacks through mixed oak woodland for 0.4 mile before intersecting the service road a final time. Stay right, going away from the road. Beyond this point the service road travels northeasterly and is dubbed the Panorama Ranch Trail, a route that connects to the Hood Mountain Summit Trail (Hike 10), which begins at the Los Alamos trailhead on the north side of the park. The footpath, now known as the Pond Trail, continues a little past the intersection and crosses a bridge before it splits again.

The most direct route to the summit is to the left, continuing on the Pond Trail. Stay left at all of the following junctions to go to Hood Mountain. However, it is worth pointing out that turning right here leads to a noteworthy destination. The

Gunsight Rock's epic view of the north end of the Sonoma Valley and the city of Santa Rosa.

path quickly deposits hikers at the edge of Merganser Pond, a scenic pond nestled in a small bowl. Following the trail on the east side of the pond leads to the primitive backpacker's camp, set amidst a nice grove of Douglas fir. The Valley View Trail climbs the ridge on the west side of pond where there is an excellent view of the Sonoma Valley. If you are looking for a shorter hiker, Merganser Pond and the Valley View Trail's semi-loop is a great destination.

Still on the route to the summit via the Pond Trail, the trail continues to climb moderately. A series of junctions appear in rapid succession: The first are trails coming up from Merganser Pond, and the last is the upper end of the Valley View Trail. At this point the Pond Trail is no longer single track but an old ranch road. It soon comes alongside Blue Heron Pond, a spring-fed pond. Past the small body of water, the trail crosses the creek again and enters Orchard Meadow. The meadow is predictably open and contains scraggly old fruit trees, true to the area's name. In the midst of the meadow, the Pond Trail reaches another junction. Approaching from the left is a spur off of the aforementioned Panorama Ranch Trail. To the right the Upper Johnson Ridge Trail begins the ascent of the hike to the summit.

The route starts out fairly straight and level, passing the upper portions of Orchard Meadow. Above the trail and to the left are the remnants of an old homestead. After 0.25 mile the Knight's Retreat Trail splits off to the right, leading to an overlook of Orchard Meadow. From there the Upper Johnson Ridge Trail steepens and begins making broad switchbacks through the forest. A bit over 0.5 mile later, the trail finally reaches the top of the ridge.

Up to this point, the route has passed through mixed oak woodland. Upon reaching the top of the ridge, it suddenly enters into the uppermost reaches of the pygmy forest that covers much of the northern side of Hood Mountain (see Hike 10). From here, the trail continues in a steep, direct line up to the summit. This part of the trail is yet another old road and climbs directly up to the summit of Hood Mountain.

The summit is a bit anticlimactic because it is just a large clearing amid dense manzanita with extremely limited views. All is not lost, however. On the west side of the clearing, the trail continues to Gunsight Rock. It descends steeply at first, passing through a tunnel cut into the thick manzanita. Eventually the trail levels out and climbs several rock formations. At the intersection with the Goodspeed-Nattkemper Trail (Hike 9), one of the three routes to the summit of Hood Mountain, stay to the right and climb gently for another 0.3 mile. The trail finally reaches Gunsight Rock, where you can enjoy one of the best views in Sonoma County, a vista that reaches from the northern Mayacamas Mountains all the way down to the Mission Peak area in San Jose.

Miles and Directions

0.0 Begin the hike at the trailhead parking area and follow the trail past some private homes and along the edge of the road.

0.5 Veer left off the road and climb some narrow switchbacks, passing some water tanks as you climb.

0.7 Merge back onto the paved road briefly and follow it for a short distance before veering off the road to the left to begin climbing a second set of switchbacks.

1.1 At the top of the switchbacks, stay right at the beginning of the Pond Trail.

1.2 Cross over a creek and then stay left at three successive forks. The trails splitting off to the right lead to Merganser Pond and the backcountry campground. The first fork begins the Valley View Trail, which passes the pond and has a great view of the Sonoma Valley before climbing back up to the Pond Trail.

1.6 After passing Blue Heron Pond, turn right onto the Orchard Meadow Trail. This path passes through the old orchard and homestead then begins to climb steeply toward the summit of Hood Mountain.

2.35 Turn right onto the Hood Mountain Trail.

2.7 Reach the summit of Hood Mountain. To get to the awesome view at Gunsight Rock, continue through the summit clearing (which has no view) and begin hiking the Goodspeed-Natkemper Trail.

2.95 Stay straight at the fork.

3.1 Arrive at Gunsight Rock. Enjoy the view! Then retrace your steps back to the trailhead.

12 Lawndale Trail

The hike on Annadel State Park's Lawndale Trail explores the park's remote southern backcountry. The trail climbs through dense forest and extensive second-growth redwood groves before arriving at the interesting Ledson Marsh area, where solitude and wildlife are abundant.

Total Distance: 6.5 miles out and back
Hiking Time: About 3 hours
Difficulty: Moderate
Elevation Gain: 775 feet
Season: All year

Canine Compatibility: Dogs are permitted on leash
Fees: None
Trail Contact: Annadel State Park, 6201 Channel Dr., Santa Rosa, CA 95409; (707) 539-3911; www.parks.ca.gov/?page_id=480

Finding the trailhead: From Kenwood, drive north on CA 12 for 0.7 mile. Turn left onto Lawndale Road. Continue on Lawndale for 1.1 miles, making a dogleg after 0.6 mile. The large, unmarked parking lot is on the right. GPS: N38°25.05617'/W122°34.51900'

The Hike

The southern half of Annadel State Park sees far less activity than the busy northern section. This is because of a combination of factors, but the most significant one is simply the southern trailhead's distance from the population center in Santa Rosa. The lighter use in no way indicates that the landscape is less scenic. The best access to this lonely area is the Lawndale Trail, which climbs up the eastern side of the park and leads to the Ledson Marsh, an interesting sibling to Lake Ilsanjo in the northern part of Annadel State Park. Boasting a scenic mix of oak woodlands, redwood forests, chaparral, and the semi-riparian marsh environment, the Lawndale Trail is a great way to enjoy Annadel State Park without having to share the trail.

At the trailhead, go uphill, climbing a wide path with little tree cover. The trail passes a home on private property on the right before quickly leaving the trappings of civilization. The grade is moderate and heads up the hill for 0.2 mile before the path makes a sharp turn to the left. Now passing through a forest of oak, madrone, and bay, the route continues to climb and soon makes switchbacks again. The trail emerges briefly from the forest at 0.65 mile, where there are some limited views of the Sonoma Valley. A picnic table along the trail is a nice place to stop and enjoy the views.

Continuing, the trail soon reenters the forest and continues to head uphill at a steady but moderate grade. Redwood trees soon begin to appear along the trail. Though none of these are particularly large, it is an enjoyable change from the usual mixed forest that dominates Annadel State Park.

Deer warily walk along the edge of Ledson Marsh.

Eventually crossing a shallow gully, the narrow path begins to round a wooded bluff and soon emerges from the forest about 1.35 miles from the trailhead. This is not a natural break in the woodlands but a clearing cut into the forest to provide access to a power line slung high overhead. Thankfully the trail switches back and immediately reenters the woods, passing more redwoods as the trail proceeds to climb moderately. After another 0.65 mile of redwood forest, the landscape suddenly shifts to a drier, chaparral-like environment. The path cuts through the brush for 0.3 mile before it reaches the power line for a second time. Trails split off on both sides of the main path, but just follow the power line, continuing straight and passing beneath the wires.

Having crossed beneath the power line, the Lawndale Trail levels off and maintains a westerly direction. At 2.75 miles from the trailhead, the path intersects the Marsh Trail. Heading straight here leads to the even more remote central part of Annadel State Park before finally connecting to the Lake Ilsanjo region. Stay left, however, passing through low brush and catching glimpses of the Ledson Marsh for the first time. After 0.2 mile from the intersection, the Marsh Trail crosses a small bridge that spans Schultz Creek, the marsh's outlet. Once across the bridge, the route skirts the edge of the marsh through oak woodland for another 0.25 mile before arriving at a picnic area. From the picnic table, a narrow use trail leads through a grassy area down to the edge of the reed-choked marsh. In the distance low ridges covered with oak and fir trees form the perimeter of the basin that contains the marsh.

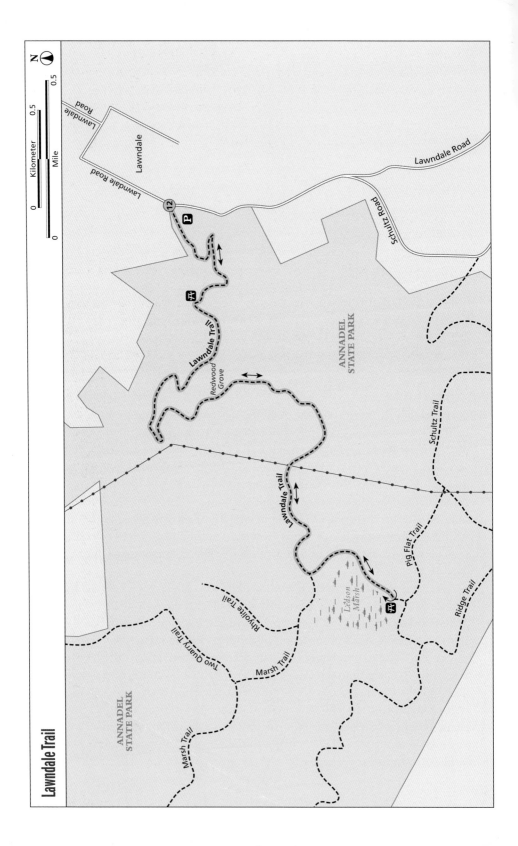

Lawndale Trail

Lawndale Road

Lawndale Road

Lawndale

12

Lawndale Road

Schultz Road

ANNADEL
STATE PARK

Lawndale Trail

Redwood
Grove

Lawndale Trail

Schultz Trail

Pig Flat Trail

Ridge Trail

Rhyolite Trail

Two Quarry Trail

Marsh Trail

Ledson
Marsh

Marsh Trail

ANNADEL
STATE PARK

N

Kilometer   0   0.5   0.5

Mile   0   0.5

In the distance the summit of Hood Mountain and its massive, craggy face—called Gunsight Rock—loom impressively beyond the marsh. Though the trail continues, this is the best place to turn around and return to the trailhead. For those looking for more exploration, the nearby Ridge Trail climbs the western rim of the marsh basin and has interesting views to the east. Inexplicably, there is no trail completely encircling the marsh, so continuing on the Ridge Trail will ultimately lead far away from the marsh and the return route.

Miles and Directions

0.0 The hike begins at the trailhead kiosk, climbing uphill.

0.25 The trail crosses a small creek and soon makes one hairpin turn.

0.65 Arrive at a small picnic area. The trail soon enters an extensive redwood forest.

1.35 After hiking through the redwoods, the trail suddenly emerges into a clearing beneath a power line. It makes another hairpin turn and reenters the redwoods.

2.3 After passing through some chaparral, the trail passes beneath the power line again. Trails follow the line in either direction. Stay straight, continuing on the Lawndale Trail.

2.75 Turn left at the junction with the Marsh Trail.

3.25 Arrive at the Ledson Marsh picnic area. Retrace your steps back to the trailhead.

13 Central Annadel Loop

This hike travels through the heart of Annadel State Park. It climbs to the park's central uplands and skirts two large meadows. After winding around Lake Ilsanjo, the nexus of many of the park's trails, it loops back through deep forests to the trailhead.

Total Distance: 5.3-mile loop
Hiking Time: About 3 hours
Difficulty: Moderate
Elevation Gain: 650 feet
Season: All year

Canine Compatibility: Dogs are permitted on leash
Fees: $6 entrance fee
Trail Contact: Annadel State Park, 6201 Channel Dr., Santa Rosa, CA 95409; (707) 539-3911; www.parks.ca.gov/?page_id=480

Finding the trailhead: Starting at the intersection of US 101 and CA 12, drive east on CA 12 for 1.5 miles. Turn left onto Farmers Lane and continue for 0.8 mile. Turn right onto Montgomery Drive. Stay on this road for 2.7 miles and then turn right onto Channel Drive. Continue on Channel Drive for 1.5 miles, passing the entrance station and parking at the signed trailhead for the North Burma Trail. GPS: N38°26.91450'/W122°37.62000'

The Hike

Annadel State Park is a wonderful natural oasis surrounded by the urban development of Santa Rosa. Bordered by the city on three sides, the 5,092-acre park is a rugged collection of high peaks, dense forests, vast meadows, and numerous creeks. Lying at the heart of the park is Lake Ilsanjo, a small reservoir that forms the nexus of an expansive trail network coursing through the park. The lake, built in the 1950s before the property became a park, is surrounded by fir-covered ridges and is one of Annadel's centerpieces. By combining a series of trails, a fantastic loop can be assembled that highlights most of the park's best features, including a boisterous creek, sweeping meadows, oak woodlands, dense fir forests, Lake Ilsanjo itself, and views of craggy Hood Mountain rising on the far side of the Sonoma Valley. This is, in many ways, the premier hike in Annadel State Park, sampling a variety of the different environs found in the park.

At the trailhead along Channel Drive, note the trail running parallel to the road; this is the return route from the loop. Heading out from the trailhead, the North Burma Trail climbs immediately through the canyon of an unnamed creek. The moderate grade is made easier by shady forest and the sounds of the creek, which still has water into the early summer.

Though it continues to climb, the path soon veers away from the creek and climbs through a pair of switchbacks before straightening out and continuing to run parallel to the creek. Soon the water and trail part ways, and the path levels

A large meadow in Annadel State Park.

off as it passes through heavy forest. The woods give way to a drier area with lots of manzanita before arriving at a junction 0.7 mile from the trailhead. Stay to the right, which is now the Live Oak Trail. Though the path stays within the woods, it maintains a course that remains close to the edge of False Lake Meadow. The large grassy plain is surrounded by oak forest and is quite scenic. Watch for wild turkeys meandering through the meadow. This part of Annadel seems peaceful and remote, yet the neighborhoods of Santa Rosa lie just on the other side of the bluff on the far side of the meadow.

As the trail continues south, it follows the crest of a very subtle ridge. Views of False Lake Meadow increasingly improve until the trail comes out of the forest and crosses a treeless divide between the large False Lake Meadow on the right and a smaller rocky meadow on the left. On the far side of the treeless area, the path arrives at a second junction 1.5 miles from the trailhead. Stay straight and proceed along the low divide.

The trail is now named the Rough-Go Trail. Leaving False Lake Meadow behind, the wide path passes through a band of trees beyond which views open up to the east, revealing another, larger meadow falling away to the left from the divide. The rugged visage of Hood Mountain towers above the oak- and fir-covered ridge on the far side of the meadow. The trail soon passes through a band of trees and then cuts across a third, smaller meadow before reentering an oak forest once again. After another 0.2 mile, the trail arrives at the edge of Lake Ilsanjo.

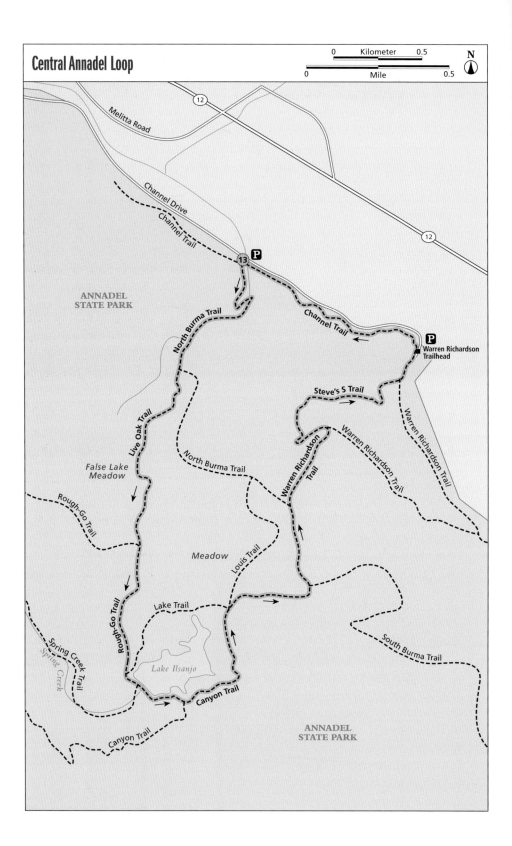

Central Annadel Loop

0 Kilometer 0.5
0 Mile 0.5

N

Melitta Road

12

Channel Drive

Channel Trail

13 P

ANNADEL
STATE PARK

North Burma Trail

Channel Trail

P
Warren Richardson
Trailhead

Live Oak Trail

Steve's S Trail

North Burma Trail

Warren Richardson Trail

Warren Richardson Trail

Warren Richardson Trail

False Lake
Meadow

Rough-Go Trail

Meadow

Louis Trail

Rough-Go Trail

Lake Trail

Spring Creek Trail

Spring Creek

Lake Ilsanjo

Canyon Trail

South Burma Trail

Canyon Trail

Canyon Trail

ANNADEL
STATE PARK

The 26-acre Lake Ilsanjo rests in a large bowl at the headwaters of Spring Creek. The impounded creek has formed a scenic, reed-lined lake with a tree-shaded shoreline. When the trail first arrives at the lake, it crosses the top of a large, deep gully that serves as a spillway when the lake is full. Though a release system has been installed to allow the lake's overflow water to exit at the earth dam and flow down Spring Creek, water still flows down the gully in the spring. Cross the wide dam, remembering that it may have a high flow in the spring. On the far side, pass through a band of trees and then cross over the dam.

Once across the dam, the path joins the Canyon Trail and proceeds around the south and east sides of the lake. Stay straight at the junction with the Canyon Trail, maintaining a course around the lake. At the northeast corner of Lake Ilsanjo, the trail comes to a four-way junction, 0.6 mile from the dam. Turn to the right onto the Warren Richardson Trail and begin a short ascent on the wide trail. Views to the west open briefly before the trail enters thicker woods and continues to the north.

After about a mile from the beginning of the Warren Richardson Trail, the path reaches a picnic area. While the Warren Richardson Trail makes a turn to the right at the picnic area, the Steve's S Trail departs to the left. Take the Steve's S Trail and descend through dense fir forest for 0.8 mile to the large staging area at the trailhead for the Warren Richardson Trail. From there hike on either Channel Drive or the footpath that runs parallel to it for 0.7 mile back to the trailhead.

Miles and Directions

0.0 Begin the hike at the trailhead, climbing almost immediately into a small drainage via the North Burma Trail.

0.95 Stay right and begin hiking on the Live Oak Trail.

1.5 At a junction, stay left. This puts you briefly on the Rough-Go Trail.

1.9 The Rough-Go Trail merges into the Lake Trail. A few yards away, the combined trail crosses over Lake Ilsanjo's spillway channel.

2.0 Arrive at the lake's dam. Cross the dam and continue hiking around Lake Ilsanjo on the Lake Trail.

2.25 The Lake Trail joins the Canyon Trail and continues around Lake Ilsanjo.

2.7 Turn right onto the wide Warren Richardson Trail.

3.65 At a picnic area, turn left onto the Steve's S Trail.

4.55 The trail ends at the Warren Richardson Trail parking lot. Hike through the parking area and turn left onto Channel Drive. Either walk on the road or the footpath just to the left.

5.3 Arrive back at the trailhead, completing the loop.

14 Lake Ilsanjo–Spring Canyon Loop

The loop through the west side of Annadel State Park is a scenic hike that samples many of the best features found in the state park, including a deep canyon, large meadows, and Lake Ilsanjo. The western entrance is less frequently used but provides access to some of Annadel's popular landmarks.

Total Distance: 5.0-mile loop
Hiking Time: About 3 hours
Difficulty: Moderate
Elevation Gain: 450 feet
Season: All year

Canine Compatibility: Dogs are not permitted
Fees: None
Trail Contact: Annadel State Park, 6201 Channel Dr., Santa Rosa, CA 95409; (707) 539-3911; www.parks.ca.gov/?page_id=480

Finding the trailhead: Starting at the intersection of CA 12 and US 101, go east on CA 12 for 1.6 miles until the freeway ends. Go straight through the signal and continue east on Hoen Avenue for 1.1 miles. Turn right onto Summerfield Road and drive 0.4 mile. Turn left onto Carissa Avenue and proceed for another 0.4 mile. Park in the pullout on the right side of the road. GPS: N38°26.22950'/W122°39.19233'

The Hike

Rising like a green-and-gold wall above the east side of Santa Rosa, the highlands of Annadel State Park form a natural barrier to the city. The park is the northernmost extension of the Sonoma Mountains, a mountain range composed of volcanic debris. Straddling the divide between the Santa Rosa Plain and the Sonoma Valley, the park consists mostly of a large plateau that is covered in a patchwork of large meadows, forested areas, and patches of chaparral. The only major peak in the park, Bennett Peak, lies on the western edge of the plateau.

An extensive trail network winds through the park, connecting a variety of destinations. The heart of the park is Lake Ilsanjo. The reservoir is at the nexus of the trail network. Even though the west side of the park is adjacent to the urban development of Santa Rosa, few trails begin on that side of Annadel. One exception is the Vietnam Veterans Memorial Trail, which serves as a backdoor to the trail network. The loop from this trail to Lake Ilsanjo features many of the best elements of the trails in Annadel State Park. It has rugged, rock-strewn prairie and meadows, Lake Ilsanjo, and a deep canyon with a raucous creek and a few errant redwoods.

The hike begins at the pullout parking area for the Vietnam Veterans Memorial Trail. Follow the trail up an open slope to the top of a hill where you pass a fantastic view of Santa Rosa along the way. At the top of the hill, a wide, rocky, very steep path drops down the far side. If this route looks unpleasant, hang a left at the top of the hill and continue on the trail for 0.1 mile, then take one of the side trails to the right.

Lake Ilsanjo.

These paths connect to the trail that descends down into Spring Creek's canyon, quickly passing the first, very steep, rocky route.

Stay on the trail for another 0.1 mile. When you arrive at a bridge and a dirt fire road, stay right and hike up the fire road. This is the beginning of the Canyon Trail, a path that leads to Lake Ilsanjo, one of Annadel State Park's most popular features. The old road climbs along one of Spring Creek's tributaries for 0.5 mile before it enters a large, rocky meadow. Continue up the trail through the grassy area until the path reaches a gate. The gate is on the park's boundary, and the area beyond it is private land. Make a sharp turn to the left here and climb through a long band of oak trees before arriving at an even larger meadow that is littered with boulders. Cross the meadow and then reenter the forest before arriving at a picnic area next to the junction with the Marsh Trail. This long trail connects to the Ledson Marsh (Hike 12) at the south end of the state park.

From the junction with the Marsh Trail, continue on the main path as it turns east and makes a slight descent to a junction with the Lake Trail, which encircles Lake Ilsanjo. Turn right and follow the path around the lake. The shore of the lake is lined with tall reeds in most places, but it is still a scenic and welcome presence in this large basin. At 2.9 miles from the trailhead, you arrive at a large junction. Stay to the left and continue to hike around the lake. As the trail rounds the north side, a large, scenic meadow opens up to the right. The wooded summit of Bennett Peak to the south makes an imposing backdrop. The route is soon joined by the Rough-Go Trail

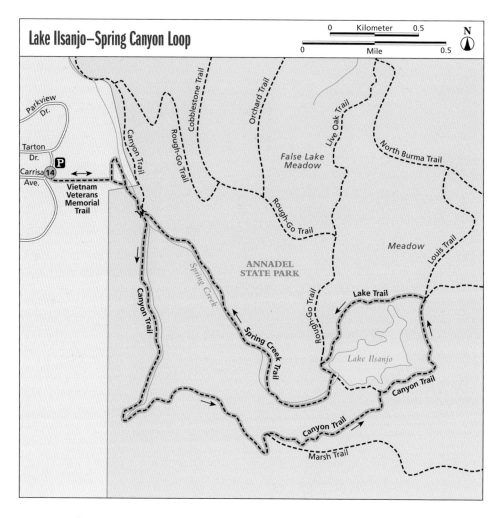

arriving from the north. Stay left and walk a little farther, crossing over the lake's spillway just before arriving at the dam, about 3.5 miles from the beginning of the hike.

Just before the dam, the Spring Creek Trail veers off to the right. Follow this path down into Spring Creek Canyon. It is very rocky as it crosses open slopes but it will soon have easier tread when it reenters the thick forest that surrounds Spring Creek Canyon. At the bottom of the grade, the trail passes through a little valley and then crosses a seasonal creek that is fed by Lake Ilsanjo's spillway. Past the small valley, the canyon is increasingly narrow, and daylight becomes scarce due to the heavy forest canopy. A few redwoods are scattered throughout the valley. The creek maintains a decent flow through most of the year and makes hiking through the canyon very pleasant. Finally, 0.65 mile after crossing the lake's outlet creek, the path arrives back at the bridge at the end of the Vietnam Veterans Memorial Trail. Turn left, cross the bridge, and retrace your steps back to the trailhead.

Miles and Directions

0.0 Begin hiking up the Vietnam Veterans Memorial Trail, enjoying good views of the city of Santa Rosa.

0.2 At a fork, either descend a steep, rocky section of trail down a slope or follow the trail to the left for about 100 feet before turning right and dropping down to a trail and proceeding to the right.

0.4 Go right at another fork by a bridge and begin hiking up the Canyon Trail. The return portion of the loop crosses the bridge on the left.

1.2 The trail arrives at a locked gate in a small, level valley. Stay to the left to continue up the trail.

1.9 Stay to the left at the junction with the Marsh Trail and continue climbing toward Lake Ilsanjo.

2.4 At the edge of Lake Ilsanjo, turn right onto the Lake Trail and follow the path around the lake.

2.9 Turn left to continue on the Lake Trail.

3.4 Stay left at the junction with the Rough-Go Trail and cross over Lake Ilsanjo's overflow channel. A short distance later, turn right onto the Spring Creek Trail, just before crossing over the dam that creates Lake Ilsanjo.

3.9 Cross over the bottom of the usually dry Lake Ilsanjo overflow channel.

4.6 Turn left and cross the bridge over Spring Creek. Once across, turn right back onto the Vietnam Veterans Memorial Trail.

5.0 Arrive back at the trailhead.

15 Spring Lake

This loop is a scenic hike around Spring Lake, a small flood-control reservoir on the edge of Santa Rosa. With natural areas interspersed with areas developed with recreational amenities, it is a great option for an easy hike just moments away from the city.

Total Distance: 2.25-mile loop
Hiking Time: About 1 hour
Difficulty: Easy
Elevation Gain: 80 feet
Season: All year
Canine Compatibility: Dogs are permitted
Fees: $7 parking fee at the trailhead
Trail Contact: Spring Lake Regional Park, 393 Violetti Rd., Santa Rosa, CA 95409; (707)

539-809; http://parks.sonomacounty.ca.gov/ Get_Outdoors/Parks/Spring_Lake_Regional_ Park.aspx
Other: The hike passes numerous picnic areas, a swimming lagoon, and concession stand. The hike can also be lengthened and made into a lollipop by starting at nearby Howarth Park and hiking in from Lake Ralphine.

Finding the trailhead: Starting at the intersection of CA 12 and US 101, go east on CA 12 for 1.6 miles until the freeway ends. Go straight through the signal and continue east on Hoen Avenue for 1.1 miles, crossing over Summerfield Road then immediately turning left onto Newanga Avenue. Stay right to continue on Newanga and proceed 0.6 mile to the park entrance station. Park at the Oak Knolls picnic area to begin the hike. GPS: 38°26.97383'/W122°39.07833'

The Hike

Despite being the fifth largest city in the San Francisco Bay Area, Santa Rosa has done an excellent job retaining a degree of small town charm. Numerous factors have contributed to this success, including the maintenance of greenbelts between it and neighboring cities like Sebastopol and Rohnert Park. The city's geography has helped as well, with hills and valleys breaking the populated areas up into distinct neighborhoods and communities.

Santa Rosa is also blessed with a significant amount of open space along its perimeter that permanently hems in development and ensures that rural and natural areas will continue to be enjoyed by future generations. One of the largest blocks of open space is the Annadel–Spring Lake–Howarth Park complex. These three parks, respectively owned by the state, county, and city, form a contiguous block of public land right on the edge of the city. Spring Lake lies at the heart of this collection of parks, a friendly, accessible oasis where you can enjoy hiking, fishing, and some fine views just moments away from the city. Spring Lake is formed by impounding Spring Creek, a tributary of Santa Rosa Creek. It begins on a high plateau in the heart of Annadel State Park, flowing out of Lake Ilsanjo and through a deep canyon before reaching Spring Lake. The trail is popular with locals, especially on weekends. Although there

Hills rise above Spring Lake.

is plenty of activity and development around the lake, there are still some beautiful, natural sections.

The trail begins at the picnic area set amid large oak trees. Follow the trail down the edge of the dam to the main loop. Turn left to begin the hike around the lake. The path is wide and paved. It stays close to the water, and there are great views to the north toward Saddle Mountain. A small island occupies the center of Spring Lake's south end. Anglers often cast from the shore along this stretch of trail, and geese are frequent visitors.

After easy walking for 0.4 mile, the trail arrives at a large boat ramp. On the far side of the concrete ramp are a few options for proceeding. One trail continues to follow the water's edge, beginning at the lowest point on the ramp. Higher up, the main path passes a large grassy area as it climbs up a low rise. Picnic areas line the trail, and restrooms are there. These are the two most popular routes. The best option is to look a few dozen yards up the ramp from the water for a narrow trail marked by a small sign. This path is the least used and the most natural. It passes through a beautiful oak forest and rocky outcroppings. After hiking on this scenic path for 0.35 mile, it arrives at a junction. Turn right and follow the trail back down to the water's edge. Turn left and continue the loop around the lake.

The main path around the lake occasionally runs parallel to narrow fishermen's trails that travel right along the water's edge. These can be great options for hiking the loop, but in the spring they can be very muddy or even completely inundated.

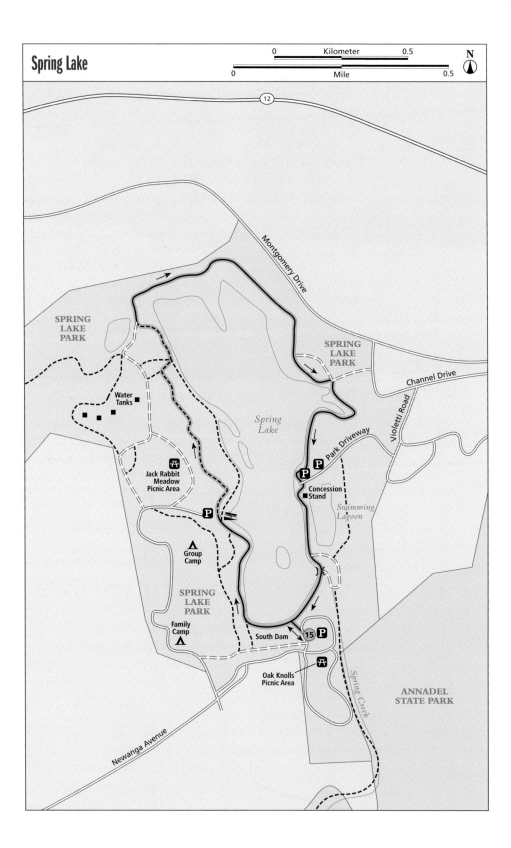

Spring Lake

Montgomery Drive

SPRING
LAKE
PARK

SPRING
LAKE
PARK

Channel Drive

Violetti Road

Water
Tanks

Spring
Lake

Park Driveway

Jack Rabbit
Meadow
Picnic Area

P

Concession
Stand

Swimming
Lagoon

P

Group
Camp

SPRING
LAKE
PARK

Family
Camp

South Dam

15 P

Oak Knolls
Picnic Area

Spring Creek

ANNADEL
STATE PARK

Newanga Avenue

N

0   Kilometer   0.5

0   Mile   0.5

About 0.9 mile from the trailhead, the loop passes a major junction with the trail coming from Lake Ralphine and Howarth Park. Stay to the right and hike along the north end of Spring Lake. Ahead lies the main dam that impounds the lake. There are smaller dams at the south end and at the northwest corner, but these are only necessary for flood control. If the water rises significantly, the lake will overflow, but the secondary dams will keep Santa Rosa from flooding. A narrow path follows the lake below the dam, but like other unofficial trails, it may be too muddy or flooded to cross. Instead, climb onto the dam and follow the path across. The wooded high country of Annadel State Park rises to the south, and Saddle Mountain and other peaks of the Mayacamas Mountains loom to the north.

On the far side of the dam, stay right at a junction with a trail coming from a parking area to the east. The path drops back down to the lake's level and continues through a cluster of trees and thick grasses of a marshy area. Soon the area opens up, and the trail skirts the edge of the parking area for the swimming lagoon. Pass the lagoon on a narrow strip of land that is flanked on the right by Spring Lake. Cross a bridge and round the south end of the lake. Turn left onto the trail that climbs back up the southern dam to complete the loop.

Miles and Directions

0.0 Begin hike at the large picnic area. Descend down the dam and turn left onto the main loop around Spring Lake.

0.4 Arrive at the boat launch. Look for the marked dirt path departing the far side of the ramp, a few dozen yards above the water.

0.8 When the trail dead-ends at a fork, turn right and then quickly turn left, rejoining the main loop around the lake.

1.0 Stay right at a fork and continue around the north side of Spring Lake.

1.2 Arrive at the top of the north dam.

1.4 Descend the east end of the dam, returning to the area adjacent to the lake.
    The trail passes the large parking area for the swimming lagoon and other activities.

1.9 Pass the swimming lagoon.

2.25 Turn left onto the trail climbing back up to the trailhead. Arrive at the trailhead, completing the hike.

16 Taylor Mountain

The hike up Taylor Mountain is possibly the best hike in the Santa Rosa area. Despite starting on the edge of the city, it quickly leaves the urban area behind and immerses hikers in beautiful, grass-covered hills and incredible views of most of central Sonoma County and the Mayacamas Mountains.

Total Distance: 5-mile reverse lollipop
Hiking Time: About 3.5 hours
Difficulty: Moderate
Elevation Gain: 1,100 feet
Season: All year
Canine Compatibility: Dogs are permitted on leash
Fees: $7

Trail Contact: Taylor Mountain Regional Park, 2080 Kawana Springs Terrace, Santa Rosa, CA 95404; (707) 539-8092; http://parks .sonomacounty.ca.gov/Get_Outdoors/Parks/ Taylor_Mountain_Regional_Park_and_Open_ Space_Preserve.aspx
Other: Cattle continue to graze on Taylor Mountain and may be encountered on the trail.

Finding the trailhead: Starting at the intersection of CA 12 and US 101, go east on CA 12 for 0.3 mile. Take the South East Street exit and merge onto Bennett Valley Road. Turn right onto Brookwood and drive 0.5 mile; Brookwood turns right and becomes Aston. Turn left onto Linwood and then right onto Brookwood again. Continue south for 0.5 mile, then turn right onto Kawana Springs Road. Go 0.1 mile, then turn left onto Meda Avenue. Turn left onto Kawana Springs Terrace, drive 0.4 mile, and then turn into the parking area on the right. GPS: N38°24.91400'/W122°41.56283'

The Hike

Taylor Mountain is one of the most recognizable landmarks on the Santa Rosa skyline. It rises over 1,200 feet above the Santa Rosa Plain, forming an impressive part of the natural barrier on the east side of the city, along with Bennett Peak and the Annadel State Park highlands. Along with these neighboring areas, Taylor Mountain is part of the Sonoma Mountains, a chain of uplands that stretch from the city of Santa Rosa south to the tidal marshes just north of San Pablo Bay.

Like the nearby Mayacamas Mountains, the Sonoma Mountains are composed of rocks deposited by ancient lava flows. The rounded summits and hills give little indication of the fiery origin of these mountains. On its east side, Taylor Mountain is separated from the bulk of the Sonoma Mountains by lovely Bennett Valley, the home of one of central Sonoma County's appellations. The hike up Taylor Mountain is a gorgeous trip, with wonderful views of Santa Rosa and Rohnert Park nearly the entire way. The trail zigzags up the side of the mountain before reaching an old road and following it the rest of the way to the top. On the return trip, an alternate trail splits off to the west and descends through a secluded valley on the way back to the trailhead.

Trail view of Santa Rosa and Mount Saint Helena.

The hike begins at the large parking area below a pair of enormous water towers. Two trails depart from the trailhead. Begin with the one on the left. It departs the trailhead and climbs gently up toward the water tanks. After you pass the tanks, head through a band of trees. As you round a bend, the north flank of Taylor Mountain comes into view. A wide dirt path runs steeply up the slope. This old ranch road is the quick option for climbing the mountain; gaining over 600 feet in 0.65 mile, it is direct and to the point. A better option is to hike 0.45 mile from the trailhead to a junction and then turn right onto a footpath that heads west. Rather than making the steep climb, enjoy a more leisurely grade as the trail follows a series of switchbacks. While this type of trail engineering can be tedious, on Taylor Mountain it heightens the enjoyment, not because it eases the grade, but because it brings so many different areas into view.

Near the junction, northeast Santa Rosa is visible to the north, but as you head west, central Santa Rosa and the west side of the Santa Rosa Plain unfold below the mountain. After a few broad switchbacks, the trail straightens out and traverses a low ridge. At 1.1 miles from the trailhead, the path arrives at a junction. Stay to the left; the route to the right is the return leg of the loop. Past the junction, the path cuts across the steep ranch road and begins a second series of switchbacks. The trail and road cross a few more times before they finally merge at the top of the long grade, about 1.7 miles from the trailhead.

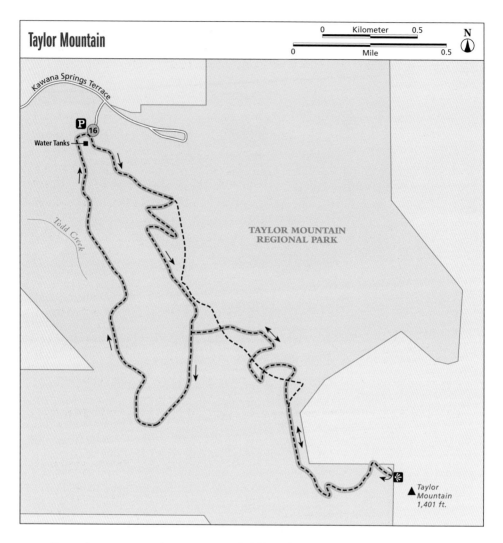

Kawana Springs Terrace

P 16

Water Tanks

Todd Creek

**TAYLOR MOUNTAIN
REGIONAL PARK**

▲ Taylor
Mountain
1,401 ft.

Once the two routes have converged, follow the old road as it climbs moderately across a naked slope. It soon passes through a long band of oak trees. The old road then makes a couple of short switchbacks and straightens out again. It ends at an old rock wall where a large breach permits the path to pass through. Beyond the wall the path climbs over grassy slopes just below the summit of Taylor Mountain. With each step the views get better. Nearly 0.15 mile past the rock wall, the trail comes to an end next to a fence. The true summit of Taylor Mountain lies beyond the fence. It may not be the highest point on the mountain, but the end of the trail lacks for nothing when it comes to grand, sweeping views.

To the west, the entire Santa Rosa Plain spreads out below the mountain and parts of Rohnert Park, Cotati, and Sebastopol are visible. Most of the city of Santa Rosa is easily observed. Mount Saint Helena towers above the city. From here it is easy to get a sense of just how much bigger that mountain is than all the other mountains in the Wine Country. To the east, Bennett Peak and the craggy face of Hood Mountain are also visible. The summit is strewn with boulders, and there are plenty of places to sit and enjoy the incredible vista.

To return to the trailhead, retrace your steps back to the trail junction between the two sets of switchbacks. This time stay left and follow the path to the west. Note the thick grass up the hill. This is fed by a seep, which may cause the trail to be muddy at times. After curving to the west, the route makes a quick turn to the north and descends down into a hidden valley. This is the headwaters of Todd Creek, a prominent waterway in southern Santa Rosa. A trail branches off and follows nascent Todd Creek. This is a nice hike if you have less time and want some solitude. After crossing the meadow-like valley floor, the trail passes through a collection of oak trees before descending back down to the large water tanks and then the trailhead, completing the return loop.

Miles and Directions

0.0 Start the hike at the large trailhead parking area. Begin on the trail to the left of the large water tanks.

0.4 Veer off of the old ranch road and begin hiking up a series of switchbacks on a narrow path through open fields. There are great views along this section of trail.

1.1 At the fork, stay left and continue climbing up the slopes of Taylor Mountain. Be sure to stay on the footpath whenever it crosses over the steep ranch road.

1.7 At the final junction of the ranch road and the switchbacking footpath, stay straight on the old road and proceed up the hill.

2.2 The old road passes through a gap in a rock wall.

2.4 Arrive at the end of the trail, just below the summit of Taylor Mountain. Enjoy the spectacular views.

3.6 After descending back down the ranch road and the switchbacks that crisscross the old road, arrive back at the trail junction (originally reached at 1.1 miles). Turn left and begin the latter portion of a loop back to the trailhead.

5.0 Arrive back at the trailhead.

17 Crane Creek Regional Park

The loop through Crane Creek Regional Park is a pleasant hike across open hills dotted with oaks and buckeyes. There are great views of vineyards, Sonoma Mountain, and Taylor Mountain.

Total Distance: 1.6-mile loop
Hiking Time: About 1 hour
Difficulty: Easy
Elevation Gain: 220 feet
Season: All year
Canine Compatibility: Dogs are permitted on leash
Fees: $7 parking fee

Trail Contact: Crane Creek Regional Park, 5000 Pressley Road, Rohnert Park; (707) 539-8092; http://parks.sonomacounty.ca.gov/Get_Outdoors/Parks/Crane_Creek_Regional_Park.aspx
Other: The park has a well-developed disc-golf course.

Finding the trailhead: Starting at US 101, take the Rohnert Park Expressway exit and drive east on the expressway for 2.4 miles. Turn right onto Petaluma Hill Road and continue south for 1.2 miles. Turn left onto Robers Road. After 1.2 miles it becomes Pressley Road. Drive another 0.6 mile and turn left into the parking lot. GPS: N38°20.65450'/W122°38.67417'

The Hike

Crane Creek Regional Park is nestled into the rolling foothills on the western slope of towering Sonoma Mountain. The giant rounded mountain forms the divide between the Sonoma Valley to the east and the Laguna de Santa Rosa and Petaluma River watershed on the west. The peak is the highest point in the Sonoma Mountains, which includes nearby Annadel State Park and Taylor Mountain.

Diminutive Crane Creek begins near the 2,463-foot summit of Sonoma Mountain and flows to the west. It contributes its waters to the expansive Laguna de Santa Rosa, the large complex of wetlands that occupies the large Santa Rosa Plain. Though Crane Creek Regional Park is small, claiming only 128 acres, it has fantastic views of the Laguna, as well as Sonoma and Taylor Mountains.

Although several short trails wind through the park, the main path is the Fiddleneck Trail, which forms a nice loop near the park's outer boundary. Adding a few more short trails makes a nice hike and adds a little length to the trek as well as a few additional opportunities to catch great views of vineyards and the Sonoma County countryside.

To begin the hike, walk west on the wide Fiddleneck Trail, climbing a gentle slope through thick grasses. Almost immediately several trails split off of the main route. Stay on the main path, which turns to the north. Follow the top of a rounded ridge with great views in all directions, including the Laguna de Santa Rosa and the city of

The trails at Crane Creek afford good views of vineyards on the flanks of Sonoma Mountain.

Rohnert Park to the west, wooded Taylor Mountain, and the meadow- and vineyard-clad heights of Sonoma Mountain. About 0.3 mile from the trailhead, a short path breaks away to the right and leads to some benches with another good vista that's highlighted by a good perspective on Taylor Mountain.

Past the vista, the trail makes a descent from the grassy ridge and winds its way through some grassy fields while coming close to the fence that marks the park's boundary. Watch for groups playing the nearby disc-golf course. The trail cuts through a small grove of oaks and crosses a seasonal creek before arriving at a fork. Stay to the left, continuing on the Fiddleneck Trail. The path runs parallel to the usually dry creek through lush fields. After another 0.1 mile, approach a second junction. Here the Fiddleneck Trail stays to the right. However, to add a bit of distance to the hike, stay to the left and proceed onto the Northern Loop Trail. The path winds through fields thick with spring wildflowers and dotted with oaks before quickly rejoining the main trail after 0.2 mile, when the trail arrives at another intersection. Take the Fiddleneck Trail to the left and cross over Crane Creek, which may be dry by midsummer.

Once on the far side of the creek, follow the wide trail on a course parallel to the creek, passing numerous oak trees. Soon a large hill rises on the left. The trail skirts the bottom edge of the hill as it heads to the east. Stay to the left at another fork in the trail that comes 0.25 mile after crossing Crane Creek. This marks the beginning of the appropriately named Buckeye Trail, which follows Crane Creek for another 0.2

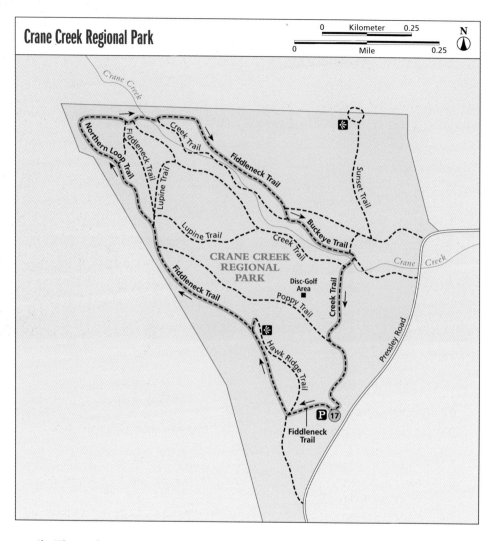

mile. The trail is appropriately named because of the presence of numerous impressive moss-draped buckeye trees. In the spring these trees bloom with spectacularly showy floral displays. The Buckeye Trail soon turns to the south and crosses over Crane Creek. Stay left when the route is joined by the Creek Trail. The wide path runs through more grassy fields with fine views of Sonoma Mountain to the east. A few other trails merge as the route continues south until the main trail itself finally arrives at the parking area, completing the loop.

A buckeye tree in full bloom along the appropriately named Buckeye Trail.

Miles and Directions

0.0 From the parking lot, hike west onto a grassy hill.

0.1 Turn right at a fork and walk across the top of the hill on the Fiddleneck Trail, with great views in all directions.

0.35 Pass a bench with a good view and descend down to the disc-golf course.

0.55 A trail merges with the Fiddleneck Trail. A few steps away the trail then forks. Stay left and continue walking to another fork a short distance away. Stay left again.

0.9 After curving through oak trees, the trail meets a third fork. Stay left again and cross over Crane Creek.

1.2 Stay right at a fork and then follow the trail to another crossing over Crane Creek.

1.5 Cross over a bridge and then turn right at a junction.

1.6 Arrive back at the trailhead, completing the loop.

18 Laguna de Santa Rosa Trail

The Laguna de Santa Rosa is an expansive wetlands complex that extends from the Russian River to the south end of the Santa Rosa Plain, near Cotati. The Laguna Trail, as it is commonly known, explores the fields and ponds of a small part of this area. A floating bridge crosses the main channel of the laguna and accesses a scenic spur trail. The trail also passes close by a lovely vineyard and has views of the Mayacamas Mountains to the north and east.

Total Distance: 4.0-mile lollipop
Hiking Time: About 2.5 hours
Difficulty: Easy
Elevation Gain: 20 feet
Season: All year
Canine Compatibility: Dogs are permitted on leash

Fees: None
Trail Contact: Sonoma County Regional Parks; (707) 433-1625; http://parks.sonomacounty .ca.gov/Get_Outdoors/Parks/Laguna_de_ Santa_Rosa_Trail.aspx
Other: There is an alternative trailhead on CA 12.

Finding the trailhead: From US 101, take the CA 12 West exit for Sebastopol and drive west for 3.0 miles. Turn right onto Fulton Road and immediately turn left onto Occidental Road. Drive west on Occidental Road for 2.4 miles. Turn left into the trailhead parking lot. GPS: N38°25.37333'/W122°48.62017'

The Hike

The Laguna de Santa Rosa is a large wetlands area that covers a significant portion of the Santa Rosa Plain. Beginning south of the city of Santa Rosa near the town of Cotati, the Laguna stretches across the west side of the plain. Flowing first into Mark West Creek, its waters ultimately contribute to the Russian River. With its abundant water, the Laguna is important habitat for birds and other wildlife. Cutting across the heart of the Laguna, the Laguna de Santa Rosa Trail is a terrific opportunity to observe the wetlands up close. Surrounded by beautiful West County farmland, the trail travels past vineyards, open pastureland, and wetlands on the way to a nice loop that brings hikers alongside the Laguna itself. On top of these highlights are nice views of the Mayacamas to the east. The Laguna de Santa Rosa Trail may not be spectacular, but it is a great Sonoma County experience.

The trail is lollipop shaped, with trailheads on Occidental Road and CA 12. The best place to start is at the Occidental Road trailhead. From there hike south on the gravel path past open fields. It soon doglegs to the right and comes alongside a beautiful vineyard with some gorgeous towering valley oaks. The path soon doglegs again but maintains its course beside the vineyard. At 0.45 mile the trail splits. Staying straight maintains a course along the main trail; however, turning left allows you to

A majestic oak rises high above the Laguna de Santa Rosa Trail.

hike around small Kelly Pond. The reed-lined body of water is pleasant and a great place to spot egrets. Watch for the summit of Mount Saint Helena poking above the trees. The trail loops 0.35 mile around three sides of the ponds and rejoins the main trail at the edge of a low bluff, where there are great views out over the Laguna.

Head down the bluff and follow the trail across wetlands, passing a gated trail on the right. This is the return route at the end of the loop section of the hike. Continuing south, the trail traverses more open wetlands, passing another fork 0.45 mile past the gated one. Stay left and hike toward CA 12, which has now become visible. To the east are views of the Mayacamas Mountains, which can be seen rising in the distance. Finally, 1.6 miles from the trailhead, the Laguna Trail arrives at the trail leading from the CA12 trailhead. Stay to the right, continuing on a path through Sebastopol's Laguna Wetland Preserve. This section travels briefly alongside the noisy highway before the trail turns back to the north and arrives at the edge of the Laguna itself. The ability to see the water improves as the trail goes north.

The path soon arrives at a fascinating floating bridge across the Laguna. The best perspective on the Laguna is from the center of the bridge. The slow-moving water looks like a wide river with no discernable current. The thick forest on either side of the Laguna gives the whole scene a bayou-like appearance. Across the bridge is a smaller trail network, which offers more close exposure to the Laguna. For the best views, turn right after the bridge and skirt the edge of some baseball diamonds. When the trail forks, stay left; you'll soon emerge at a large clearing with numerous

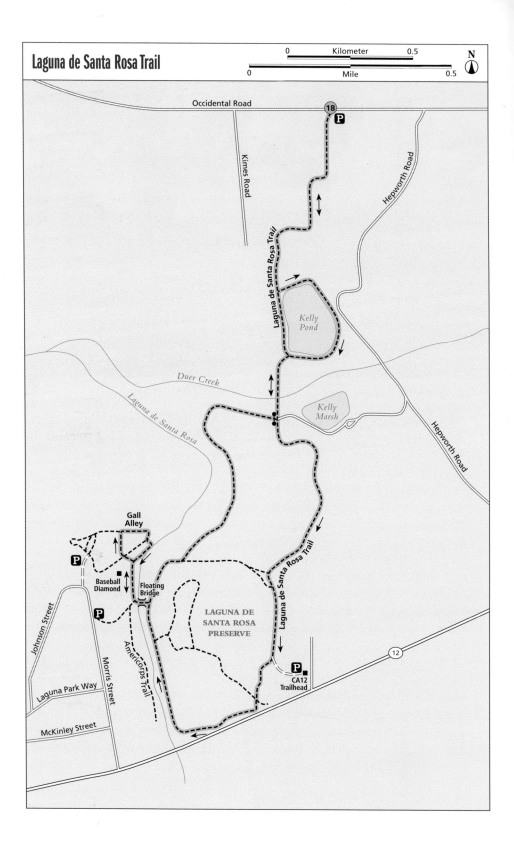

Laguna de Santa Rosa Trail

0   Kilometer   0.5
0   Mile   0.5

N

Occidental Road

18
P

Kimes Road

Hepworth Road

Laguna de Santa Rosa Trail

Kelly Pond

Duer Creek

Laguna de Santa Rosa

Kelly Marsh

Hepworth Road

Gall Alley

P

Baseball Diamond

Floating Bridge

LAGUNA DE SANTA ROSA PRESERVE

Laguna de Santa Rosa Trail

P

Johnson Street

Morris Street

Americorps Trail

Laguna Park Way

McKinley Street

P

CA12 Trailhead

12

trails branching off in many directions. Stay straight across the clearing. The trail soon makes a right-hand turn and then passes some pastures with cattle before it comes alongside the Laguna. Stay left at a fork before completing a loop and rejoining the trail by the baseball diamonds. Return across the bridge.

Back on the main loop, turn left and proceed along the edge of the Laguna for 0.1 mile. When the path turns toward the east, away from the Laguna, look for a trail branching off to the left. Though not adjacent to the water, the trail maintains a course parallel to the water, separated by a thick band of trees. The trail veers away from the trees and crosses an open field before passing through a gate and rejoining the main trail. From here turn left and follow the main trail back to the trailhead on Occidental Road.

Miles and Directions

0.0 The hike begins at the trailhead parking lot. Head south on the wide trail, passing through a field.

0.45 Turn left onto a short loop around Kelly Pond.

0.8 Turn left, rejoining the main trail.

0.9 Stay left at a junction, passing a gated trail on the right. This is the end of the loop section of the trail.

1.4 Stay left at another junction.

1.6 Continue onto Sebastopol's Laguna Wetland Preserve Trail, staying right at a junction with the spur leading from the Laguna Trail's CA 12 trailhead. Stay left at a second junction a short distance away.

2.15 Turn left to cross the bridge and hike the 0.45-mile spur loop along the Laguna.

2.75 Turn left onto the final leg of the loop, passing through fields.

3.3 Rejoin the main trail and turn left.

4.0 Arrive back at the trailhead.

19 West County Trail

A pleasant passage through rural, western Sonoma County, the West County Trail offers hikers an opportunity to experience the area's venerable apple industry. Connecting the small communities of Forestville and Graton, the hike is a unique combination of historical, agricultural, and natural highlights.

Total Distance: 6.6 miles out and back
Hiking Time: About 4 hours
Difficulty: Easy
Elevation Gain: None
Season: All year
Canine Compatibility: Dogs are permitted on leash

Fees: None
Trail Contact: Sonoma County Regional Parks; (707) 433-1625; http://parks.sonomacounty .ca.gov/Get_Outdoors/Parks/West_County_ Regional_Trail.aspx
Other: The hike requires a short section of hiking on a bike path along a road.

Finding the trailhead: From US 101, take the River Road exit and drive west on River Road for 7.9 miles. Turn left onto Mirabel Road and continue for 1.4 miles. Turn left onto Front Street and park in the large dirt parking area on the south side of the road. An open space filled with oak trees is adjacent to the parking area. GPS: N38°28.40717'/W122°53.59267'

The Hike

Western Sonoma County, particularly the greater Sebastopol area, is a beautiful, pastoral region that exemplifies rural life on the coastal side of the county. Although it is not flat, the terrain is much more subdued than the mountainous eastern part of the county. This is, in many ways, the agricultural heartland of the county, especially in terms of produce not related to wine making. Apples, particularly the Gravenstein, were the primary product in this area for most of the twentieth century. The Gravenstein was initially brought to the area by Russian fur traders operating out of Fort Ross on the coast. Despite apples being the dominant produce, grapes have had a long history in this area as well, particularly the area north of Sebastopol, along Green Valley Creek. Today apple production is in decline, and grape growing is becoming more common.

Explore the lush countryside along the West County Trail, which is a "rails to trails" conversion. The trail was once a rail line belonging to the Petaluma & Santa Rosa Railroad. It connected the small communities of Graton and Forestville. Now it is a very scenic trail that runs through the heart of the West County, passing vineyards, apple orchards, wineries, and small farmhouses in a peaceful, rustic setting as well as offering a close look at one of the last apple-processing plants in the county. Another highlight of the hike is the opportunity to explore the small towns at both ends of the

Apple orchards and grape vines along the West County Trail.

trail. However, it can be hiked from either Graton or Forestville, and it is not necessary to hike the entire distance to enjoy the beautiful countryside.

Begin the hike at the large dirt parking lot in downtown Forestville. The trail used to follow the dirt road on the east side of the parking lot, going behind a small winery before reaching the official beginning of the West County Trail. An alternate route has been constructed and begins in the center of the parking lot and heads into the open field directly to the south. The oak-dotted field is a small city preserve, and a trail has been constructed through it. Both routes lead to the same place. Once on the main path, you head south on a level course. It passes a few houses and a water treatment plant and then leaves the trappings of the small town behind. It threads its way through vineyards and wooded areas and over some small creeks. This section of the trail has a thick forest canopy, but views out into the countryside can still be had. When they are in season, watch for blackberries growing along the path.

At 1.15 miles the trail runs into Ross Branch Road. Turn left and then immediately turn right onto Ross Station Road. Walk past the small parking lot and onto the trail, which now runs parallel to a blackberry farm on the left. This section of the trail is open with great views of vineyards, orchards, and farms. Watch for the sign for Ektimo Vineyards next to a paved driveway 0.4 mile from the second parking area. The driveway leads to the vineyard's tasting room, which shares a location with Ross Road Custom Crush, a company that makes wine for small vineyard owners. If the tasting room is open, be sure to stop by. Another 0.4 mile away, the trail passes a

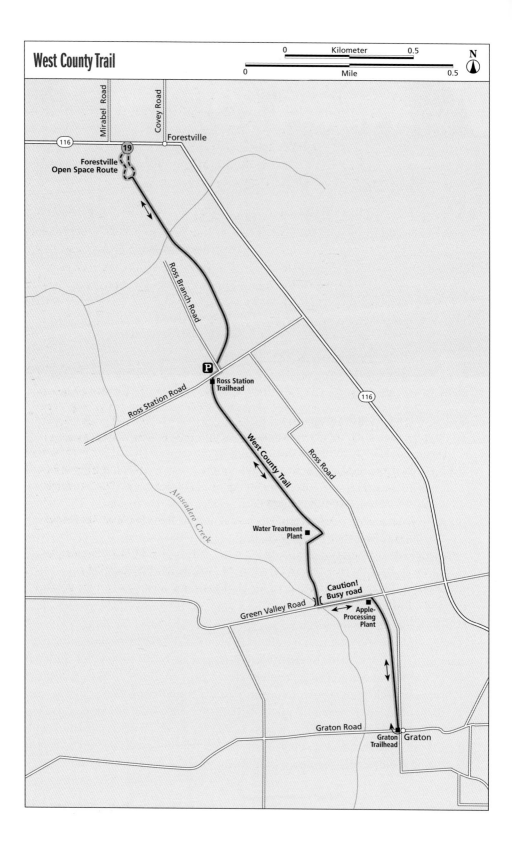

West County Trail

0   Kilometer   0.5

0   Mile   0.5

N

Mirabel Road

Covey Road

116

Forestville

19

Forestville
Open Space Route

Ross Branch Road

P

Ross Station
Trailhead

Ross Station Road

116

West County Trail

Ross Road

Atascadero Creek

Water Treatment
Plant

Caution!
Busy road

Green Valley Road

Apple-
Processing
Plant

Graton Road

Graton
Trailhead

Graton

second water treatment plant. The trail bends around the edge of the facility before heading south again. Passing beneath another thick forest canopy, the path crosses a long causeway before coming to an end on Green Valley Road.

Turn right and follow the bike path next to Green Valley Road for 0.25 mile, passing attractive vineyards and apple orchards. A hundred yards before the intersection with Ross Road, cross Green Valley Road and pass the large apple-processing plant of Manzana Products, one of the few apple processers left in the West County. Manzana makes applesauce, apple juice, and apple cider vinegar. The smell of the apples is intense and delicious.

Look for the West County Trail just past Manzana's plant. The trail runs south, next to the large structure. The trail continues south for another 0.65 mile before coming to an end at the edge of downtown Graton. Although Graton was once a sleepy village surrounded by apple orchards, the ever-expanding wine industry has brought investment to the community, and its quaint old downtown is now filled with restaurants and shops. Enjoy a stroll through town and possibly stop for a snack or a meal before retracing your steps back to Forestville.

Miles and Directions

0.0 The hike starts at the large dirt parking area in downtown Forestville. There are two options at the outset. One is to walk east and turn right onto a dirt road that passes a private residence and proceeds behind a small winery. At the back end of the winery's storage yard is the official beginning of the West County Trail. The other option is to find the wide dirt path in the field directly south of the parking lot. This trail connects to the West County Trail as well.

1.15 The trail stops at Ross Branch Road. Turn left and then immediately turn right onto Ross Station Road. Another trailhead parking lot lies just a few yards ahead. Walk through the parking lot and resume hiking on the trail.

2.4 After crossing a long wooden causeway, the trail ends at Green Valley Road. Turn left and walk along the road on the bike path.

2.6 Cross Green Valley Road and walk along the front of the large apple-processing plant. At the far end of the plant, turn right and continue hiking on the West County Trail.

3.3 Arrive in downtown Graton. Enjoy walking around town and then retrace your steps back to the beginning of the hike.

20 Steelhead Beach Loop

The best access to the Russian River is found along the short loop at Steelhead Beach. The loop offers hikers the opportunity to enjoy two beaches and a section of trail along the river. The trail also passes beneath a towering riparian canopy and historic ruins of a large gravel dispenser.

Total Distance: 1.1-mile loop
Hiking Time: About 1 hour
Difficulty: Easy
Elevation Gain: None
Season: All year
Canine Compatibility: Dogs are permitted on leash

Fees: $7 parking fee
Trail Contact: Sonoma County Regional Parks; (707) 433-1625; http://parks.sonomacounty.ca.gov/Get_Outdoors/Parks/Steelhead_Beach_Regional_Park.aspx
Other: Beach access along the Russian River

Finding the trailhead: From US 101, take the River Road exit and drive west on River Road for 8.2 miles. Turn right into the driveway leading to the Steelhead Beach parking area. GPS: N38°29.89117'/W122°53.99300'

The Hike

The Russian River is one of the most important physical features in the Wine Country. The river has a significant influence on the weather in the region and on the vineyards that surround it. For most of its journey through Sonoma County, the river passes through a series of broad valleys. For the final leg of its trip to the sea, it enters a redwood-covered canyon that winds slowly around a series of ridges. Steelhead Beach Regional Park is one of the popular public access points on the river. It is generally used for picnicking and for its boat launch that allows small craft to be put in and taken out of the river. The park also has one of the few hiking trails that provide access to the river. While it is not a long trail, the path leads through majestic forests to a hidden beach on the Russian River, which makes for a great spot to relax and enjoy the cool water.

To begin the hike, walk north from the parking area on the main park road. Near a smaller gravel parking lot, cross the road and walk around a gate onto a dirt road, which is signed as the Osprey Trail. This wide road winds through the forest, which is dominated by a high, open canopy of large willow trees, a typical denizen of riparian areas in Sonoma County. Though the sound of traffic from nearby River Road is at times audible, the scenic forest is a good distraction. Some of the willows are right by the trail, and their girth is impressive.

About 0.3 mile from the parking lot, the path passes a closed trail. Stay to the left, maintaining a course on the main route. After hiking through the forest for 0.5

The Russian River flows past Children's Beach.

mile, the trail splits. Stay to the left and arrive almost immediately at a second fork. Stay left once again and dip down through a gully that may be muddy or even filled with water in the spring. On the far side, pass through a tunnel of low bushes before emerging on the sandy bank of the Russian River at Children's Beach. The river is flanked by short trees and bushes, but tall redwood trees can be seen rising high above them. It is a scenic and secluded spot, worth the time to sit and enjoy the large river.

When it is time to return, head back across the beach and climb up the south side of the gully to the main trail. Hang a left and head through another tunnel of trees and bushes. If this section of trail is too muddy in the spring, simply head back up the main trail to the first fork and hang a left on the wide trail. Both routes meet at the same spot, but the one that passes through the tunnel of trees stays closer to the river and has a few good views of the water.

Once the two routes converge, the trail, now referred to as the Willow Trail, follows the river upstream. The river is often obscured from the trail by large trees, so there are not as many views as one might expect. Nearly 0.3 mile from Children's Beach, a narrow trail splits off to the left. This is a seasonal path that stays closer to the river and ends at Steelhead Beach. If this area is open when the spring waters have receded, this is the more scenic path and a good option.

Continuing on the main trail, the path soon arrives at the driveway leading down to the boat launch at Steelhead Beach. Cross over the road and continue on the path through a picnic area before arriving at the concrete carcass of a gravel-screening

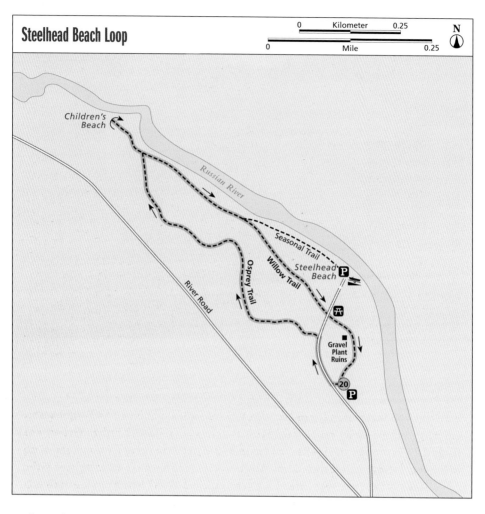

plant. The old facility used to sort gravel and load it into waiting trucks. The parking lot (and the end of the hike) is immediately adjacent to the old edifice.

Miles and Directions

0.0 Begin at the large parking area. Follow the main road toward the driveway down to Steelhead Beach. Near a small gravel parking area, cross the road and go around a gate marked for the Osprey Trail.

0.5 Stay left at a junction and follow the short spur out to Children's Beach. To get back to the trailhead, return to the junction and stay left, continuing on the loop.

0.8 A seasonal trail branches off to the left and follows the river to Steelhead Beach.

1.0 Cross over the road leading down to Steelhead Beach. Follow the path through a picnic area toward the large gravel plant ruins.

1.1 Arrive back at the parking area.

21 Riverfront Regional Park

A moderate trail that has many of the best features of the Wine Country, including redwoods, vineyards, the Russian River, views of tall peaks, and a large lake, stocked for fishing.

Total Distance: 2.5-mile lollipop
Hiking Time: About 1.5 hours
Difficulty: Easy
Elevation Gain: None
Season: All year
Canine Compatibility: Dogs are permitted on leash

Fees: $7 parking fee
Trail Contact: Sonoma County Regional Parks; (707) 433-1625; http://parks.sonomacounty .ca.gov/Get_Outdoors/Parks/Riverfront_ Regional_Park.aspx
Other: There is a large picnic area in a beautiful redwood grove.

Finding the trailhead: From US 101, take the Central Windsor exit. Go west on Old Redwood Highway, which becomes Windsor River Road on the west side of US 101. Continue on Windsor River Road for 2 miles. Turn left onto Eastside Road and continue for 1.8 miles. Turn right into the signed driveway for Riverfront Regional Park. Follow the signs to the trailhead. GPS: N38°31.12383'/W122°51.27217'

The Hike

Riverfront Regional Park is a pretty, friendly park located on the west side of Sonoma County. The trail has a number of the best features of hiking in the Wine Country all arranged in a convenient package. There are vineyards, redwoods, views of towering peaks, the Russian River, and a large lake at the heart of the park. Lake Benoist is the centerpiece of the park. The lake, along with nearby Lake Wilson in an undeveloped part of the park, was once a gravel quarry that is now filled with water. Although swimming is not allowed in the lake, it is stocked with fish, which makes it a popular place with anglers.

The main park trail begins by vineyards, passes the redwood grove, and then circles the lake. Side trails provide access to the Russian River. These features are perfectly arranged, making the park a great place for a relaxing hike through the rustic Sonoma County countryside.

The parking area for Riverfront Regional Park is along the edge of a large, picturesque vineyard. The trail begins near the center of the parking lot and heads west, passing the large redwood grove. A branch of the main trail enters the grove, where there are several picnic tables, a large barbecue pit, horseshoe pits, and a volleyball net. A trail leads through the redwood grove and loops back to the main trail. This makes a scenic alternative to the initial part of the hike. Both routes eventually lead along the long linear path to a little bluff above Benoist Lake.

Mount Saint Helena lines the horizon beyond Lake Benoist.

The trail forks and begins the loop around the lake. Stay to the left. Some use trails descend the high embankment to the edge of the lake and continue along the water through some brush before rejoining the main trail. The route continues along the entire length of the lake. At the far western end, about 1.1 miles from the trailhead, is a bench with a great view out over the water. In the distance the brooding mass of Mount Saint Helena rises above the water. Late in the afternoon and evening, the mountain's reflection is cast upon the lake. It is a great spot to sit and enjoy the beauty.

Continuing on the loop, the path veers away from the trail a bit and passes through some wetlands before arriving at a large rock pile. Here the trail splits. The path to the right stays low, following the lakeshore. The path to the left climbs onto a levee and runs parallel to the lake. Stay to the left and climb onto the levee. After hiking on the elevated trail for 0.3 mile, a narrow path splits off to the left. This trail leads down to the Russian River and follows close to the water. Near one of the river depth gauges, the trail climbs back up the levee and rejoins the main trail at a clearing overlooking the Russian River. Walking over to the edge reveals a nice view of the river and the Mayacamas Mountains in the distance. A wide path continues along the river but is closed to the public because this section of the park is awaiting development. Returning to the main loop around the lake, the path passes along some pleasant picnic areas before arriving at the beginning of the loop.

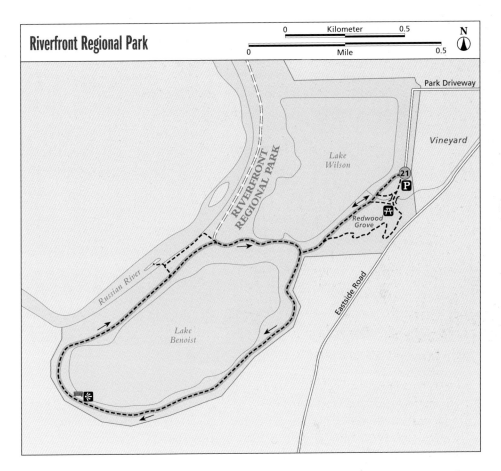

Riverfront Regional Park

Kilometer
Mile

N

Park Driveway

Vineyard

Lake Wilson

RIVERFRONT REGIONAL PARK

21

P

Redwood Grove

Russian River

Eastside Road

Lake Benoist

From the junction at the beginning of the loop, return to the parking area via the wide main path. For those wanting to lengthen the hike and add some vertical terrain, look for the Redwood Hill Trail heading off to the right. It enters the redwood grove and climbs 120 feet up the side of the hill. On the summit the trail leaves the redwoods behind and switchbacks down the back side. After leveling off, it reenters the redwood grove at the large picnic area. From there it is a short walk back to the trailhead.

Miles and Directions

0.0 The hike leaves the parking area on a wide, level path. Spurs lead into the large redwood grove on the left. Paths through the grove reconnect to the main trail.

0.3 The trail arrives at the beginning of the loop. Turn left and follow the path above the lake. Narrow tracks drop down to the water's edge.

1.1 A bench by the water provides a fantastic view of Mount Saint Helena looming above Lake Benoist.

1.3 The trail splits by a large pile of concrete boulders. The route on the left climbs onto a levee. The right-hand path stays close to the water before joining the upper trail.

1.6 A spur branches off of the main trail and leads down to the Russian River. From here you can follow a seasonal trail along the river before rejoining the main route.

2.2 Arrive at the end of the loop and follow the path back to the trailhead.

2.5 Arrive back at the trailhead.

22 Shiloh Ranch Regional Park

This hike is a diverse loop through the Mayacamas Mountains near Windsor. The trail passes vineyards and large forests before climbing up to a fantastic vista above the Russian River Valley. It then drops down to a small pond and travels down a narrow canyon along a beautiful creek.

Total Distance: 4.0-mile loop
Hiking Time: About 2.5 hours
Difficulty: Moderate
Elevation Gain: 550 feet
Season: All year
Canine Compatibility: Dogs are not permitted

Fees: $7 parking fee
Trail Contact: Sonoma County Regional Parks, (707) 433-1625; http://parks.sonomacounty .ca.gov/Get_Outdoors/Parks/Shiloh_Ranch_ Regional_Park.aspx

Finding the trailhead: From US 101, take the Shiloh Road exit. Drive west on Shiloh Road for 1.3 miles. Turn right onto Faught Road and continue 0.1 mile before turning left into the trailhead parking lot. GPS: N38°31.53717'/W122°45.74667'

The Hike

Shiloh Ranch Regional Park is an 860-acre natural oasis in the foothills of the Mayacamas Mountains. Located just east of the city of Windsor, the park is at the nexus of the small Chalk Hill appellation area and the expansive Russian River Valley area. Typical of mountains in the Wine Country, the park has a mix of densely wooded areas interspersed with open grassy hillsides. A network of trails explores the former cattle ranch, and it is possible to hike a number of loop variations. The best option passes through most of Shiloh Ranch's different environments. It connects heavily wooded areas with bare hills while climbing to a grand overlook above the Russian River Valley that is then followed by a narrow canyon drained by a scenic creek.

The main parking lot for Shiloh Ranch lies across a road from a large complex of vineyards, indicative of the park's location on the edge of the beautiful Russian River Valley. Take the Big Leaf Trail to the south, running along the base of the hills. The spectacle of the vineyards stretching across the valley makes this section of the hike easygoing. After passing a small vineyard on the right, the trail plunges into a deep, dark forest and begins to climb steeply. The trail, an old dirt road, continues to climb, but the grade quickly becomes more moderate.

Entering a small canyon, the path clings to the steep slope. After crossing a seasonal stream, the trail briefly traverses the south side of the canyon before veering away and climbing out onto open hillsides. At 1.0 mile it is joined at a hairpin turn by a trail leading from a secondary parking lot. After the tight turn, walk across grassy

Vista point view of the Russian River Valley.

slopes before quickly arriving at another junction. Take the trail to the left, which is now called the South Ridge Trail.

As the trail reenters the forest, the grade steepens. The path rounds the head of the narrow canyon as it climbs the opposite side. Just after passing beneath power lines, a spur trail branches off to the left. The path leads past some benches on a narrow shoulder of the mountains to a great vista point overlooking the Russian River Valley. Vineyards spread out below the park while the city of Windsor is visible just to the north. The broad Santa Rosa Plain and its perimeter ring of hills and mountains lie to the south. Looking north, the Mayacamas Mountains form the horizon. The pyramidal Geyser Peak is among the most prominent summits visible from here.

To resume the loop, head back to the South Ridge Trail and hike to the northeast. The path soon rounds the upper portion of a second small canyon before intersecting the Ridge Trail. If you are looking for a short hike, turn left here and follow the Ridge Trail 0.6 mile back to the trailhead. To stay with the recommended loop, turn right onto the Ridge Trail.

Now on the top of a long ridge, the Ridge Trail runs through an open area before being enveloped again by a shadowy forest. It begins to lose elevation. Passing through the trees, the trail reemerges into a lawn-like valley. A narrow path, the Creekside Trail, splits off to the left and leads down toward a small pond. The Pond Trail also leads to the small pond, though it is less direct as it rounds the upper end of the small valley. Both trails meet at the small pond, which is occupied by geese. A small earthen dam forms the little pond. Walk past the dam and continue west on the Creekside Trail. It passes a small gully before the valley narrows into a tight little canyon. The trail hugs the cliff above the creek as it gently descends beside the creek.

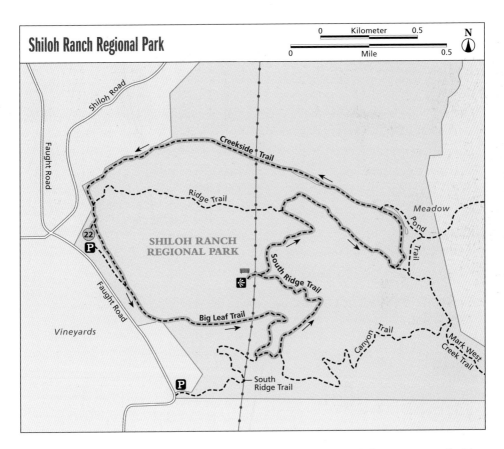

Shiloh Ranch Regional Park

SHILOH RANCH
REGIONAL PARK

Vineyards

The entire canyon is quite scenic. The trail runs beside the creek for an entire mile. In the lower reaches of the canyon, the trail crosses a bridge before climbing gently and rejoining the Ridge Trail. Stay to the right at the junction and continue the last little bit of the trail back to the trailhead, completing the loop.

Miles and Directions

0.0   Begin the hike by leaving the trailhead on the Big Leaf Trail. Head south, with views looking out over the vineyards of the Russian River Valley.

1.0   Stay left at a junction with a trail climbing up from an alternate trailhead.

1.1   Stay left again and begin climbing up the South Ridge Trail.

1.7   Follow the spur branching off to the left to a great panoramic vista overlooking the Russian River Valley.

2.1   Turn right onto the Ridge Trail.

2.6   Turn left onto the Creekside Trail.

2.8   Pass the dam at the end of a small pond, staying to the left and continuing on the Creekside Trail.

4.0   Arrive back at the trailhead, completing the loop.

23 Foothill Regional Park

The loop through Foothill Regional Park is a pleasant trail with just enough length and steep terrain to make it feel like it penetrates deep into the Mayacamas backcountry without having to travel too far from the trailhead. It passes three small ponds on the way to great views of the Russian River Valley and Mount Saint Helena.

Total Distance: 3.0-mile loop
Hiking Time: About 1.5 hours
Difficulty: Moderate
Elevation Gain: 400 feet
Season: All year
Canine Compatibility: Dogs are permitted on leash

Fees: $7 parking fee
Trail Contact: Sonoma County Regional Parks, (707) 433-1625; http://parks.sonomacounty .ca.gov/Get_Outdoors/Parks/Foothill_ Regional_Park.aspx

Finding the trailhead: From US 101, take the Arata Lane exit. Drive east on Arata Lane for 1.3 miles. Turn left into the trailhead parking lot. GPS: N38°33.67133'/W122°47.86733'

The Hike

Secreted away in the hills of the Chalk Hill area, just east of the city of Windsor, is small Foothill Regional Park. Encompassing 211 acres, it is one of the smaller inland parks in Sonoma County's excellent regional park system. Despite its small size, the park is home to surprisingly rugged terrain, deep forests, a trio of small ponds, and far-reaching vistas. Like many of the smaller parks in the Wine Country, Foothill Regional Park has a web of trails coursing through it, allowing numerous hike combinations to be assembled. The best permutation at Foothill follows the perimeter of the park. This enables hikers to get the longest trip possible despite the park's relatively small size. At the same time, it hits the park's three highlights: the three ponds, the hushed recesses of the thick oak forest, and the sweeping views.

From the parking lot, begin hiking up the wide path to the east. The wide trail curves around some trees and makes a short climb up to the corner of a small dam that forms the first of the three ponds. At a fork by the dam, stay to the right and enter a thick oak forest. Some homes are visible at the edge of the forest on the right. Hike through the woods, emerging from beneath the canopy as the trail joins another trail at the edge of a second dam, 0.3 mile from the trailhead. Stay to the right and cross the dam, which holds back the waters of the second pond. This small body of water is far more attractive than the first. For those looking for a little more distance, follow the short loop trail that encircles the pond. The trail passes through some grassy areas and passes a handicapped-accessible parking area before arriving at the third of Foothill's three ponds. This trail is ringed with grassy hills.

Oak trees line the trail in Foothill Regional Park.

The main trail stays on a levee overlooking the pond, while a narrow, parallel route drops down and hugs the water. Whichever trail you take, the paths reconvene at a trail junction. Stay on the wide trail that departs to the right, or east. This is the Alta Vista Trail.

Once on the Alta Vista Trail, the climbing begins in earnest. During the climb a couple of narrow use trails branch off the main route. Disregard these and keep climbing. Fortunately the trail enters the oak woodland again, and the climb is moderated a little bit by the shade. Finally, after climbing 320 feet in 0.4 mile, the trail reaches the top of the hill, and an expansive view to the southwest opens up. Windsor lies immediately below the vista, while Santa Rosa and the flat plain of the Laguna de Santa Rosa spread out to the south, hemmed in by the rolling hills of the North Coast Range. When it is time to continue hiking, follow the Alta Vista Trail north, descending the back side of the vista point. The trail weaves through the forest as it descends. The trail bends to the west and crosses a narrow use trail before reorienting to the north and continuing through the oaks.

The path makes an attractive course through the small trees before the trees part a bit and the views open up to the north. A large pond lies in the midst of a lush meadow just beyond the park boundary. Rising impressively above the scene is the enormous bulk of Mount Saint Helena, the most significant mountain in the Wine Country. Pressing on just a short distance leads to a large junction with the Oakwood Trail about 1.45 miles from the trailhead.

Foothill Regional Park

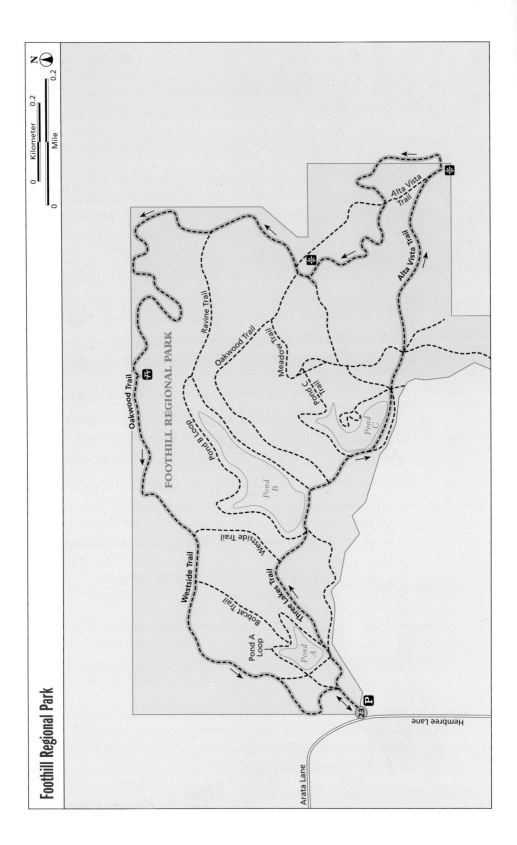

Turn right onto the Oakwood Trail and follow it to the east, with its views of the small pond partially filtered by the trees. The trail continues to skirt the scenic pond on its north side before veering away and heading north. From this point the trail rarely emerges from the forest cover. The path winds circuitously through the rounded, oak-dotted hills that make up the remote Foothill backcountry. Eventually the trail turns to the west and undulates over the hills on the north side of the park, running roughly parallel to the boundary.

The forest canopy opens up 2.35 miles from the beginning of the hike. Picnic tables are scattered around the area. Pressing on down the trail, the path finally arrives at a junction with the Westside Trail, which forms a loop at the western end of Foothill Regional Park. Turning left here leads to the second lake and a quick return back to the trailhead. A short distance down the Oakwood Trail is another junction, this one for the Bobcat Trail. This path also leads back to the trailhead, though it does so while passing the first pond. Both of these are scenic options for the hike. To get the longest possible hike, stay right at both junctions and proceed west along the upper section of the Westside Trail. The trail soon drops down through oak and some light chaparral before depositing hikers back at the trailhead.

Miles and Directions

0.0 Three trails depart from the trailhead. Take the one farthest to the right—the Three Lakes Trail—passing the first trail almost immediately. Several paths branch off the main trail. Stay on the Three Lakes Trail at these early junctions.

0.35 Reach the second pond and cross the dam at its south end.

0.45 Arrive at the third pond.

0.6 At the far end of the pond, stay right at a fork and begin hiking the Alta Vista Trail. Ignore the numerous small paths that branch off the main trail.

1.0 After a steep climb, enjoy the view to the west and south from the highest point on the trail.

1.45 Turn right onto the Oakwood Trail. The trail will soon pass a great view of Mount Saint Helena rising to the east.

1.6 Stay to the right on the main trail when a pair of trails breaks away to the left.

2.45 Stay to the right and begin hiking on the Westside Trail.

3.0 Arrive back at the trailhead.

24 Healdsburg Ridge Open Space Preserve

This beautiful loop is a hidden gem on the edge of the upscale town of Healdsburg. Traveling through open hills and beautiful forests, the highlight is a great view of a secluded section of the vineyard-flanked Russian River and the towering Mount Saint Helena.

Total Distance: 2.4-mile loop
Hiking Timing: About 1.5 hours
Difficulty: Easy
Elevation Gain: 300 feet
Season: All year
Canine Compatibility: Dogs are permitted only on the All-the-Oaks Trail
Fees: None

Trail Contact: Sonoma County Agricultural Preservation and Open Space District, 747 Mendocino Ave., Ste. 100, Santa Rosa, CA 95401; (707) 565-7360; www.sonomaopen space.org/Content/?p=10045/preview.html
Other: The parking area is in a private neighborhood; please be respectful of homeowners.

Finding the trailhead: From US 101, take the Dry Creek exit on the north end of Healdsburg and drive east on Dry Creek Road for 0.3 mile. Turn left onto Healdsburg Avenue and drive north for 0.8 mile. Turn right onto Parkland Farms Boulevard and continue for 0.7 mile. Turn left onto Bridle Path and park on the side of the street with no houses. GPS: N38°38.41800'/W122°51.64867'

The Hike

The small town of Healdsburg boasts the enviable position of being at the nexus of three of Sonoma County's great grape-growing regions. Situated on the banks of the Russian River, the town lies at the northern head of the Russian River Valley American viticulture area (AVA), at the eastern end of the Dry Creek Valley AVA, and at the southern tip of the Alexander Valley AVA. All three of these regions lay claim to distinguished wineries and are prime centers of Sonoma County's viticulture industry, both in terms of wine production and tourism. Healdsburg has parlayed this location to great success, and although the town once was a sleepy agricultural community, it is now the thriving center of tourism for the northern half of Sonoma County.

While Healdsburg's location in the broader context of northern Sonoma County is fantastic, the town's more immediate location is also quite scenic. Flowing south from Mendocino County, the Russian River enters Sonoma County at the north end of Alexander Valley. At the lower end of the valley, the river makes a winding passage through the foothills of the Mayacamas Mountains before emerging into the broad, flat Russian River Valley.

Healdsburg sits on the banks of the river, right at the edge of the low foothills. While much of the area is privately owned, a hidden gem of a park is tucked away

Mount Saint Helena gazes down on the Russian River.

into the hills at the north end of town. At only 161 acres, the Healdsburg Ridge Open Space Preserve is a tight, compact area, but it claims a diverse landscape and many scenic vistas. It makes a perfect afternoon hike after a day enjoying the numerous attractions around Healdsburg.

From the parking area on Bridle Path, walk across the street and head south down the paved driveway. Turn left onto the Murray's Road Trail at the beginning of the preserve's trail network. Immediately veer left at a fork, which marks the start of the Nancy's Hill Trail. The wide path crosses a bridge that spans the outlet of small Fox Pond. Climbing up a single switchback, the trail begins to make an arc around the base of a grassy knob. A use trail climbs to the top of the knoll for some nice views.

Back on the main trail, the path winds lazily through the rolling, grassy hills. Though the trail climbs, it has a very moderate grade and plenty of good views of the lower section of the preserve. Soon the route makes a short descent to the spring-fed stream that feeds into Fox Pond, crossing the water at about 0.7 mile from the trailhead. Beyond the stream the trail cuts across a meadow before arriving at a junction. A quick side trip to the left leads to the top of a grassy summit with a nice view of Fox Pond. Return back to the junction and stay straight, beginning the Ridge Trail.

Almost immediately the Ridge Trail reaches another fork, this time joined by the Murray's Road Trail. Stay left at this point and continue on the Ridge Trail, which passes under the forest canopy. Oak, bay, and madrone, the usual denizens of most of Sonoma County's inland forests, are all present. As the trail climbs through the woods,

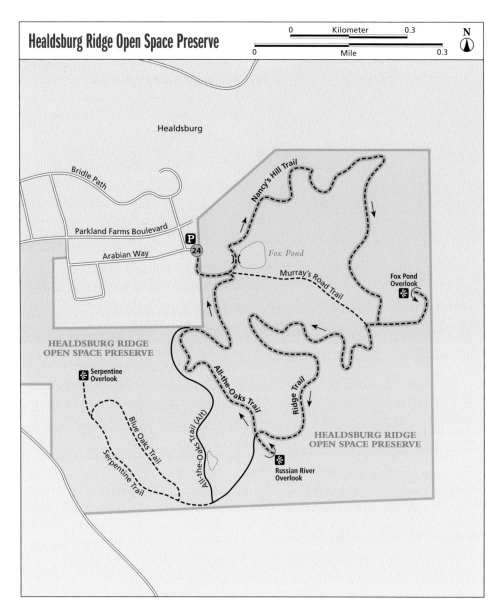

it skirts the edge of a grassy clearing in the woods. At the far end of the clearing, the trail makes a wide switchback, turning back to the east as it heads uphill at an easy grade. At the far end of the clearing, the trail turns to the south and follows the top of the ridge. Views are minimal along this section of the trail because of the dense forest cover. The trail finally arrives at another junction, about 1.8 miles from the beginning of the hike. A short spur leads to the Russian River overlook. Although some power lines cut across the field of view, it is an inspiring sight. On the horizon is the brooding mass of awesome Mount Saint Helena, the dominant peak of the Wine Country.

Below the ridge lie expansive vineyards planted alongside the meandering Russian River. This secluded valley is a northern outlier of the Russian River Valley AVA, the majority of which lies to the south of Healdsburg. It is a classic Wine Country vista. When it is time to move on, return to the junction and follow a road for a few yards before veering to the right and hiking north on the All-the-Oaks Trail. This trail reenters the forest and makes a few wide switchbacks as it descends 0.5 mile back to the beginning of the trail system by Fox Pond. From there retrace your steps back to the parking lot.

Miles and Directions

0.0 Begin the hike by crossing the street from the parking area and walking up the paved driveway, turning left onto the marked beginning of the Murray's Road Trail. After a short distance, cross a bridge and begin the Nancy's Hill Trail.

0.85 After winding around beautiful, bare hills, the trail arrives at a junction. To the left is a short path that leads to an overlook above Fox Pond. Stay right to continue the loop.

1.85 At a small clearing on top of a hill, turn left and follow the spur to the great overlook above the Russian River. To continue to the trailhead, return to the clearing and proceed down the All-the-Oaks Trail.

2.4 Turn left onto the Murray's Road Trail, then turn right back onto the paved driveway, completing the loop.

25 Woodland Ridge Trail

The short Woodland Ridge Trail is a quick hike with varied terrain, a great introduction to the Lake Sonoma area, and it offers a great opportunity for hikers to enjoy a quick jaunt in the beautiful Dry Creek Valley.

Total Distance: 1.1-mile loop
Hiking Time: About 1 hour
Difficulty: Easy
Elevation Gain: 370 feet
Season: All year
Canine Compatibility: Dogs are permitted on leash

Fees: None
Trail Contact: US Army Corps of Engineers, Lake Sonoma Visitor Center, 3288 Skaggs Springs Rd., Geyserville, CA 95441; (707) 431-4533; www.spn.usace.army.mil/Missions/Recreation/LakeSonoma.aspx

Finding the trailhead: From US 101, take the Dry Creek exit on the north end of Healdsburg and drive west on Dry Creek Road for 10.2 miles. As you approach Warm Springs Dam, Dry Creek Road curves left and becomes Skaggs Springs Road. Continue for another 0.3 mile. The trailhead is located in a large pullout just past the visitor center. GPS: N38°42.93850'/W123°00.00383'

The Hike

Lake Sonoma is a large reservoir in north-central Sonoma County. It lies at the head of Dry Creek Valley, a premier wine-making appellation. The lake impounds Dry Creek, which begins in southern Mendocino County and runs 43 miles to its confluence with the Russian River near Healdsburg. The Warm Springs Dam is located at the head of Dry Creek Valley and was completed in 1982. The US Army Corps of Engineers built the dam as well as the extensive recreational infrastructure that surrounds Lake Sonoma. The center of much of the activity at the lake is the visitor center and fish hatchery, which are located at the base of Warm Springs Dam. Located just a stone's throw away is the trailhead for the Woodland Ridge Trail, a short loop that explores a diverse area near the lake. For hikers looking for a short, interesting hike near world-class attractions, this introductory loop is a great option.

The trailhead for the Woodland Ridge Trail is just north of the visitor center parking lot. Cross a wide bridge and turn to the left. The trail quickly enters a beautiful dark redwood grove. Quickly leaving the cool copse, the trail merges onto an old roadbed and begins climbing through the region's typical mixed forest that includes oak, bay, madrone, and fir. The grade steepens noticeably as the trail climbs. It soon makes a turn to the north and continues climbing up the hill. A few clearings punctuate the trail as it passes through the woods. At one clearing is a picnic table and a bit of a view to the northeast, where the Mayacamas Mountains can be seen looming in the distance. Although much of this section of the hike passes through wooded area,

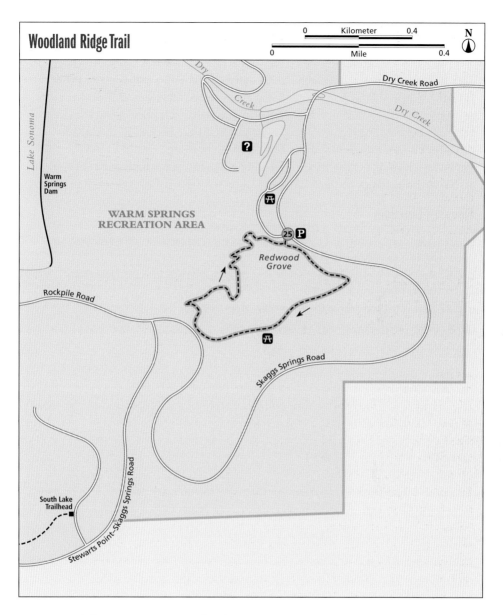

occasional drier spots are more brushy in nature. The trail proceeds a little farther until it finally levels off and comes alongside the road leading from the visitor center to Lake Sonoma.

Fortunately the trail does not linger near the noisy road and soon reenters the woods and begins its descent back down to the trailhead. As the forest closes in, the trail makes a horseshoe turn back to the east. A narrow goat trail once led from this point to the west, ending at a clearing where there was a good view of Warm Springs

Dam. The remnants of the trail are still visible, but the path has been condemned and is now overgrown.

The main trail continues down into a narrow gully where redwoods reappear. Although this is not a tight grouping like the redwood grove at the beginning of the hike, the trees in this canyon are good specimens and add a great scenic quality to this section of the trail. Once in the canyon, the path makes a traverse along the flank of the gully before initiating a series of switchbacks. At the bottom of the hill, the trail turns back to the east as it enters a large clearing. A bridge crosses a drainage channel before crossing a grassy area. The trail then rejoins the beginning of the loop. Go across the bridge, back to the trailhead.

Miles and Directions

0.0 Cross over the bridge and turn left at the beginning of the loop. The trail immediately enters a beautiful redwood grove.

0.5 Reach the top of the hill, where there is an opportunity to see the peaks of the Mayacamas Mountains to the north.

0.65 Begin a series of switchbacks descending to the trailhead.

1.1 Arrive back at the trailhead, completing the loop.

26 South Lake Trail

Lake Sonoma's South Lake Trail is a long path that stretches deep into the lake's backcountry for many miles. While most of the trail is the domain of the few backpackers that hike out to camp at several primitive campsites, the first 2.75 miles make a great day hike. The trail maintains a fairly level course as it travels high above the lake with good views of the water and surrounding hills. The trail then veers away from the lake and travels through isolated gullies before arriving at the Skaggs Springs Vista, which has a panoramic view of Lake Sonoma.

Total Distance: 5.5 miles out and back (optional lollipop)
Hiking Time: About 4 hours
Difficulty: Moderate
Elevation Gain: 550 feet
Season: All year
Canine Compatibility: Dogs are permitted on leash

Fees: None
Trail Contact: US Army Corps of Engineers, Lake Sonoma Visitor Center, 3288 Skaggs Springs Rd., Geyserville, CA 95441; (707) 431-4533; www.spn.usace.army.mil/Missions/ Recreation/LakeSonoma.aspx

Finding the trailhead: From US 101, take the Dry Creek exit on the north end of Healdsburg and drive west on Dry Creek Road for 10.2 miles. As you approach Warm Springs Dam, Dry Creek Road curves left and becomes Skaggs Springs Road. Continue for another 1.8 miles. Turn left to stay on Skaggs Spring Road and drive another 0.5 mile. Turn right into the large parking lot at the trailhead. GPS: N38°42.42182'/W123°00.56683'

The Hike

Lake Sonoma, the largest body of water in Sonoma County, is divided into two main sections. The Dry Creek Arm is the largest part of the lake and is the area directly adjacent to the Warm Springs Dam. Connected to the Dry Creek Arm by a strait running beneath the Warm Springs Bridge is the Warm Springs Arm. Although it is the smaller of the two sections, this section is the more heavily used part of the lake. The lake's main marina is located here, and it is a popular area with water skiers. This area also has the most well-developed trail network at Lake Sonoma. With a long, isolated trail around most of the Warm Springs Arm and scattered backcountry campsites for backpackers, this is a great area for hikers to explore.

The South Lake Trail at Lake Sonoma contains a classic section of the trail network around Lake Sonoma. It follows the western end of the Warm Springs Arm. With views of the lake, some interesting geology, and a remote terrain, this is a great but fairly easy trip that has a little bit of everything. The trip ends at the Skaggs Springs Vista, where a shuttle car can be left, halving the distance of the hike.

The view from the Skaggs Springs Vista.

The large South Lake trailhead is located several hundred feet above the lake. Here are views to the west of the Warm Springs Bridge and of the craggy Pritchett Peaks, the most impressive of the crags around Lake Sonoma. The trail initially climbs to the west before beginning a long descent. After crossing the paved road that leads down to the marina, the trail continues downhill for 0.5 mile. The hillsides are covered in chaparral and gray pines, so the views, while not great, are fairly constant and interesting.

Directly across the lake is the rounded, wooded summit of Bummer Peak. After reaching a low point, the path turns to the south and maintains a fairly level course through the thick brush. Undulating in and out of gullies, the trail finally leaves the chaparral behind 1 mile from the trailhead when it enters a cool oak forest.

Shortly after the trail enters the forest, watch for a short route leading down to a ledge. From this spot is a great panoramic view of much of Lake Sonoma's Warm Springs section. From here the trail winds its way through a series of small drainages as it leaves the lake behind and climbs up a small canyon. Even though Skaggs Springs Road is nearby, the steep terrain keeps this area very isolated. The path begins to climb more earnestly, but the canyon is heavily wooded so there is plenty of shade along the way. The trail eventually crosses the canyon's small, seasonal creek. It then climbs up to a small saddle.

From the saddle, the trail begins to descend into a second, larger canyon. It passes through some open, grassy areas before making a single switchback to the

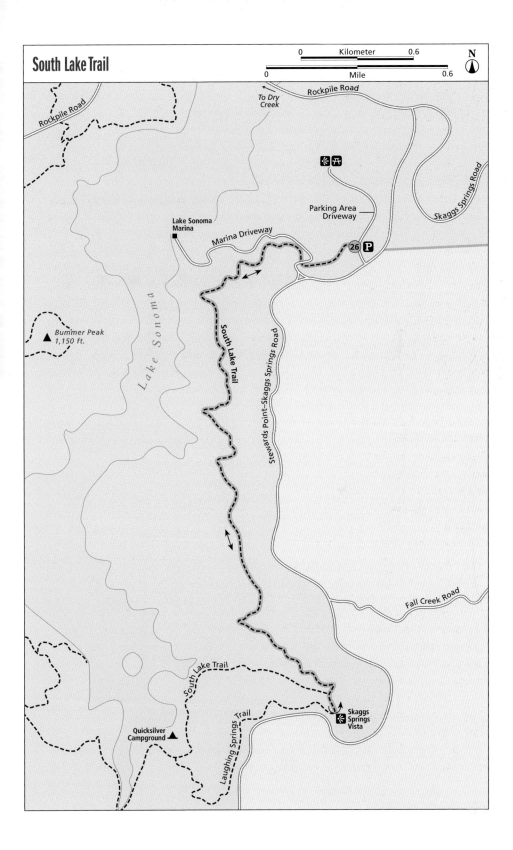

South Lake Trail

Rockpile Road

Rockpile Road

To Dry Creek

Skaggs Springs Road

Parking Area Driveway

Lake Sonoma Marina

Marina Driveway

26 P

Lake Sonoma

Bummer Peak 1,150 ft.

South Lake Trail

Stewards Point–Skaggs Springs Road

Fall Creek Road

South Lake Trail

Laughing Springs Trail

Quicksilver Campground

Skaggs Springs Vista

east. Following the switchback, the path makes a long traverse of the second canyon, alternating between wooded and open areas. The trail finally crosses another seasonal stream and arrives at a fork.

Going to the right begins the Laughing Springs Trail, which drops steeply down 500 feet to the water and the primitive Quicksilver Campground. Stay to the left for a climb up close to Skaggs Springs Road. The South Lake Trail soon arrives at the Skaggs Springs Vista, where there is a panoramic view of the Warm Springs arm of the lake and the surrounding area. The oak-dotted hills are a great contrast to the lake's blue water. The craggy Pritchett Peaks are visible rising above the Rockpile area, one of Sonoma County's smallest and most obscure wine appellations. Some of Rockpile's vineyards are visible in the distance, clinging to hillsides.

If you are up for a longer trip, look for the Laughing Springs Trail at the vista point. Follow the trail down toward the water where it comes to another fork, 0.6 mile from the vista. The trail heading off to the left is a continuation of the South Lake Trail, which goes deep into the Lake Sonoma backcountry before looping around the west end of the lake and connecting to the extensive trail network in the Rockpile area. To continue the Laughing Springs Trail, stay to the right and follow the trail for 0.8 mile as it first runs parallel to the lake and then climbs up a canyon, where it finally rejoins the South Lake Trail just after the crossing of the second seasonal creek. Be sure to watch for the path leading to the Quicksilver Campground. Once on the South Lake Trail, retrace your steps back to the trailhead.

Miles and Directions

0.0 The South Lake Trail begins at the south end of the large trailhead parking lot.

0.15 The trail crosses over the road to the Lake Sonoma Marina.

1.1 Follow a short side trail down to an overlook with a sweeping vista of Lake Sonoma. Past this point the trail moves away from the lake.

1.85 After climbing up a long drainage, the trail crosses over a saddle and begins to descend back down toward the lake.

2.5 Stay left at a junction to reach Skaggs Springs Vista.

2.75 Arrive at the vista and enjoy the panoramic views. From here you can either hike the 1.4-mile Laughing Springs Trail back to the South Lake Trail or just retrace your steps.

27 Half-a-Canoe Trail

The beautiful Half-a-Canoe Trail is Lake Sonoma's best hike. Consisting mostly of a loop through remote parts of Lake Sonoma's backcountry, the trail has panoramic views, oak forests, lake access, and open, grassy hillsides. A pair of primitive campsites makes this a possible overnighter for backpackers.

Total Distance: 5.0-mile lollipop
Hiking Time: About 4.5 hours
Difficulty: Moderate
Elevation Gain: 700 feet
Season: All year
Canine Compatibility: Dogs are permitted on leash

Fees: None
Trail Contact: US Army Corps of Engineers, Lake Sonoma Visitor Center, 3288 Skaggs Springs Rd., Geyserville, CA 95441; (707) 431-4533; www.spn.usace.army.mil/Missions/Recreation/LakeSonoma.aspx

Finding the trailhead: From US 101, take the Dry Creek exit on the north end of Healdsburg and drive west on Dry Creek Road for 10.2 miles. As you approach Warm Springs Dam, Dry Creek Road curves left and becomes Skaggs Springs Road. Continue for another 1.8 miles. Where Skaggs Springs Road turns left, continue straight onto Rockpile Road and proceed another 1.8 miles. Park at the No Name Flat trailhead on the left side of the road. GPS: N38°42.85550'/W123°02.13350'

The Hike

The Half-a-Canoe Trail is a loop through the heart of the Lake Sonoma area. It is arguably the best trail at the lake, boasting panoramic vistas, remote backcountry, lake access, and the rare opportunity for backpacking in the Wine Country. It highlights the best of the hiking potential around Lake Sonoma. Traveling across a long peninsula that lies between the two arms of the lake, it crosses some rugged terrain without demanding too much effort. The peninsula is a part of the area that makes up the Rockpile appellation. The vineyards cling to steep hillsides in a seldom-traveled part of Sonoma County. Though there are no vineyards along the trail, they lie just down the road from the trailhead.

To reach the Half-a-Canoe Trail, it is necessary to hike the short No Name Flat Trail. This begins at the like-named trailhead. The path immediately descends into a shady forest before quickly emerging into the open and crossing grassy slopes. Cross a pair of bridges and enter a narrow gully. As the trail nears the end of the gully, look for a bay tree that has grown in a prone position and sprouts more than a dozen branches growing vertically, creating its own little forest. After 0.4 mile the No Name Flat Trail intersects the Half-a-Canoe Trail. Turn left, beginning the loop.

Half-a-Canoe backcountry at Lake Sonoma.

Although the Half-a-Canoe Trail is technically considered a fire road, it nevertheless resembles a trail far more than a road. The trail runs east along the top of a long ridge, passing the North Slope Trail shortly after beginning the loop. Stay to the right. Views of Lake Sonoma alternate with perspectives of the Warm Springs Bridge and the marina area as the trail undulates across the ridge. It is also possible to see peaks of the Mayacamas Mountains rising to the east.

Stay right at a junction with the Bummer Peak Trail at 0.65 mile. The trail then cuts through a long grove of oaks growing along the crest of the ridge. After coming into the open again, the Crowley's Lake Trail crosses and then quickly recrosses the Half-a-Canoe Trail. Continue along the grassy ridge, where the views once again resume. At the end of the long ridge, the trail makes a sharp turn to the right and descends into the Bummer Peak Camp, a backpacker's campground. Nestled just below the summit of the peak in a grove of oak trees, it is a great spot for a weekend overnighter.

Past the Bummer Peak Camp, the trail begins its descent down to the edge of Lake Sonoma. Initially crossing grassy hillsides, the route soon enters a ravine with a seasonal stream. Once again under a canopy of trees, the trail passes small rocky outcroppings on the way to a junction just above the lake but 500 feet below the Bummer Peak Camp. The spur to the left leads to scenic Lone Pine Camp, another secluded backpacker's camp located on the lake's shore. Turn right and begin to follow the folds of the small gullies that drop down into the lake. Around 2.35 miles

Half-a-Canoe Trail

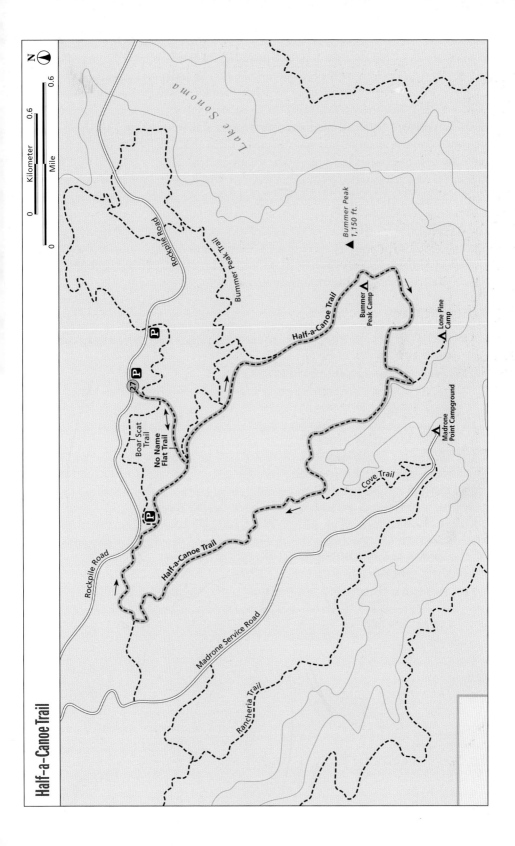

from the trailhead, begin to climb away from the lake. The trail rounds the end of one of Lake Sonoma's fingers before leaving the lake behind and entering a long valley.

Once in the valley, the trail begins to climb steadily. Stay right at a junction with the Cove Trail. Like much of the Half-a-Canoe Trail, this section of the route continues to alternate between open areas with views and wooded areas that provide welcome shade. Numerous side trails branch off the main path. Stay on the main trail. Nearly a mile into the climb up the valley, the trail curves around a small side drainage before being joined by the Outcrop Trail, which connects the Half-a-Canoe Trail with the Liberty Glen Campground. Stay to the right and continue climbing an open hillside with great views back down the valley to the lake. Near the top of the climb, pass a side trail that leads to the Lone Rock trailhead before pulling alongside Rockpile Road. The road and trail quickly diverge, and the trail continues along a steep slope with more great views. A short distance later is the junction with the No Name Flat Trail. Follow it back to the trailhead.

Miles and Directions

0.0 The trail descends from the No Name Flat trailhead into a thick forest before crossing over onto an open hillside.

0.35 Turn right to begin the loop on the Half-a-Canoe Trail.

1.4 Over the course of the first mile of the loop, a narrow path crisscrosses the main trail several times. Stay on the wide, primary trail.

1.5 The trail passes through the Bummer Peak Camp. Past the camp, the trail begins its descent down to Lake Sonoma.

2.1 Turn right at a fork just above the water. The trail to the left leads to the Lone Pine Camp, another great option for backpackers.

2.85 After 0.75 mile of following the shore of Lake Sonoma, the trail turns to the north and begins climbing up a long gulch that leads back toward the trailhead.

3.9 Near the top of the climb, the trail is joined by a path coming from the Liberty Glen Campground area. Turn right at the junction to continue the loop. There are great views down to Lake Sonoma from along this stretch of trail.

4.6 Turn left onto the No Name Flat Trail.

5.0 Arrive back at the trailhead.

28 Clover Springs Preserve

The hike through the lightly developed Clover Springs Preserve is the best hike through Sonoma County's Alexander Valley, one of the Wine Country's premier grape-growing regions. The first part of the hike follows perennial Porterfield Creek and then climbs high above the valley through dense forest to views of the north end of the valley.

Total Distance: 3.0-mile loop
Hiking Time: About 2 hours
Difficulty: Moderate
Elevation Gain: 650 feet
Season: All year
Canine Compatibility: Dogs are permitted on the trail
Fees: None

Trail Contact: Sonoma County Agricultural Preservation and Open Space District, 747 Mendocino Ave., Ste. 100, Santa Rosa, CA 95401; (707) 565-7360; www.sonomaopen space.org/Content/?p=10164/preview.html
Other: The trailhead is located in a neighborhood; please be considerate of the residents.

Finding the trailhead: From US 101, take the South Cloverdale exit. Drive west, under the freeway, and turn right onto South Cloverdale Boulevard. Drive north for 0.6 mile. Turn left onto Del Webb Drive. Immediately turn left onto Clover Springs Drive and continue for another 0.6 mile. Turn left onto Skyview Drive and drive to the end of the road. Park on the side of the road near the gate. GPS: N38°47.32317'/W123°01.72217'

The Hike

The Alexander Valley is one of Sonoma County's most prestigious wine-making areas. The Russian River flows through the entire length of the nearly 20-mile-long valley, winding its way through vineyards and past quaint towns and villages. The valley is flanked by tall hills and mountain peaks, at times rising more than 1,500 feet above the fertile land. It is a striking place and quite beautiful. Unfortunately, there is very little public land in the Alexander Valley, so opportunities to explore the great beauty of the area are limited. The best place to hike in the mountains around the valley is Cloverdale's Clover Springs Preserve. Protecting a small portion of the hills in the northwest corner of the Alexander Valley, the preserve is a park in development. Little has been done to improve Clover Springs, but work has begun to formalize existing, unofficial trails and to construct new paths. While an official trail network is not yet complete, plenty of hiking is still to be had. Old, narrow roads are the most traveled paths, but a growing network of hiking trails now penetrate deep into the preserve's backcountry. Despite still being a primitive park, this is a great place to hike, with beautiful forests, a scenic and perennial creek, and great views of the Alexander Valley.

All the trails into the Clover Springs Preserve begin at the end of Skyview Drive. Go around the gate and take the wide, unpaved path to the right, passing through a small meadow. As the trail rounds a small hill, it enters the woods and soon arrives at an attractive wooden pedestrian bridge crossing Porterfield Creek. The small creek has a good flow all year and pours through interesting bedrock chutes.

Across the bridge, the old road runs beside the creek, the sound of racing water filling the otherwise quiet forest. After following the creek closely, the trail arrives at a three-way fork 0.5 mile from the trailhead. The left-hand trail follows the creek a little farther until fading away at a wide spot along the creek; this is a great place to sit and enjoy the running water. The right-hand path does not yet lead anywhere; it's the beginning of an as-yet-undeveloped trail system. Take the middle trail, climbing above the creek. The trail heads uphill for another 0.2 mile before making a sharp turn to the right. A narrow path breaks away to the left and leads to an overlook above Porterfield Creek's canyon.

Continuing on the main path, it soon turns to the left again and maintains its upward trajectory, climbing moderately. The forest persists a little farther before giving way to chaparral. The presence of inhospitable serpentine is one reason that the heartier chaparral brush grows along this section of trail. The path grows narrower and rougher and climbs a little high until it arrives at a fence marking the end of the preserve. Looking back to the east reveals a good view of the northern part of Alexander Valley. Many high peaks, including Cobb Mountain, Geyser Peak, and Mount Saint Helena, are all visible from this vantage. Keen observers may even discern a few large structures below Cobb Mountain. These buildings are part of the vast Geysers geothermal complex that lies along the Sonoma County and Lake County line. This amazing project generates more than 60 percent of the electrical needs of coastal California between San Francisco and the Oregon border, an area with nearly one million residents. The unique geology of the region allows the power plants to harness super-heated subterranean steam to generate electricity. It is powerful testimony to the region's volcanic geology.

At the point where the trail arrives at the fence, there is an obvious, well-established trail branching to the north, passing through some manzanita. This is the beginning of another trail that is still in development. It is possible to follow the trail to a fork and, bearing right, return to the main trail after 0.25 mile. However, the best option is to simply head back 0.1 mile downhill to a band of trees that shade the trail between brushy chaparral thickets on either side. On the north side of the trail, the aforementioned loop rejoins the trail.

On the south side, another trail descends into the upper reaches of Porterfield Creek's canyon. The route is narrow but well-constructed. Red paint blazes have been placed on trees every 30 to 40 feet to mark the way. This trail makes a terrific loop with many interesting features and great views. The red-blazed trail quickly drops down to Porterfield Creek. Cross over the rocky channel and then climb back out of the canyon to the south. Once on top there is a small but lovely little redwood

An open section of trail reveals the Mayacamas Mountains and Cloverdale.

grove followed quickly by a serene, rocky hollow. From there the trail makes a fairly level traverse of the hillside for 0.35 mile. There are occasional filtered views to the northeast, but most of the route stays within a dense mixed forest.

The narrow trail finally emerges from the woods and merges onto a rough old road on a brushy hillside. The views from here are fantastic, with far-reaching vistas to the south and to the east. The city of Cloverdale spreads out at the base of the hill, while the Mayacamas Mountains make a formidable bulwark to the east. From here the course of the Russian River can be observed as well as large vineyards that fill in the eastern side of the Alexander Valley.

When it is time to head back down to the trailhead, hike downhill on the rocky road. The road heads off to the south, away from the trailhead, so be sure to turn left on the road, heading down toward Cloverdale and a cluster of large water tanks. The views remain great during the descent. After 0.15 mile is a subtle split in the trail. The red paint blazes return and mark the point where the trail breaks away from the old road. This path descends back into the canyon, where it eventually rejoins the main trail a few hundred yards from the trailhead. The other option continues down the old road to the large water tanks. From there, follow the paved access road back to the trailhead. Both are about 0.6 mile and are good options for completing the loop through the Clover Springs Preserve.

Clover Springs Preserve

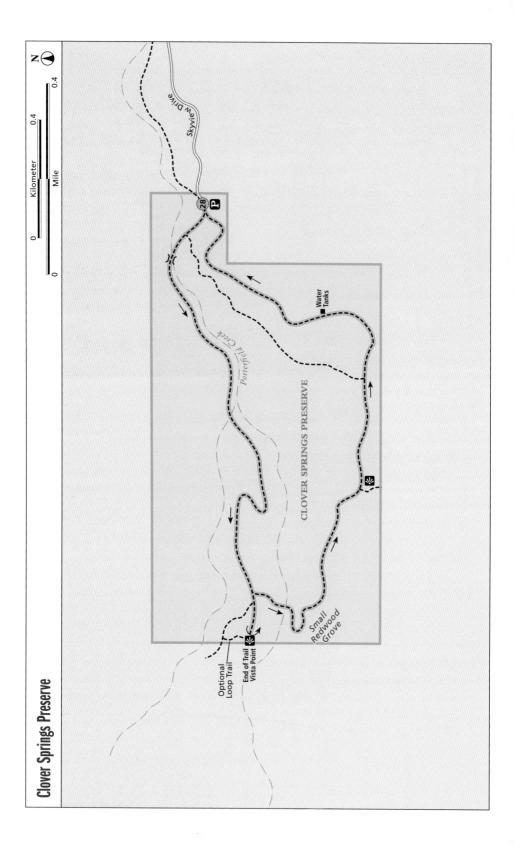

N

0   Kilometer   0.4

0   Mile   0.4

Skyview Drive

28

P

Porterfield Creek

CLOVER SPRINGS PRESERVE

Water Tanks

Small Redwood Grove

Optional Loop Trail

End of Trail Vista Point

Miles and Directions

0.0 From the end of the road, go around the gate and follow the dirt trail to the right.

0.2 Cross the wooden pedestrian bridge and hike up the canyon alongside Porterfield Creek.

0.6 The trail comes to a three-way junction. The path on the left leads down to the creek and makes a nice place to sit and enjoy the quick-moving water. To continue the hike, take the middle trail and continue climbing up the canyon.

0.85 A short path to the left leads to a nice view of the increasingly deep canyon.

1.25 The trail comes to a dead end at the preserve's boundary line. A trail branches off to the north and leads to a short 0.3-mile loop that rejoins the main trail 0.1 mile back down the path.

1.55 At the end of the loop, cross over the main trail and pick up the narrow but well-built path marked by red blazes. This is the route that returns to the trailhead.

1.7 After crossing the creek, the trail passes through a small redwood grove and a rocky glen.

2.15 The narrow path emerges from the forest and joins an old, rocky road on a bluff that offers a great view of Cloverdale, the Alexander Valley, and the Mayacamas Mountains. Turn left and follow the road down the hill.

2.3 The red-blazed trail breaks away to the left. This is one option to return to the trail, but there a few more views if you stay to the right and follow the old road.

2.5 The trail ends at a cluster of large water tanks. Follow the paved road back down to the trailhead.

3.0 Arrive back at the trailhead.

29 Cloverdale River Park

Of all the trails in the Wine Country, this short hike has the most and best access to the Russian River. It follows the riverbank, passing through forests and meadows. This section of the river still retains its swift-moving mountain-river character, and numerous little rapids and rocky chutes are found along the hike.

Total Distance: 2.3 miles out and back
Hiking Time: About 1 hour
Difficulty: Easy
Elevation Gain: None
Season: All year
Canine Compatibility: Dogs are permitted

Fees: None
Trail Contact: Cloverdale River Park, 31820 McCray Rd., Cloverdale, CA 95425; (707) 565-2041; http://parks.sonomacounty.ca.gov/Get_Outdoors/Parks/Cloverdale_River_Park.aspx
Other: Park hours are 6 a.m. to 8 p.m. daily.

Finding the trailhead: From US 101, take the Citrus Fair exit. Turn east onto Citrus Fair Drive. Turn left onto Asti Road. Continue 0.5 mile and turn right onto East 1st Street / Crocker Road. After only 0.1 mile, turn left into the driveway of the cemetery and park in the parking area by a concrete retaining wall. GPS: N38°48.49400' / W123°00.58317'

The Hike

The Russian River begins its 110-mile journey to the sea in the mountains of the North Coast Range, northwest of Clear Lake. The river makes a scenic passage through the canyons and valleys of the North Coast Range before finally reaching the sea at the small village of Jenner. Nearly the entire length of the Russian River travels through private land, making it largely off-limits to hikers. Of the few trails that do have trail access to the river, the path through the Cloverdale River Park offers the longest and the most scenic and interesting opportunity to enjoy this Wine Country waterway. Anchoring the northern end of the famed Alexander Valley, the town of Cloverdale was initially a railroad stop that developed a significant timber industry. Although both of those economic bases have faded, grape growing has increased in importance. Cloverdale River Park is more of an urban park than a nature park, and the proximity of a water treatment plant and US 101 do detract from the setting. Nonetheless, much of the park is peaceful, natural, and quite scenic, especially along the Russian River.

The trail through the Cloverdale River Park can be hiked from either its northern or southern terminus. The northern is much more scenic and makes a better destination than the southern end. The parking area is not actually in the park but just a short walk away from the trail. From the parking area by an old cemetery, walk a short distance down 1st Street. Turn left and walk down the paved driveway just before the bridge over the Russian River. Follow the road for a few hundred yards until a paved path branches off to the right, immediately before the entrance to the water

Spring wildflowers at the Cloverdale River Park.

treatment plant. The path continues north, passing between the water treatment plant on the left and the river's wide, rocky floodplain on the right. The Russian River's channel is on the far side of the floodplain.

Past the treatment plant, the trail cuts across a grassy area and then makes a short, slight descent down toward the river, which has swung to the west and now runs immediately parallel to the trail. A fairly dense riparian forest covers much of the route in this area. Use trails run from the trail through thick vegetation down to the water, where there are occasional riffles that give the river a boisterous character. Watch for a creek joining the river on the opposite bank. This is Big Sulphur Creek, which begins to the east in the Mayacamas Mountains and flows through the heart of the Geysers, the largest geothermal facility in the world; the area's unique geology has produced a significant steam resource that has been harnessed to make electricity. Soon the trail crosses over Oat Valley Creek via a large metal bridge. The small creek, which is often dry in the summer, begins to the northwest, along the highway that leads to Mendocino and the Pacific Ocean.

On the far side of the bridge, the trail continues along the river and through the thick woods before arriving at a large grassy meadow. A seasonal trail goes left here, making a wide loop across the meadow and through the oak woodland on the far side. The main path maintains its course to the north, passing alongside the edge of the meadow area. In the spring, wildflowers are abundant along this section of the trail. Narrow use trails continue to provide access to the Russian River.

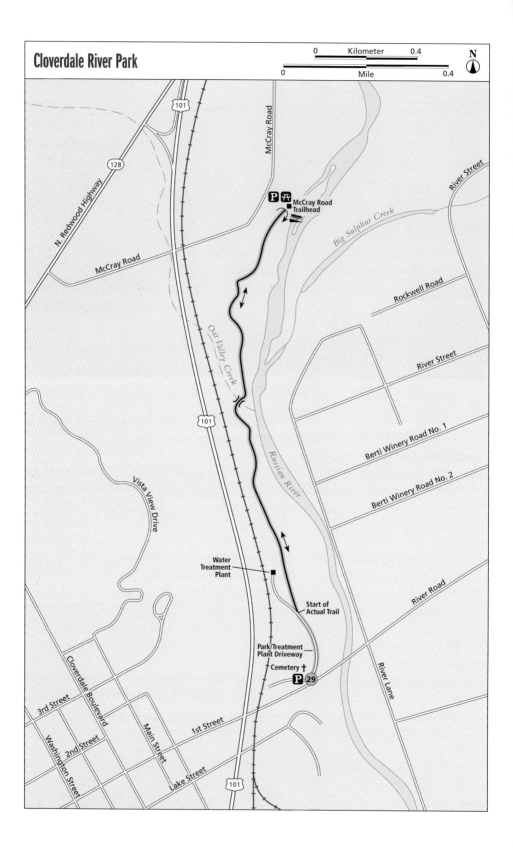

Cloverdale River Park

0   Kilometer   0.4

0   Mile   0.4

N

101

128

McCray Road

N. Redwood Highway

McCray Road

McCray Road Trailhead

Big Sulphur Creek

River Street

Rockwell Road

River Street

Oat Valley Creek

Russian River

Berti Winery Road No. 1

Berti Winery Road No. 2

101

Vista View Drive

Water Treatment Plant

Start of Actual Trail

River Road

Park/Treatment Plant Driveway

Cemetery †

River Lane

P 29

Cloverdale Boulevard

3rd Street

2nd Street

Washington Street

Main Street

1st Street

Lake Street

101

Finally the path reaches the north trailhead on McCray Road. Picnic facilities are available in addition to a boat launch, which provides great access to the river. However, the real pleasure in this area, aside from the journey getting there, is the views of the peaks to the north, which mark the uppermost wall of the Alexander Valley as well as the boundary between Sonoma and Mendocino Counties. The top of the ridge and the area to the northeast is included in the Pine Mountain–Cloverdale Peak American viticulture area (AVA), which sits astride the border of the two counties. When it is time to head back, retrace your steps back to the trailhead.

Miles and Directions

0.0 Leave the little parking area and briefly walk on East 1st Street. Turn left at the entrance to Cloverdale River Park and follow the driveway toward the water treatment plant.

0.25 Veer right and begin hiking on the paved trail.

0.5 A few unofficial trails provide good access to the Russian River as it races through some riffles.

0.7 Cross a large bridge that spans a seasonal creek.

0.9 A seasonal loop departs to the left.

1.15 Arrive at the picnic area at the north end of the trail. Retrace your steps back to the trailhead.

30 Armstrong Redwoods

This is the finest collection of redwoods in the Bay Area. Towering giants line the trail, and numerous noteworthy specimens highlight features of these unique trees, including notable girth and height, large burls, and great age. This is the best Wine Country hike in the redwoods.

Total Distance: 2.0-mile loop
Hiking Time: About 1 hour
Difficulty: Easy
Elevation Gain: None
Season: All year
Canine Compatibility: Dogs are not permitted
Fees: None

Trail Contact: Armstrong Redwoods State Natural Reserve, 17000 Armstrong Woods Rd., Guerneville, CA 95446; (707) 869-2015; www .parks.ca.gov/?page_id=450
Other: There is a free parking area just outside of the entrance gate.

Finding the trailhead: From US 101, take the River Road exit and drive west on River Road for 15.2 miles. In the town of Guerneville, turn right onto Armstrong Woods Road. Drive 2.2 miles and park in the visitor center parking area just before the entrance station. GPS: N38°31.94283' / W123°00.17067'

The Hike

Armstrong Redwoods State Natural Reserve contains the grandest collection of coast redwoods in the Wine Country. The 805-acre park was first preserved in the 1870s by Colonel James Armstrong, a prominent lumberman in the region. After his passing, his family lobbied the public to conserve the redwoods, and in 1917 Sonoma County purchased the land for the purpose of making it a park. The land was deeded to the State of California in 1934, when it became a part of the state park system. Today the land is managed as a reserve, indicating the state's focus on the grove's preservation. The trees are a grand natural monument. Walking through the redwoods often takes longer than the short mileage would indicate, not because it is a difficult trail but rather because people often walk slowly, gazing upward and commenting in hushed voices on the majesty of these mighty trees; indeed, these trees often create the atmosphere of a cathedral rather than a forest. The nature trail that passes through the grove is an easy hike but a magical experience.

Although it is possible to drive into the grove on the narrow park road, doing so requires paying an entrance fee. However, the park has a parking lot next to the visitor center that provides free parking. Begin the hike there, staying to the left of the small visitor center. Cross the park road, keeping the entrance booth to the left. Once on the trail, you head north, penetrating the heart of the dense redwood forest. The tall trees soar hundreds of feet overhead and form a dense, nearly impenetrable canopy.

Fife Creek flows through the redwoods.

On the left side of the trail is Fife Creek, which has a decent flow well into summer, though it does dry up later in the summer or during dry years. Low wooden fences keep hikers on the trail so the trees remain undisturbed. After 0.1 mile the wide path crosses a service road near the large Parson Jones Tree, the tallest tree in the

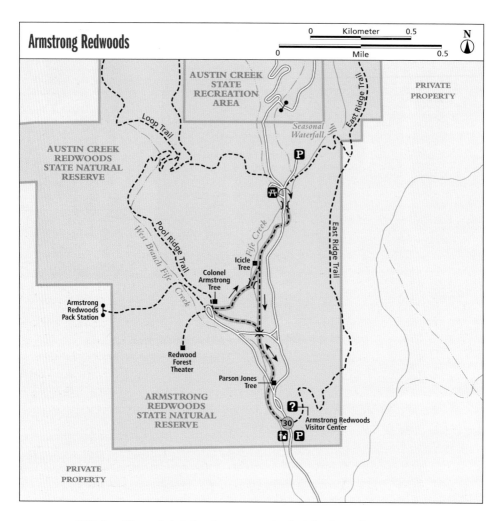

0   Kilometer   0.5

0   Mile   0.5

N

AUSTIN CREEK
STATE
RECREATION
AREA

PRIVATE
PROPERTY

Loop Trail

Seasonal
Waterfall

East Ridge Trail

AUSTIN CREEK
REDWOODS
STATE NATURAL
RESERVE

West Branch Fife Creek

Pool Ridge Trail

Fife Creek

East Ridge Trail

Icicle
Tree

Colonel
Armstrong
Tree

Armstrong
Redwoods
Pack Station

Redwood
Forest
Theater

Parson Jones
Tree

ARMSTRONG
REDWOODS
STATE NATURAL
RESERVE

30

Armstrong Redwoods
Visitor Center

PRIVATE
PROPERTY

grove at 310 feet. Though it is hard to gauge the height from the ground, especially when measured against all the other tall trees, the Parson Jones Tree's impressive girth gives hikers a sense of its enormous proportion.

Past the Parson Jones Tree, the trail continues through the quiet forest, running parallel to Fife Creek. The forest floor is covered with a thick blanket of clover-like sorrel and dotted with ferns. After 0.3 mile the trail arrives at a junction by the Burbank Circle. This is a group of large trees that seem to be arrayed around what would have been a tremendous redwood. However, the remains of the central tree are absent, leaving the growth pattern of these trees a mystery. At the junction, stay to the left, crossing over Fife Creek and then continuing parallel to another service road. Soon the trail encounters a small boardwalk that offers a chance to walk all the way around a particularly large tree. Another 0.1 mile later, the trail reaches the base of the Colonel Armstrong Tree, the oldest and largest tree in the park. At 308 feet high and 14.5 feet in diameter, the tree is awe-inspiring. It is estimated to be over 1,400 years old.

After pausing to enjoy the Colonel Armstrong Tree, continue on the trail, which is now called the Icicle Tree Trail. It now heads east, back toward Fife Creek. The path hugs the hillside and has a very short, easy climb, which is the only significant elevation gain on the hike. When the trail reaches the creek, the path turns back to the north, still staying close to the hillside. It passes beside an enormous fallen redwood before crossing Fife Creek again, arriving at the Icicle Tree. The tree is so named because of the massive, seemingly dripping burls hanging off of the trunk and branches.

Beyond the Icicle Tree, the trail continues north through the grove, passing several large trees. The trail briefly crosses the main park road and then crosses over Fife Creek one more time before arriving at the park's main picnic area. This is typically the end of the hike. If Fife Creek has significant flow, hikers can head right to the eastern half of the picnic area and pick up the Waterfall Trail, which switchbacks up through some gargantuan redwoods before passing a scenic cascade on the creek. Past this point the trail continues to climb up to the East Ridge Trail, which accesses the reserve's backcountry and the remote Austin Creek State Recreation Area.

To return to the trailhead from the picnic area, retrace the route back to the Icicle Tree. Rather than returning to the Colonel Armstrong Tree, stay left at the junction and head south on the main trail back to the Burbank Circle. From there follow the trail back to the visitor center.

Miles and Directions

0.0 Cross the road by the entrance station and start hiking on the main park trail.

0.2 Walk across a road as you pass the Parson Jones Tree, the tallest in the reserve.

0.35 At a junction, begin the hike's loop by turning left and walking through enormous, ancient trees.

0.55 Arrive at the Colonel Armstrong Tree, the largest and oldest in the reserve. From the tree, follow the path as it heads back to the east, following the bottom of a hill.

0.75 Pass alongside an enormous, fallen redwood.

0.85 The path rejoins the main trail. Continue to the left, hiking through more redwoods.

1.1 The trail ends at an extensive picnic area. Turn around here and begin the hike back to the trailhead.

1.40 Returning to the junction, stay left to complete the loop through the grove.

1.6 Stay straight at the junction with the trail coming from the Colonel Armstrong Tree.

2.0 Arrive back at the trailhead.

31 Armstrong Ridges Loop

Climbing the ridges that surround the Armstrong Redwoods State Natural Reserve, this trail offers the opportunity to explore the redwoods while taking a longer hike. The ridges are blanketed in fir forests but open up at the highest point of the hike, yielding awesome views to the south. On the return, hike through idyllic little redwood groves along Fife Creek and pass a nice seasonal waterfall.

Total Distance: 6.0-mile lollipop
Hiking Time: About 4 hours
Difficulty: Moderate
Elevation Gain: 1,100 feet
Season: All year
Canine Compatibility: Dogs are not permitted
Fees: None

Trail Contact: Armstrong Redwoods State Natural Reserve, 17000 Armstrong Woods Rd., Guerneville, CA 95446; (707) 869-2015; www.parks.ca.gov/?page_id=450
Other: There is a free parking area just outside of the entrance gate.

Finding the trailhead: From US 101, take the River Road exit and drive west on River Road for 15.2 miles. In the town of Guerneville, turn right onto Armstrong Woods Road. Drive 2.2 miles and park in the visitor center parking area just before the entrance station. GPS: N38°31.94283'/W123°00.17067'

The Hike

While most visitors who come to the Armstrong Redwoods State Natural Reserve do so to enjoy the spectacular redwoods, hikers looking for a longer, more challenging trail will be pleased by the great loop trail encircling the canyon that is home to the magnificent trees. Not only does this hike still offer a chance to wonder at the stunning trees but it also climbs through some remote backcountry and offers tremendous views of both the seldom-traveled portions of the North Coast Range and the Russian River country.

From the visitor center parking lot, cross the main park road near the tollbooth and head out on the wide path through the redwoods. In spring the waters of Fife Creek break the cathedral-like silence of the grove. The trail proceeds for 0.3 mile, passing the Parson Jones Tree on the way to a junction just after it crosses a road. Stay to the left and continue through the beautiful grove until the path arrives at the Colonel Armstrong Tree, the largest redwood in the park.

Continue past the tree and a small handicapped-accessible parking lot and follow signs for the Pool Ridge Trail, staying right at another junction. Going left here follows a park service road until it reaches a gate at the boundary. The trail narrows quickly and begins to climb in earnest along the west branch of Fife Creek. As the path climbs, the redwoods are left behind, and the forest becomes dominated by oaks,

Southern Sonoma County can be seen from the ridges high above Armstrong Redwoods.

bay, and firs. Although the trail climbs more than it did at the canyon bottom, it still maintains a reasonable grade. A little more than 0.5 mile after leaving the Colonel Armstrong Tree, the trail crosses the small creek and begins a long series of switchbacks up the end of the drainage. The grade is still moderate and climbs a bit less than 200 feet in 0.5 mile. It finally tops out at a saddle, where there is another trail junction. The trail to the right descends back down into the redwood grove and ends near a picnic area where hikers can resume the main park trail.

Staying to the left, the trail descends briefly before it resumes the climb up Pool Ridge Trail. The path soon emerges from the dense forest cover and climbs through a brushy area with views to the south. After diving back into the forest cover, the trial climbs even more steeply before emerging briefly into a clear area. Once back in the forest, the path levels off briefly before climbing again. Stay right at the junction for a short loop trail and continue uphill as the path rounds a forest-covered bluff and enters into a canyon that contains a seasonal tributary of Fife Creek. The trail traverses the slope of the canyon and soon crosses the small stream, which is typically dry by summer.

Still climbing, the route heads out of the canyon, rounds a corner, and heads into another canyon that contains a small tributary of Fife Creek. The trail then crosses a pair of bridges and makes the final, shadeless ascent to the top of the ridge, 2.9 miles from the visitor center parking lot. Fantastic views to the south are the reward for the steep climb to the ridge. The redwood-blanketed Russian River area lies immediately to the south. Note the pocket of vineyards in a small level area amid the green ridges. These belong to famed champagne-maker Korbel. Farther to the south are the domed peak of Mount Burdell and the long ridge of iconic Mount Tamalpais in distant Marin County.

When it is time to resume the journey, turn right on the gravel road and head east a short distance to the Gilliam Creek trailhead. This area is technically in the Austin Creek State Recreation Area, and the Gilliam Creek Trail is one of the main access routes to this area's scenic backcountry. Look for signs marking the East Ridge Trail and follow this trail through a grove of trees, up a short set of stairs, and then across a paved road. This road leads to the area's Bullfrog Pond Campground.

On the far side of the road, the trail turns to the north and parallels it for a short distance before turning to the east again and climbing up to the top of a treeless knoll. This is the highest point on the loop, and it is graced with spectacular views to the south. In addition to the highlights visible from the previous vista, the view now takes in the summit of nearby Mount Jackson, the southern end of massive Sonoma Mountain, and much of the city of Santa Rosa. It is a scenic high as much as it is the highest altitude on the trail.

From the vista knoll, the path begins its long descent back to the canyon bottom. Though exposed initially, the trail down soon reenters the forest cover and runs parallel to a small, spring-fed stream as it continues to head downhill. Be sure to note two old houses near the trail before finally entering the lovely little redwood grove, with Fife Creek running through the center of it. Even if the creek is dry in the main part of the grove, it is often still running in this area. It is an idyllic spot that is broken up only by the gravel fire road passing through.

Cross the bridge and climb a few short switchbacks, leaving the redwoods behind. From here the trail makes a gradual descent to the south for 0.55 mile to a trail junction. To the left, the path continues to head down to the visitor center parking lot, which is 1.2 miles away. This path is the most direct but not nearly as scenic as the option to the right. Staying right will lead down the Waterfall Trail, which switchbacks down through some mammoth redwoods to the canyon bottom and the park's picnic area. On the way down, keep an eye out for Fife Creek as it drops over a series of cataracts forming the aforementioned waterfall. Once down at the picnic area, follow the main park road over a bridge and hike up the foot path that winds through the majestic grove. Follow this path through the forest cathedral back to the trailhead at the visitor center.

Miles and Directions

- **0.0** Cross the road by the entrance station and start hiking on the main park trail.
- **0.2** Walk across a road as you pass the Parson Jones Tree, the tallest in the reserve.
- **0.35** At a junction, begin the hike's loop by turning left and walking through enormous, ancient trees.

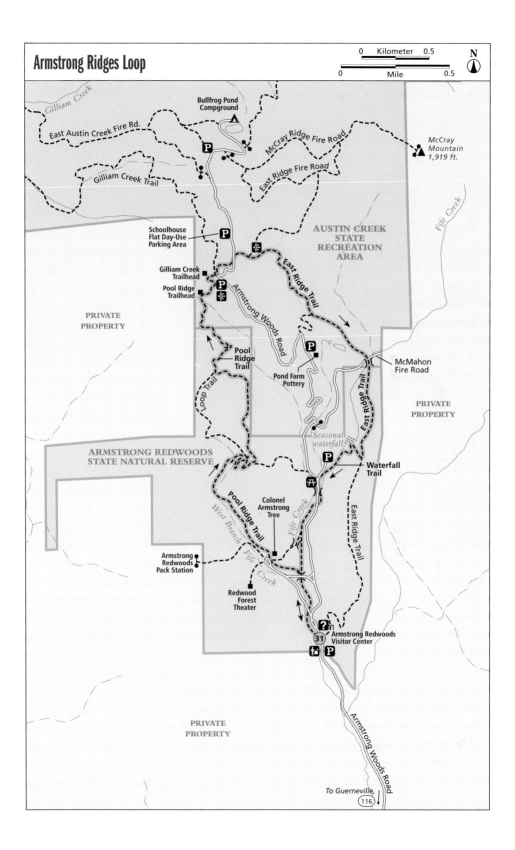

Armstrong Ridges Loop

Gilliam Creek

East Austin Creek Fire Rd.

Bullfrog Pond Campground

McCray Ridge Fire Road

McCray Mountain 1,919 ft.

Fife Creek

Gilliam Creek Trail

East Ridge Fire Road

Schoolhouse Flat Day-Use Parking Area

AUSTIN CREEK STATE RECREATION AREA

Gilliam Creek Trailhead

Pool Ridge Trailhead

Armstrong Woods Road

East Ridge Trail

PRIVATE PROPERTY

Pool Ridge Trail

Loop Trail

Pond Farm Pottery

McMahon Fire Road

PRIVATE PROPERTY

East Ridge Trail

ARMSTRONG REDWOODS STATE NATURAL RESERVE

Seasonal waterfall

Waterfall Trail

Pool Ridge Trail

West Branch Fife Creek

Fife Creek

Colonel Armstrong Tree

East Ridge Trail

Armstrong Redwoods Pack Station

Redwood Forest Theater

31

Armstrong Redwoods Visitor Center

PRIVATE PROPERTY

Armstrong Woods Road

To Guerneville,
116

0   Kilometer   0.5

0   Mile   0.5

N

0.55 Arrive at the Colonel Armstrong Tree, the oldest and largest in the reserve. Continue past the tree, following a dirt road a short distance to the beginning of the Pool Ridge Trail.

1.5 After a series of switchbacks, the trail reaches a junction where there is a nice view looking down on the redwood grove. Stay left at the junction and continue climbing up the ridge.

2.9 The trail reaches the top of the high ridge south of the redwood grove. The view to the south is good, and the bench is ideal for a little rest. To resume the hike, turn right onto the paved road and follow it around the bend to the Gilliam Creek trailhead. Two trails depart from there. Take the right-hand path, which is the East Ridge Trail.

3.1 Cross over a paved road and continue hiking to the top of a grassy knoll, where the best vista of the hike awaits. Just below the knoll, the trail splits. Stay to the right.

4.2 Amid a small redwood glen, cross a road and Fife Creek to resume hiking on the East Ridge Trail.

4.75 Turn right onto the Waterfall Trail and switchback down to the bottom of the valley, passing a seasonal waterfall and enormous redwoods as you descend.

5.15 After walking along a short section of access road in the picnic area, find the main park trail through the redwood grove and continue hiking.

6.0 Arrive back at the trailhead.

32 Austin Creek

This loop through the backcountry in Austin Creek State Recreation Area is one of the longest and most isolated trails in the Wine Country. With several creek crossings and two fords of large East Austin Creek, this is wild country, far removed from civilization. The trail has many panoramic vistas of the rugged North Coast Range and primitive backpacker camps, making this a great option for overnight trips.

Total Distance: 9.1-mile loop
Hiking Time: About 6 hours
Difficulty: Strenuous
Elevation Gain: 1,350 feet
Season: All year
Canine Compatibility: Dogs are not permitted
Fees: $8 entrance fee
Trail Contact: Austin Creek State Recreation Area, 17000 Armstrong Woods Rd., Guerneville,

CA 95446; (707) 869-2015; www.parks.ca .gov/?page_id=450
Other: This trail makes several creek crossings; in winter and spring, it is best to check with rangers about water levels. If the water is too high and crossings are dangerous, especially on East Austin Creek, this hike should not be attempted.

Finding the trailhead: From US 101, take the River Road exit and drive west on River Road for 15.2 miles. In the town of Guerneville, turn right onto Armstrong Woods Road. Drive 2.2 miles to the entrance station. Pass the entrance station and continue driving through the redwood grove for 0.7 mile. At the picnic area, Armstrong Woods Road veers right and begins a steep, narrow climb. The road passes incredibly tight turns that are not passable in RVs or even some longer trucks. After climbing for 0.9 mile, stay left when the road splits and immediately turn to the right into the Gilliam Creek trailhead parking area. GPS: N38°33.35967'/W123°00.71017'

The Hike

Hidden in the tangled ridges of northwest Sonoma County's isolated North Coast Range backcountry, Austin Creek State Recreation Area is one of the largest blocks of public land in the Wine Country. Contiguous with Armstrong Redwoods State Natural Reserve but a world away from the well-loved redwood groves, the park boasts numerous creeks running through steep canyons. The rugged terrain has contributed significantly to the park's secluded qualities. An excellent loop weaves its way through the park's deep canyons and offers hikers the chance to enjoy sections of East Austin Creek, one of the largest creeks in Sonoma County.

This is also one of the few trails in the Wine Country where it is possible to backpack. Primitive campsites are located in lonely corners of the park, giving backpackers a chance to enjoy backcountry solitude. However, the journey is not without its drawbacks. First, the loop requires several creek crossings, including two bridgeless crossings of East Austin Creek. In the spring these may be impassable; it is best to check in at the visitor center at Armstrong Redwoods to find out trail

Austin Creek flows through wild terrain.

conditions. Even when the creeks are low enough to cross, the hike ends with the long climb up infamous Panorama Grade, a shadeless 1,000-foot ascent. Thankfully, despite these obstacles, the loop through Austin Creek State Recreation Area rewards the effort.

Two trails begin at the Gilliam Creek trailhead. Take the trail on the left, which is the Gilliam Creek Trail, located next to the small trailhead display. The trail on the right is the return route. Once on the Gilliam Creek Trail, the path begins to descend immediately through thick forest cover. The trail soon levels off and winds its way through the trees for 0.2 mile. It then passes onto a grassy hillside with views to the west. The most notable feature is the barren wall of Red Oat Ridge and the nearby pinnacle, the Black Rock. Views of these features will improve later in the hike. Behind Red Oat Ridge lies the Cedars, a large pluton of ultramafic rock, mostly serpentine, that is a distinct outlier from the other rock types that compose the Coast Range. During World War I, a narrow-gauge railroad was built along East Austin Creek to access magnesite mines in the Cedars.

As the trail heads west, it snakes its way through small drainages and back onto grassy hillsides, where the great views are once again revealed. At 0.75 mile from the trailhead, the trail makes a sharp turn to the north and begins a precipitous descent. As the trail turns back to the west, still dropping steeply, look to the right across the small canyon and note the road climbing along a ridge on the other side. That is the infamous Panorama Grade, which is the return leg of the loop.

As the trail continues to descend, observe a subtle shift in the vegetation to a more chaparral type of environment. This coincides with the trail's crossing over a band of ultramafic serpentine rock, identifiable by its smooth surface and variations of blue and green color. The rocks are most evident in the soils exposed by trail construction. The band of serpentine is a long stem branching off of the main serpentine pluton that forms the Cedars. It creates a poor soil that most plants find inhospitable and that results in the transition to more hearty, chaparral plants. After crossing over the serpentine band, the trail turns to the south again and makes its final descent down to Schoolhouse Creek, crossing the creek about 1.5 miles from the trailhead.

Once the trail has arrived at Schoolhouse Creek, the Gilliam Creek Trail heads west once again. Running parallel to the creek, the trail passes through a wonderfully scenic area where the nearly impenetrable forest canopy filters out most of the sunlight and the trail becomes comfortably shady. Schoolhouse Creek often dries up later in the summer, but even its dry creek bed, filled with rocks, is attractive. A few creek crossings and 0.65 mile later, the trail arrives at the confluence of Schoolhouse Creek and Gilliam Creek, as well as at the first trail junction. Stay to the left. Going right here will connect to the far side of the loop just before beginning the long climb up the Panorama Grade.

Unlike Schoolhouse Creek, Gilliam Creek has a perennial flow, and even late in the summer of dry years, there will be some running water. The trail runs alongside the creek for nearly 1.4 miles. Initially traveling on the south side of Gilliam Creek, astute observers will notice the trail on the opposite side of the creek. The loop constricts here, with the two sections of the hike running alongside Gilliam Creek for 0.2 mile. After the trail across the creek has veered away, the Gilliam Creek Trail begins a series of creek crossings. There are nine in total, and hikers are ultimately left on the north side of the creek, where the trail eventually angles away from the creek and finally makes a short descent to East Austin Creek. Just before arriving at the creek, a picnic table marks the site of the abandoned Gilliam Creek Camp, formerly one of the park's primitive camping areas.

East Austin Creek is a large, year-round stream with a significant flow throughout the summer. It is a stark contrast to the small creeks encountered thus far on the hike. In the spring, when the creek is swollen with runoff, crossing it may be impossible, and it is best to be prepared to turn around and return to the trailhead if that is the case. However, lingering at the creek is an imperative, as numerous small rapids add interest to it, and redwood trees near the water make a great place to relax and enjoy the scenery.

When it is time to continue, it is necessary to cross the creek, which may be a challenge. There are no bridges, and there are few rocks to aid in keeping feet dry. Hop across the creek on what few rocks there are or take off your shoes and wade. Fortunately, East Austin Creek is wide and shallow here, so fording it is fairly easy. On the far side, the narrow trail actually runs downstream, climbing up a small rise. It then makes a sharp turn to the right, merging with an old roadbed, possibly the

The Panorama Grade climbs through Austin Creek State Recreation Area.

site of the narrow-gauge railroad that accessed the mines in the Cedars at the beginning of the twentieth century. Another 0.2 mile down the trail leads to a maintained dirt road and another trail junction. Turning to the left leads up the Fox Mountain fire road. Stay to the right, following the seldom-used fire road that runs parallel to, though well above, East Austin Creek. The sound of the creek pouring over cataracts far below highlights this section of trail, as do occasional glimpses of the creek and its deep canyon.

Eventually, after following East Austin Creek for 1.25 miles, the fire road drops down to the creek, and it is necessary to ford East Austin Creek one more time. Like the previous crossing, there are few rocks to help keep feet dry, but it is wide and shallow and easy to ford. Large redwood trees highlight this area.

On the far side of the creek is another fork in the trail. Going left here heads upstream and leads to the primitive campsites at Mannings Flat. Stay to the right and follow the trail downstream, staying close to East Austin Creek for 0.3 mile. Cross a bridge over perennial Thompson Creek and begin to climb a steep grade. Stay right at a fork; the path to the left leads to the Tom King camp, the final primitive camping area in the Austin Creek backcountry. A little more climbing completes the ascent, and far-reaching views open up for the first time since descending into Schoolhouse Creek's canyon. However, the views do not last, and the road drops back down to Gilliam Creek, where it runs parallel to the Gilliam Creek Trail for 0.3 mile. A short distance later, the wide path crosses a bridge and arrives at the junction with a spur off of the Gilliam Creek Trail. Going right here leads back to main part of the Gilliam

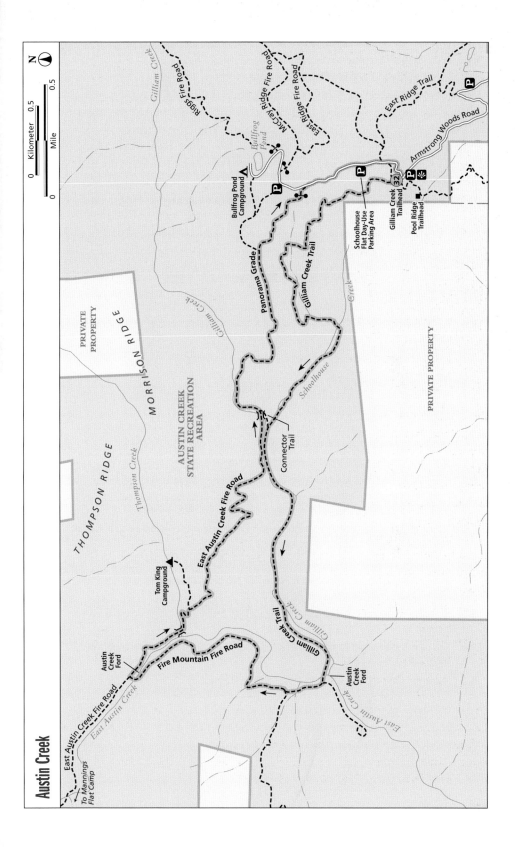

Austin Creek

N

0   Kilometer   0.5
0   Mile   0.5

Gilliam Creek

Riggs Ridge Fire Road

McCray Ridge Fire Road

East Ridge Fire Road

Bullfrog Pond

East Ridge Trail

Bullfrog Pond Campground

Armstrong Woods Road

Panorama Grade

Gilliam Creek Trail

Schoolhouse Flat Day-Use Parking Area

32

Gilliam Creek Trailhead

Pool Ridge Trailhead

Gilliam Creek

Schoolhouse Creek

THOMPSON RIDGE

MORRISON RIDGE

PRIVATE PROPERTY

AUSTIN CREEK STATE RECREATION AREA

Gilliam Creek

Thompson Creek

Tom King Campground

East Austin Creek Fire Road

Connector Trail

Gilliam Creek Trail

PRIVATE PROPERTY

Austin Creek Ford

Fire Mountain Fire Road

Gilliam Creek Trail

Gilliam Creek

East Austin Creek

Austin Creek Ford

East Austin Creek Fire Road

To Mannings Flat Camp

East Austin Creek

Creek Trail and the confluence of Schoolhouse and Gilliam Creeks. Stay straight and begin the climb up the steep Panorama Grade.

Climbing 1,000 feet in 1.25 miles, the Panorama Grade is the payment required for all of the easy downhill and level hiking that has characterized the majority of the loop through Austin Creek State Recreation Area. The difficulty of the climb is mitigated somewhat by the increasingly excellent views, particularly to the west. Once again, Red Oat Ridge and the dark spire of the Black Rock are the highlights of the view.

The grade finally comes to an end at a gate, where it merges with a paved road that leads to a car-accessible campground. Go right on the road and follow it for 0.4 mile. Turn right at a series of wooden steps and descend to the single track trail. Follow the path through some redwoods and around some rocks back to the Gilliam Creek trailhead, completing the long loop.

Miles and Directions

0.0 Two trails begin at the Gilliam Creek trailhead. Take the trail on the left, which is the Gilliam Creek Trail.

0.75 The trail begins to descend into the Schoolhouse Creek canyon.

1.5 Arrive at Schoolhouse Creek.

2.1 At the confluence of Schoolhouse Creek and Gilliam Creek, the trail splits. Turn left and begin hiking along Gilliam Creek.

3.65 The trail fords large East Austin Creek, which is large and has a strong flow. Early in the year, when the rains have increased the water volume, it can be impassable.

3.9 Stay right at the junction with the Fox Mountain fire road.

5.2 Ford East Austin Creek a second time in a grove of large redwoods. On the far side of the creek, the trail splits. To the left it follows the creek to the Mannings Flat primitive campsites. Stay right here and head downstream alongside East Austin Creek.

5.6 Shortly after crossing a bridge over Thompson Creek, a spur trail branches off to the left and leads to the Tom King primitive campsite.

6.75 Arrive back alongside Gilliam Creek, now on the opposite side from the first section of trail.

7.0 After crossing Gilliam Creek, stay left at the fork and begin the long climb up the Panorama Grade. Enjoy the views on the long climb!

8.5 The grade finally ends at the paved road leading to Bullfrog Pond. Turn right and walk on the road.

9.0 Turn right and descend some wooden steps on the East Ridge Trail. At the bottom of the steps, the trail levels off.

9.1 Reach the Gilliam Creek trailhead and complete the loop.

33 Fort Ross

This is a beautiful hike on the Sonoma Coast that explores coves, high cliffs above the surf, and sandy beaches. The highlight of the hike is amazing Fort Ross, the nineteenth-century Russian outpost that once thrived here. The fort has a large wooden stockade, numerous buildings, and a rustic Orthodox church, all set high a coastal bluff beside the sea.

Total Distance: 3.25 miles out and back
Hiking Time: About 2 hours
Difficulty: Easy
Elevation Gain: 135 feet
Season: All year
Canine Compatibility: Dogs are not permitted
Fees: $7 entrance fee

Trail Contact: Fort Ross State Park, 19005 Coast Hwy., Jenner, CA 95450; (707) 847-3437; www.fortross.org/
Other: The historic buildings are closed on Tuesday, Wednesday, and Thursday, and the park entrance is gated. Hikers are allowed to park at the entrance along CA 1 and walk into the park.

Finding the trailhead: At the intersection of CA 1 and CA 116 near Jenner, drive north on CA 1 for 8.3 miles. Turn left into the driveway for Fort Ross State Historic Park. GPS: N38°30.97267'/W123°14.79083'

The Hike

Perched on a lonely, wind-swept plateau above the Pacific Ocean, Fort Ross is a fascinating remnant of European colonialism. Established by the Russian-American Company, a Russian mercantile operation established to colonize Alaska, Fort Ross marked the southernmost point of Russia's colonial incursion into North America. In a way, this was the high-water mark of European colonization. Fort Ross and the nearby Spanish settlements on the interior of Sonoma County mark the point where the Russians, moving across Asia and the Pacific and expanding southward, met the Spanish, coming across the Atlantic and up from Mexico. The Russians maintained the fort from 1812 to 1841. It was a center for seal hunting and was also a gathering point for several agricultural operations that supplied food for the Russian settlements in Alaska. When Fort Ross's importance waned, it was sold to John Sutter, a Swiss pioneer who established the first European settlement in California's great Central Valley.

Today the restored fort is part of Fort Ross State Historic Park, which includes not only the fort but also a significant portion of the surrounding countryside. While there are a few hiking opportunities in the park, the best option is the Reef Trail. As it passes the fort on the way to exploring three beaches and skirting along the edge of high bluffs overlooking the Pacific Ocean, the trail is a great opportunity

Fort Ross is situated on a bluff above Fort Ross Cove.

to explore both Sonoma County's unique Russian history as well as the awesome Sonoma coastline.

From the visitor center, follow the sidewalk along the south side of the building heading toward a small gully. As the trail turns to the right, pass through the opening in the fence and onto a dirt trail that runs parallel to the small gully. The forest here is mostly cypress, but there are also massive eucalyptus trees, native to Australia, on the right-hand side of the trail. The path soon emerges from the woods, crosses a picnic area, and merges with a gravel road. Turn left on the road and head toward the wooden stockade of Fort Ross. The white farmhouse on the left was the residence of the Call family, who owned the land from the 1870s until it became a state park in the 1970s.

At the fort's south gate, turn right and follow the road toward the sea. The road makes a hairpin turn near the edge of the bluff and descends to a small parking area, roughly 0.5 mile from the visitor center. At the parking area, the trail splits. One route enters a tunnel formed of dense vegetation. It crosses a bridge over small Fort Ross Creek and then ascends a shallow gully to the old Russian cemetery, about 0.2 mile away. To continue the hike, head south from the parking lot toward the sound of the surf. The path deposits hikers on the beach of Sandy Cove, where Russian shipwrights once worked. Turn left and walk across the beach, skirting the edge of Fort Ross Creek. The creek does not usually reach the sea but sinks beneath the sand instead.

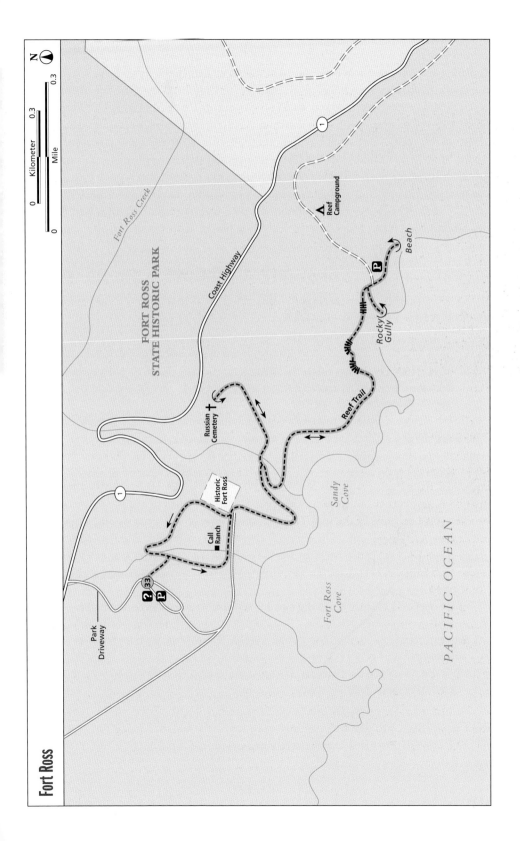

Fort Ross

PACIFIC OCEAN

On the far side of the cove, a series of wooden steps climb to the top of the bluffs. A marker indicates that this is the route of the Reef Trail. Following the path across the grassy bluffs, views back toward the fort are fantastic, and the sound of the surf crashing against the rocks below is loud and ubiquitous. The trail now runs along the edge of the cliffs. It is classic coastal terrain. Small wooden bridges provide passage across narrow gullies. After hiking along the bluffs for 0.4 mile, the trail descends a narrow draw to a second gravel parking lot, marking the end of the trail. A campground is adjacent to the parking lot. Just before the parking area, a path splits off to the right and descends a short canyon to a great vista overlooking an incredibly craggy beach. Returning to the parking lot, turn right and find another trail that descends to a big rocky beach littered with large pieces of driftwood. There is ample room for exploring on this lonely beach.

Return to the visitor center by retracing your steps. Just past the south gate at Fort Ross, turn right at the corner of the stockade and follow the wooden walls to the fort's main entrance. After checking out the fort, head back to the visitor center via the cement path, passing a community garden along the way.

Miles and Directions

0.0 Begin the hike at the visitor center. The trail departs to the right, beside the building. Near the rear entrance, turn right onto a dirt path and follow it as it travels above a gully surrounded by towering eucalyptus trees.

0.1 Turn left onto a road. Walk past an old farmhouse before nearing Fort Ross's stockade.

0.33 Near the west entrance of the stockade, turn right and follow the road toward the ocean.

0.6 The trail arrives at a little parking area and divides. On the east side, a trail crosses a bridge and enters a little gully; in 0.3 mile, this trail leads to the old Russian cemetery.

0.9 After visiting, return to the junction.

1.5 To continue the hike from the junction at the parking area, head south and follow the footpath toward the beach. When you get to the surf, turn left, walk across the cove, and climb up the steps on the far side.

1.6 Arrive at the top of the coastal bluff. Proceed south, along the edge of the cliffs.

2.0 After walking along the edge of coastal bluffs, the trail descends to another parking area. To the right a path leads down a narrow gap to a beautifully craggy beach. After exploring the small area, return to the parking area and cross over to the south side, where a trail leads down to a large beach.

2.85 After exploring the beach, retrace your steps back to the west entrance to the Fort Ross stockade.

3.25 Turn right and follow the trail to the main entrance to the fort. From there follow the path back to the visitor center.

34 Kortum Trail

Coastal bluffs, great views of the coast, and craggy rock formations are all highlights of this easy yet beautiful hike on the Sonoma Coast. The ocean is in view for nearly the entire hike, and there is beach access at a few points on the trail.

Total Distance: 4.3 miles out and back
Hiking Time: About 2.5 hours
Difficulty: Easy
Elevation Gain: 120 feet
Season: All year

Canine Compatibility: Dogs are not permitted
Fees: None
Trail Contact: Sonoma Coast State Park, Salmon Creek, Jenner, CA 95450; (707) 875-3483; www.sonoma-coast-state-park.com

Finding the trailhead: At the intersection of CA 1 and CA 116 near Jenner, turn left onto CA 1 and drive south for 2.5 miles. Turn right onto Carlevaro Way. Drive 100 yards, then turn right, and park at the end of the road. GPS: N38°24.74767'/W123°06.00717'

The Hike

The Sonoma Coast is an extraordinarily scenic region, with high cliffs plunging into the roiling surf, grassy meadows, lovely beaches, and rugged rock formations. A significant portion of the coastline falls under the jurisdiction of Sonoma Coast State Park. This diverse park offers access to numerous beaches as well as hiking paths both along the sea and in the high hills to the west.

The dramatic coast naturally attracts hikers, and for them the best route to explore this spectacular area is the Kortum Trail. An easy, level path that runs parallel to the beaches at the bottom of sheer cliffs, the Kortum Trail offers tremendous payoff for minimal effort. Along with great views in all directions, the trail affords easy access to beaches as well as interesting rock formations to explore.

Unlike most hikes in the Wine Country, the Kortum Trail has numerous trailheads and no single destination. Consequently, a few different options are available to hikers. The most frequently used access points are pullouts on the side of the road to Goat Rock, the Shell Beach parking lot, and the Wright's Beach parking area. However, a seldom-used trailhead on Carlevaro Way makes a great place to start the hike. Doing so adds 0.75 mile of scenic hiking while skipping some of the sections near Wright's Beach that veer away from the coast and run closer to CA 1.

From the parking area on lonely Carlevaro Way, take the wide path from the end of the road and hike to the west. Almost immediately, begin a descent into Furlong Gulch, dropping down more than 75 feet to a bridge that crosses Furlong Creek. A narrow path splits off the main trail and heads down to the large beach at the mouth of the gulch. After crossing the bridge, the Kortum Trail climbs back up to the broad plateau that runs parallel to the coastline and continues to the north. The trail then

The Sunset Boulders along the Kortum Trail.

veers away from the cliffs that mark the edge of the plateau and crosses another bridge over a small creek. Though the sounds of the gurgling stream are audible, it is difficult to see the water through the nearly impenetrable vegetation. After the bridge, the trail turns back toward the sea and finally arrives at the Shell Beach parking lot, about 0.75 mile from the beginning of the hike.

At the Shell Beach parking lot, a short spur leads down to the beautiful, rocky beach while the Kortum Trail continues to the north. About 0.15 mile from the Shell Beach parking lot, another spur branches off to the left and quickly leads to a dramatic overlook at the edge of the cliffs. Be careful around the precipice. Back on the main trail, hike to the north through open meadows with great views of the Pacific Ocean to the west and the hills of the Coast Range to the east. The route briefly swings away from the coast before once again running parallel to the cliffs that rise above the surf. Another short descent leads to a bridge across a small, spring-fed stream.

On the north side of the crossing, the route maintains its course, running parallel to the edge of the cliffs. Hills line the horizon to the north. Below the hills, a pair of large rock formations erupts from the flat grasslands crossed by the Kortum Trail. The first formation is a solitary crag rising about 35 to 40 feet above the ground. A sign indicates that the area around the first crag is closed to allow the vegetation to recover. The second formation is not a single crag but a cluster of rocks known collectively as the Sunset Boulders. The Kortum Trail swings close to these boulders, and numerous tracks lead up to the rocks where one can scramble around the tall, upright stones.

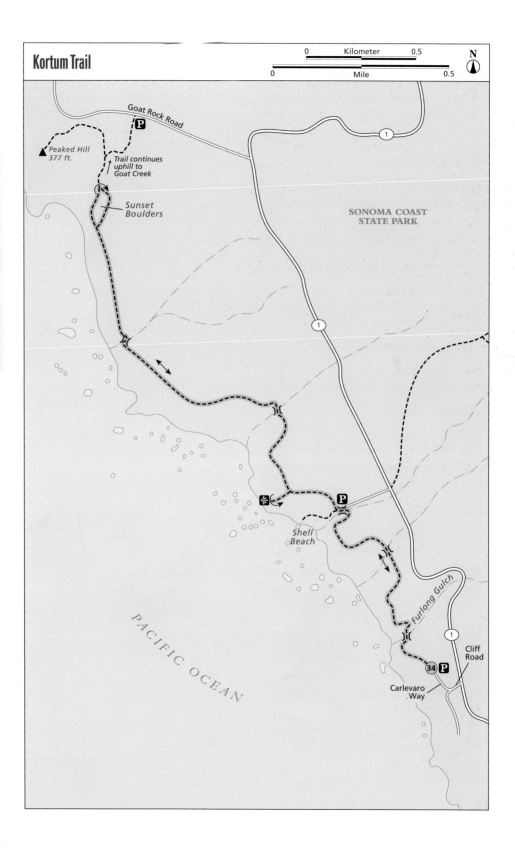

Kortum Trail

0   Kilometer   0.5

0   Mile   0.5

N

Goat Rock Road

P

▲ Peaked Hill
377 ft.

Trail continues
uphill to
Goat Creek

Sunset
Boulders

SONOMA COAST
STATE PARK

1

1

P

Shell
Beach

Furlong Gulch

1

Cliff
Road

34 P

Carlevaro
Way

PACIFIC OCEAN

A short loop encircles the Sunset Boulders and connects back to the main path. For hikers looking for a longer trip, the Kortum Trail climbs up the hill just to the north of the Sunset Boulders and ultimately leads to Goat Rock. However, the boulders make a good destination with interesting exploration potential and plenty of views. From there retrace your steps back to the trailhead at Carlevaro Way.

Miles and Directions

0.0 A connector trail departs from the trailhead, passing through some brush before connecting to the main stem of the Kortum Trail.

0.1 Cross over Furlong Gulch. Beach access is to the left.

0.75 Arrive at the Shell Beach parking area. A trail splits off to the left and leads down to the beach.

0.9 A spur leads to a nice overlook above the surf.

2.15 Reach the Sunset Boulders. The trail continues to climb the hillside, but this makes a good place to turn around. Retrace your steps back to the trailhead.

35 Pomo Canyon–Red Hill Loop

The hike from Pomo Canyon to Shell Beach is an epic loop that combines panoramic vistas, redwoods, rugged rock formations, and the beautiful Sonoma Coast.

Total Distance: 7.6-mile loop
Hiking Time: About 5 hours
Difficulty: Strenuous
Elevation Gain: 1,500 feet
Season: All year
Canine Compatibility: Dogs are permitted

Fees: None
Trail Contact: Sonoma Coast State Park, Salmon Creek, Jenner, CA 95450; (707) 875-3483; www.sonoma-coast-state-park.com
Other: Willow Creek Road may be closed because of flood conditions.

Finding the trailhead: At the intersection of CA 1 and CA 116 near Jenner, turn left onto CA 1 and drive south for 0.3 mile. Turn left onto Willow Creek Road. Follow this road for 2.6 miles to a wide spot on the road by a gate. Park near the gate. GPS: N38°25.81233' / W123°04.21100'

The Hike

Highlighting many of the greatest features of western Sonoma County, the Pomo Canyon Trail is one of the best hikes in the Wine Country. The route forms a great loop running from redwood forests, along coastal hillsides with good views, to the Shell Beach parking lot with easy access to the surf. On the way back, the loop climbs high over expansive meadows and scenic rock formations to the summit of Red Hill and some of the most spectacular views in the Wine Country.

The Pomo Canyon Trail used to begin at the beautiful Pomo Canyon Campground. Tucked away in a beautiful redwood forest, it was once a great place to enjoy camping in a redwood forest. Unfortunately the campground has been shuttered due to budget cuts. Adding insult to injury, the last 0.5 mile of the access road has been gated, requiring an additional 0.5 mile of hiking along the gravel road. The road ends at the old campground parking lot.

The beginning of the proper Pomo Canyon Trail is just to the right of the campground information board and a pair of restrooms. You will begin to climb immediately through the redwoods. Note the ringed arrangement of the redwoods in this area. These are "fairy rings," where several small sprouts generate off of a dead tree trunk. In this case the original forest was cut, and the fairy rings have regenerated the forest. The path passes many of these trees as it climbs first to the north and then to the west. After climbing for 0.25 mile, the redwoods give way to a normal mixed forest of oak, fir, and bay. The trail's grade maintains a steep grade as it traverses a steep cliff choked with dense vegetation.

At 1.2 miles from the beginning, the trail arrives at a fork. Those hikers looking for a shorter hike can go left here and simply hike to the top of Red Hill for a great,

The first view of Red Hill Loop from the trail.

albeit abbreviated, outing. To stay on the main loop, proceed to the right, passing some small open areas before once again entering the woods. This pattern of alternating open and wooded sections continues for a mile, with some occasional views to the north. Eventually you cross a long grassy area with constantly improving views. After heading down a short, lazy switchback, the trail levels off as it heads west. A short path branches off to the right and leads to a small knoll with a great view looking down on the Russian River and the small seaside community of Jenner. From there the main trail continues to the west through open terrain with improving views of the Pacific Ocean to the west.

About 0.3 mile from the vista point, the path arrives at a junction with the route leading down from Red Hill, which makes up the latter part of the loop. For hikers not interested in heading down to Shell Beach, go left here and make the journey back to Pomo Canyon. To get to Shell Beach, continue downhill on the wide path, which by now has become an old road. Excellent views of the Pacific, the coastal bluffs, and distant landmarks Bodega Head and Point Reyes are found here.

Along the bluffs the Kortum Trail is visibly hugging the precipice along the cliffs. At the bottom of the hill, you will reach a gate. Here the trail ends at the edge of CA 1, directly across the road from the driveway leading to Shell Beach. Cross the road carefully and walk down the driveway about 300 yards to the trailhead leading down to Shell Beach. It is a short descent down to the surf.

The Pomo Canyon–Red Hill Loop affords dramatic views of the Russian River's passage to the sea.

To return to Pomo Canyon, cross back over CA 1 and make the climb to the junction with the route that leads to Red Hill. Stay right here and continue climbing through open, grassy terrain with great views. The trail passes between a pair of large, lonely rock towers. The northern tower is easy to climb and has good views. After skirting the rocks, the route swings to the north and then back to the east. The grade is constant but moderate, and the hiking is excellent. Following a small gully, the trail turns to the south. After you cross the gully, resume hiking on an eastward trajectory. The open, grassy hillsides are beautiful, and the great scenery makes the uphill grade pleasant. The path soon nears the edge of a large wooded area, passing through a tunnel beneath the low trees. On the other side, the trail crosses more grassy slopes, but now the views have shifted to the east. It is just a short distance farther before arriving at another junction. Turn right and begin the final climb to the summit of Red Hill.

The route to the summit of Red Hill first travels through a small rock garden set amid the grassy hillside. It turns to the west and climbs toward a large redwood grove. This grove, situated on the top of a prominent mountain, is unusual in that it is in an open, windy spot rather than at the bottom of a protected valley. The trail enters the grove and winds through the dark redwood forest before reemerging on the grassy flanks just below the summit of Red Hill.

The trail makes the final loop up to the summit, revealing one of the most spectacular vistas in the Wine Country. To the east, a long tangle of ridges leads inland. On the horizon, the Mayacamas Mountains, the backbone of the Wine Country, can

Pomo Canyon—Red Hill Loop

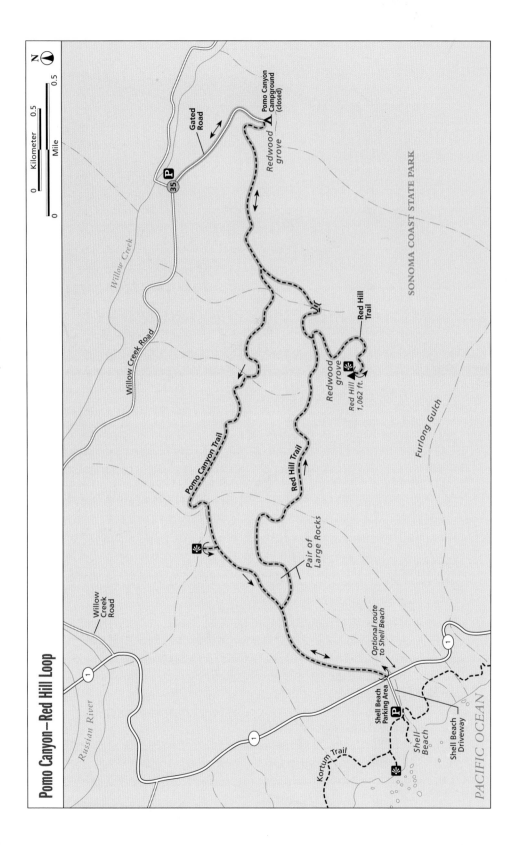

Willow Creek Road

Russian River

Willow Creek

Willow Creek Road

Gated Road

P 35

Pomo Canyon Campground (closed)

Redwood grove

SONOMA COAST STATE PARK

Pomo Canyon Trail

Red Hill Trail

Red Hill Trail

Redwood grove

Red Hill 1,062 ft.

Red Hill Trail

Furlong Gulch

Pair of Large Rocks

Optional route to Shell Beach

Shell Beach Parking Area

P

Shell Beach

Shell Beach Driveway

Kortum Trail

PACIFIC OCEAN

1

1

1

N

0   Kilometer   0.5

0   Mile   0.5

be seen, highlighted by the towering summits of Cobb Mountain and Mount Saint Helena. The northern vista includes high coastal peaks and cliffs above the pounding surf, but the real apogee of the northern perspective is the Russian River's arrival at the Pacific Ocean. The small village of Jenner clings to the side of the river's canyon just above the estuary. It is an inspiring sight, though the view to the south is nearly as impressive. On the coast, Bodega Head and Point Reyes jut prominently into the sea. On clear days, the distant Farallon Islands are discernable nearly 30 miles off the coast. Inland, a vast expanse of hills, ridges, and valleys extend to the south. It is a spectacular view in all directions.

When it is time to return to the trailhead, head back down the summit trail to the main trail. Turn right and head downhill across more grassy hillsides. The trail crosses a bridge over a scenic stream that is quite noisy in the spring. After the bridge, continue down the hill to a fence, where a wooden pass-through permits hikers to continue to the other side. Beyond the fence it is only 0.2 mile down to the Pomo Canyon Trail. Stay to the right and retrace your steps to the Pomo Canyon Campground and then back along the access road to the parking area.

Miles and Directions

0.0 From the parking area on the side of Willow Creek Road, walk around the gate and begin hiking down the dirt road.

0.5 At the old trailhead in the old Pomo Canyon Campground, turn right to begin hiking on the Pomo Canyon Trail.

1.2 Stay right to continue on the Pomo Canyon Trail. The left fork here marks the return route.

2.5 A short spur leads to a great overlook above the Russian River.

2.9 Stay straight at the junction with the Red Hill Trail.

3.4 The trail ends at CA 1. Cross the highway and walk down the driveway to get to Shell Beach.

3.9 After climbing back up from CA 1, turn right onto the Red Hill Trail to begin the return section of the loop.

5.15 Turn right on the spur that leads to the summit of Red Hill.

5.6 Arrive at the summit of Red Hill and enjoy one of the best views in the Wine Country.

6.05 Back at the main trail, turn right to finish the loop.

6.5 Turn right back onto the Pomo Canyon Trail.

7.1 The trail ends at the old Pomo Canyon Campground. Continue down the gravel road.

7.6 Arrive back at the trailhead.

36 Bodega Head

The short hike around Bodega Head is a classic trip on one of the most interesting and historic sections of the Sonoma Coast. In addition to beautiful views and a lovely beach surrounded by craggy rock formations, the trail offers a unique look into the massive geologic forces at work along the coast.

Total Distance: 1.75-mile loop
Hiking Time: About 1 hour
Difficulty: Easy
Elevation Gain: 150 feet
Season: All year
Canine Compatibility: Dogs are permitted
Fees: None

Trail Contact: Sonoma Coast State Park, Salmon Creek, Jenner, CA 95450; (707) 875-3483; www.sonoma-coast-state-park.com
Other: Steep cliffs above the surf are close to some sections of the trail; be wary of the exposure.

Finding the trailhead: Driving north on CA 1 through the small town of Bodega Bay, turn left onto Eastshore Road. Drive 0.3 mile, then turn right onto Bay Flat Road. After 0.4 mile, it becomes Westshore Road. Continue for 3.2 miles to the parking lot at the end of the road. GPS: N38°18.22233'/W123°03.85800'

The Hike

Bodega Head is one of the most dramatic features on the Sonoma County coast. Most of the coastline consists of rolling hills leveling off to a narrow bench, followed by cliffs plunging into the surf. In contrast, Bodega Head is a prominent peninsula protruding 2 miles out from the coastline. While the presence of a large finger of land extending into the sea is interesting, a quick examination of a map reveals a larger and eminently more fascinating picture. Bodega Head is, in fact, a result of the San Andreas Fault. A result of tectonic activity, the fault exists at the point where the Pacific and North American plates meet. For most of its length, the San Andreas Fault runs inland from the coast and is responsible for many of the most dominant geographic features in Southern California, including the Imperial Valley and the Transverse Range. Heading toward central California, it runs closer to the coast and finally dives into the sea at San Francisco. However, north of the Golden Gate Bridge, the fault resurfaces. The San Andreas dips inland again and forms the Olema Valley, which separates the Point Reyes Peninsula from the rest of Marin County. North of the valley lies Tomales Bay, where the fault runs underwater again briefly before emerging one more time at Bodega Head. The fault line is evident to the naked eye. It's also easy to see that Point Reyes and Bodega Head are part of a different geologic region than the rest of the coast.

A fishing boat passes dramatic cliffs at Bodega Head.

Interestingly, Bodega Head and the northern part of the Point Reyes Peninsula are composed of granite, a rock type that does not appear anywhere else in the Wine Country, which mostly consists of cherts, shales, sandstones, and volcanic rocks. Bodega Head itself is composed of granite, while the neck that connects the head to the mainland is a complex of sand dunes. While Bodega Head was once an island, dunes, which lie right on the fault, have built up over the millennia, eventually connecting the head to the mainland. Consequently, a hike on Bodega Head is a hike on the tectonic plate that is also home to points as far away as the South Island of New Zealand. Whatever its geologic history, the Bodega Head Trail offers exceptional scenery that includes high sea cliffs and views of the Sonoma Coast's Tomales Bay and Point Reyes.

The Bodega Head Trail begins at the large parking lot just above a small but exceptionally scenic beach. The exposed, weathered granite is sculpted into spires and crags and makes a great backdrop to the pretty little beach that's tucked into its small cove. A short trail descends into the cove and offers a chance to enjoy the beach or climb on the rocks.

To find the Bodega Head Trail, look for the wide path immediately adjacent to the bathrooms. It sets out to the south and right away encounters a fork. (It should be noted that the Bodega Head Trail is riddled with hiker-made use trails.) To stay on the main trail and enjoy the best scenery, be sure to follow the main trail as it stays close to the edge of the cliffs. At the fork, stay to the right and follow the trail toward the

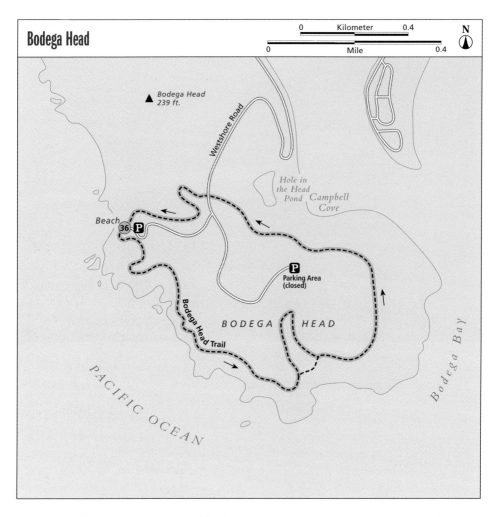

Bodega Head 239 ft.

Westshore Road

Hole in the Head Pond

Campbell Cove

Beach

36 P

P Parking Area (closed)

Bodega Head Trail

BODEGA HEAD

Bodega Bay

PACIFIC OCEAN

0 Kilometer 0.4

0 Mile 0.4

N

cliffs as it makes a sweeping switchback. As you approach the precipice, watch for the ship-shaped monument to seafarers. Once the path arrives at the edge of the cliff, it swings back to the east and follows them above a small, secluded cove.

The trail rounds the cove and turns to the south, still hugging the edge of the cliffs. The views are fantastic in all directions, and the sound of the surf pounding the rocks at the base of the cliffs is both ubiquitous and awesome. The path proceeds to climb for 0.1 mile up a grade until a pair of trails split off to the east. Stay straight, following the cliffs, continuing up the moderate grade to the south. The path hugs the cliffs as it rounds the southern tip of the head. Views improve as more of Point Reyes, the Sonoma Coast, and Bodega Bay come into view. The bay is formed by Bodega Head at the north and Tomales Point, the northernmost point of the Point Reyes Peninsula, to the south. As the trail reaches its highest point on the south side of the head, the full vista to the south and east unfolds. The sounds of seas lions barking from nearby Bodega Rock add to the cacophony of the waves far below. It is an amazing spot.

The trail now swings to the north, and Bodega Harbor, formed by Bodega Head and the sandy spit of Doran Beach, comes into view. The harbor is filled with small fishing vessels, and the quaint seaside village of Bodega Bay sits on a bluff just above the water. It is a classic coastal scene. As the trail heads north, it veers inland, away from the cliffs. These are less dramatic on the leeward side of the head, since the powerful sea waves do not batter them. Finally, about 1.15 miles from the beginning of the hike, the trail turns west and comes close to some old bathrooms beside an abandoned parking lot. A short spur connects to these. Stay to the right and continue to follow the main path.

Just below the low bluffs to the right of the trail is the famed Hole in the Head, which was dug in preparation for the construction of the first commercial nuclear power plant in the United States. The threat to Bodega Bay's rural way of life and, more importantly, the location on top of the active San Andreas Fault ultimately led to the project's cancellation. The "Hole" has now filled with water and is a scenic pond, almost indistinguishable from the natural setting. A little farther down the trail, the path crosses the main access road and makes a quick switchback through thick growth, finally returning to the trailhead next to the short trail that drops down to the beach, thus completing the loop.

Miles and Directions

0.0 The hike starts near the restrooms at the trailhead. Hike south, staying on the main trail and avoiding several unofficial paths.

0.1 Pass a sailor's monument at an overlook above the sea.

0.5 The trail reaches the highest point on the hike, with awesome views to the south of the Point Reyes Peninsula, Tomales Point, and Tomales Bay.

1.0 Enjoy a picnic table with a nice view from above Bodega Bay's ship channel.

1.15 Stay to the right at a junction with a trail leading to a closed parking area.

1.45 Cross the road and continue hiking the trail. A little more hiking leads to an overlook with a bench. A narrow track departs from this point and travels north toward the Horseshoe Cove overlook.

1.75 Arrive back at the trailhead, next to the path leading down to the beautiful beach.

37 Helen Putnam Regional Park

The short loop through pretty Helen Putnam Regional Park offers a brief introduction to the terrain of southern Sonoma County's Petaluma Gap. The hike has a nice mix of forests and grass-covered hillsides, as well as some fine views, including a wonderful vista of the city of Petaluma and tall Sonoma Mountain.

Total Distance: 2.0-mile loop
Hiking Time: About 1.5 hours
Difficulty: Easy
Elevation Gain: 400 feet
Season: All year
Canine Compatibility: Dogs are permitted on leash

Fees: $7 parking fee
Trail Contact: Sonoma County Regional Parks; (707) 433-1625; http://parks.sonomacounty .ca.gov/Get_Outdoors/Parks/Helen_Putnam_ Regional_Park.aspx

Finding the trailhead: From US 101 in Petaluma, take the East Washington exit and drive west on East Washington Street for 1.2 miles; on the west side of downtown, it becomes Bodega Avenue. Continue for another 0.7 mile. Turn left onto Bantam Way and drive 0.3 mile. Turn right onto Western Avenue and continue for 0.8 mile. Turn left onto Chileno Valley Road, driving another 0.8 mile. Turn left into the large, signed trailhead parking lot. GPS: N38°12.77033'/W122°39.83067'

The Hike

The Petaluma Gap is a low elevation depression in the North Coast Range that runs inland 30 miles from Bodega Bay to the mouth of the Petaluma River at San Pablo Bay, which is the northern half of San Francisco Bay. Elevations to the north and south of the gap often exceed 1,000 feet and frequently climb even higher. This is in stark contrast to the elevation in the Petaluma Gap, where the elevation is often close to sea level and rarely exceeds 500 feet. The gentle topography of the gap creates something akin to a natural wind tunnel and draws strong winds off the coast and funnels them down toward San Pablo Bay.

The area is distinct visually. Where most of the North Coast Range is heavily wooded, the gap is generally a hilly, grassy region punctuated by occasional trees. This is Sonoma County's dairy land, and carefree cattle are ubiquitous. With the marine winds also comes a copious amount of coastal fog, which has a significant impact on grape growing in the area, especially along the Petaluma River, where vineyards are abundant.

Most of the land in the Petaluma Gap is privately owned. One small exception is Helen Putnam Regional Park, which lies a few miles west of Petaluma. The park is in a transitional area on the southern fringe of the gap, but it still displays much of the

Helen Putnam view of Sonoma Mountain and Petaluma.

gap's distinctiveness. The trail system at Helen Putnam Regional Park is well developed and explores the park's different ecosystems. It also boasts great views of the windswept Petaluma Gap as well as a fantastic vista overlooking the city of Petaluma.

The trail, initially called the Panorama Trail, begins at the far end of the parking lot, right next to the bathrooms. Climb up a steep, open hill on a wide dirt path. Stay to the left at a fork almost immediately past the trailhead. Views of the rolling hills of the Petaluma Gap to the west are terrific. Be sure to glance to the south during the climb and spot the rounded peak of Mount Burdell, a high mountain along the Marin County line. Once on the top of the hill, two trail junctions appear in quick succession. Stay to the right at the first junction, which puts you on the Pomo Trail. Go straight through the second one. The trail then enters an oak woodland before arriving at a third junction. Stay to the left, which marks the beginning of the Fillaree Trail.

This path weaves its way through the forest as it makes a gradual descent. The forest canopy is thick, and while there are no views, the woods are pleasant and the hiking is easy. Finally, the trail emerges from the woods and merges onto a wide trail 1 mile from the trailhead. Hang a left on the trail and then immediately look for a spur trail branching off to the left. Take this out to a magnificent vista overlooking Petaluma. The city spreads out 350 feet below the hill while massive Sonoma Mountain looms on the far side of the valley. To the north the view is even grander. The high peaks of the Mayacamas Mountains mark the horizon, including conical Geyser Peak

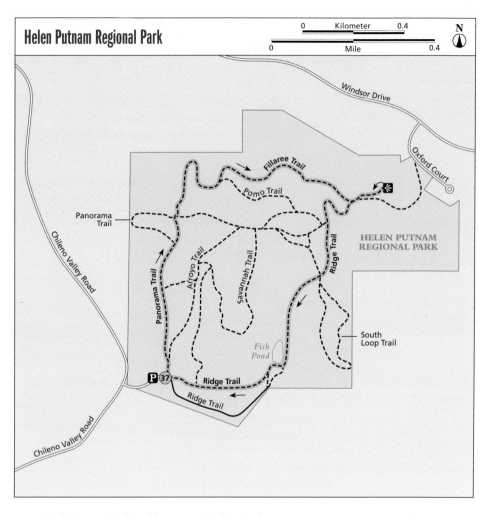

Kilometer 0 0.4

Mile 0 0.4

N

Windsor Drive

Oxford Court

Fillaree Trail

Pomo Trail

Panorama Trail

Chileno Valley Road

HELEN PUTNAM REGIONAL PARK

Panorama Trail

Arroyo Trail

Savannah Trail

Ridge Trail

South Loop Trail

Fish Pond

P 37

Ridge Trail

Ridge Trail

Chileno Valley Road

on the left, rounded Cobb Mountain (the highest point in Sonoma County), and the mammoth Mount Saint Helena.

To continue the hike, return to the main trail and turn right, heading back up the hill. Go straight past the end of the Fillaree Trail and climb the hill as the wide path passes through a cluster of oak trees. A side trail to the right leads to a grassy knoll with great views to the west and south. From here the route begins the long descent down to the trailhead. It first follows a small creek through a shallow gully before arriving at small Fish Pond. An impoundment on the small creek, the diminutive pond is ringed with reeds and is a popular place for young anglers to cast a line. Cross over the small dam and take the unpaved Ridge Trail. Crossing a lovely, open hillside, the trail makes its final drop down to the trailhead, completing the loop.

Miles and Directions

0.0 The trail begins near the restrooms at the far end of the parking area. It begins climbing steeply right away. Stay left at a junction a short distance from the beginning of the hike, which marks the beginning of the Panorama Trail.

0.25 Stay left at another junction.

0.35 At a junction, veer to the right off of the Panorama Trail and begin hiking on the Pomo Trail. A short distance later, stay straight, crossing over the Panorama Trail and continuing on the Pomo Trail.

0.5 Turn left and begin hiking on the Fillaree Trail.

1.0 Turn left onto a paved trail and immediately veer to the left onto a short spur that leads to a fantastic vista above Petaluma. Return to the paved trail and turn right, hiking up the hill.

1.5 At a five-way intersection, stay straight and continue hiking on the Ridge Trail.

1.7 At the far end of Fish Pond, turn right onto the hiking trail that crosses the little dam. Continue on the trail past the tank and across a grass-covered hillside.

2.0 Arrive back at the trailhead.

38 Petaluma River

Passing through tidal marshes, beside levees, and next to the Petaluma River, the hike connecting the Alman Marsh to a loop through Schollenberger Park is a pleasant, easy trip along southern Sonoma County's Petaluma River.

Total Distance: 4.25-mile lollipop
Hiking Time: About 2.5 hours
Difficulty: Easy
Elevation Gain: None
Season: All year
Canine Compatibility: Dogs are permitted on leash
Fees: None

Trail Contact: City of Petaluma Parks and Recreation, 320 N. McDowell Blvd., Petaluma, CA; (707) 778-4380; http://cityofpetaluma.net/parksnrec/parks-pages/shollenberger.html
Other: Though not connected to the trail, the Rocky Memorial Dog Park is located in Schollenberger Park.

Finding the trailhead: From US 101 in Petaluma, take the CA 116 exit and drive east on CA 116 for 0.2 mile. Turn right onto Baywood Drive, which immediately enters the Sheraton Hotel parking lot. Drive past the hotel's main entrance to the south end of the parking lot. Park in the spaces near the trailhead sign next to a footbridge. GPS: N38°13.81500'/W122°36.72283'

The Hike

The Petaluma River drains a significant part of southern Sonoma County. Rising at the northern end of the Petaluma flood plain, the river travels 18 miles to San Pablo Bay. Most of the river is a long tidal estuary, heavily governed by the tide. The lower 14 miles, beginning in downtown Petaluma, are navigable, and barges and private boats frequently travel the river. Even though sections of the river are developed and the fringes of the city cling to its banks, the Petaluma is still a very scenic and undervalued natural landmark. A few trails near the downtown area offer good access to parts of the river and strike a pleasant balance between the proximity to urban development and quiet natural areas. The best way to explore the river is to combine the trails. The first trail crosses the Alman Marsh and provides scenic, backdoor access to the loop around Shollenberger Park. Both trails have attractive sections along the Petaluma River, as well as views of the Sonoma Mountains to the east. Of course, they both have views of a freeway and the edge of the urban area. Shollenberger Park has a separate trailhead from Alman Marsh and can be hiked independently of the first trail.

The Alman Marsh Trail begins at the far end of the hotel parking lot. Cross a bridge over a slough. The trail turns to the west and runs parallel to the creek before reaching the river. Here you can observe the freeway bridge and old railroad bridge over the water and the nearby marina next to the hotel. Following the river downstream, the trail crosses a long boardwalk across marshy areas before turning away

The Petaluma River.

from the river. A second bridge crosses Adobe Creek, one of the Petaluma River's largest tributaries. The trail continues inland for 0.4 mile, crossing a third bridge over a swampy channel. As the trail approaches a large white building, it turns to the right and runs beside a fence before arriving at a junction with the trail leading from Shollenberger Park's trailhead parking area to the main loop. Turn right here and cross a wide bridge to the beginning of the Shollenberger loop, 1.1 miles from the Alman Marsh trailhead.

To start the loop, turn right and follow the wide path back toward the Petaluma River. To the right is a large tidal flat. This area was once filled with the silt dredged out of the Petaluma River. Now it is a vast, muddy area that fills with water when the tide is in. The loop trail encircles this flat area. When the trail reaches the river, it makes a turn to the left. A large wooden observation deck extends over the water and offers great views of the muddy river as well as the surrounding area. Dilapidated maritime buildings line the opposite side of the river. They seem strangely out of place this far inland, bounded by rolling hills. From the observation deck, the wide trail follows the Petaluma River for 0.55 mile before turning inland. The trail follows a levee across the tidal flats for 0.5 mile. The trail then forks. To the right is a trail that leads to reclaimed areas around a water treatment plant. Go left and follow the trail back to the bridge at the beginning of the Shollenberger loop. From here retrace your steps to the parking lot at the beginning of the Alman Marsh Trail.

Petaluma River

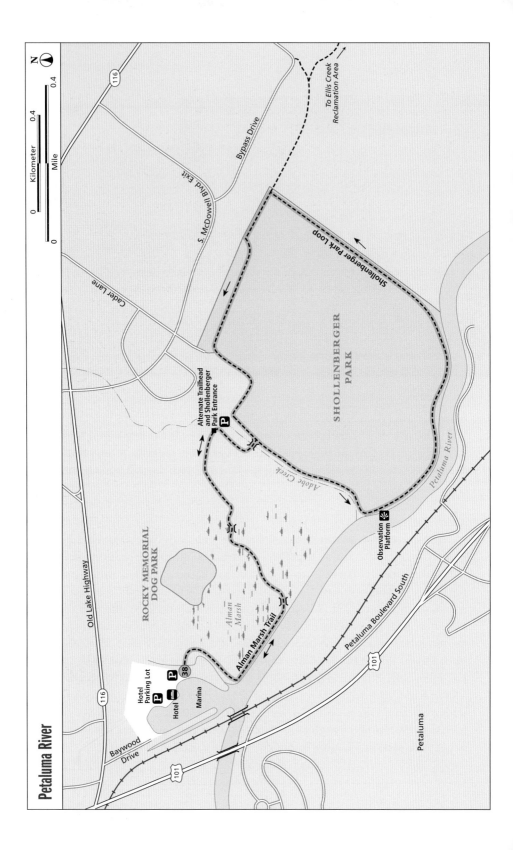

N

Kilometer
0   0.4

Mile
0   0.4

116

Old Lake Highway

116

Baywood Drive

Cadet Lane

S. McDowell Blvd. Exit

Bypass Drive

To Ellis Creek
Reclamation Area

Shollenberger Park Loop

SHOLLENBERGER PARK

Petaluma River

Adobe Creek

Observation
Platform

Alternate Trailhead
and Shollenberger
Park Entrance

P

ROCKY MEMORIAL
DOG PARK

Alman Marsh

Alman Marsh Trail

Hotel Parking Lot

P

P

Hotel

38

Marina

Petaluma Boulevard South

101

101

Petaluma

Miles and Directions

0.0 From the south end of the Sheraton Hotel parking lot, walk across the footbridge and begin hiking on the trail through Alman Marsh.

0.2 The trail turns to the south and runs parallel to the Petaluma River.

0.45 After veering away from the river, the trail crosses a little bridge and turns inland.

1.0 Merge onto the trail coming from the main Shollenberger Park trailhead.

1.1 Arrive at the beginning of the Shollenberger Park loop. Turn right to begin the loop.

1.4 The trail reaches the Petaluma River and begins to travel alongside it. A nice observation platform sits over the water.

2.0 The path veers from the river and begins to head inland across a levee.

2.5 At a trail junction, turn left.

3.2 Complete the loop and turn right back onto the trail to Alman Marsh. Retrace your steps to the trailhead.

4.25 Arrive back at the trailhead.

39 Tolay Lake Regional Park

This is an excellent hike around the headwaters of Tolay Creek in the southern Sonoma Mountains. The high hills of the park are contrasted against vast meadows and old forests. With great views of Tolay Lake's valley, vineyards, and San Francisco Bay, this is a dramatic but lightly hiked trail.

Total Distance: 7.25-mile loop
Hiking Time: About 4.5 hours
Difficulty: Moderate
Elevation Gain: 530 feet
Season: All year
Canine Compatibility: Dogs are not permitted
Fees: $7 parking fee
Trail Contact: Tolay Lake Regional Park, 5869 Cannon Lane, Petaluma CA; (707) 539-8092;

http://parks.sonomacounty.ca.gov/Get_Outdoors/Parks/Tolay_Lake_Regional_Park.aspx
Other: The park is currently in the development phase and not regularly open to the public. It can be hiked once you have a permit. To receive a permit, you must take a 1-hour orientation.

Finding the trailhead: From US 101 in Petaluma, take the CA 116 exit and drive east on CA 116 for 4.4 miles. Continue straight onto Lakeville Highway and proceed for 1.3 miles. At the signed turn for Tolay Lake Regional Park, turn left onto Cannon Lane. Drive 1.3 miles to the park entrance gate. Using the code on your permit, pass through the gate and drive down the hill to the parking area. GPS: N38°12.28433'/W122°31.23433'

The Hike

Tolay Lake Regional Park is sublime corner of southern Sonoma County's quiet agricultural backcountry. For many years the park was a working ranch, and it still has many of the trappings of ranch life, including the presence of cattle that graze the park's lands at times. Likewise, ranch buildings are found at the trailhead, and most of the park trails are old ranch roads. However, though the park itself was once a ranch, much of the land around it has been overtaken by the American viticulture area (AVA). Although vineyards now lurk around the park's boundaries, the transformation of the ranch into a county park has permanently halted the vines' advance, and it is now a pastoral oasis.

Tucked away in a secluded valley at the southernmost tip of the Sonoma Mountains, Tolay Lake Regional Park highlights lush, grassy hills and wetlands. The namesake lake, though it is often reduced to a marshy area, lies at the headwaters of Tolay Creek. The lake's level is dependent on the quantity of rainfall over the winter. Tolay Creek is the southernmost significant creek to spring from the Sonoma Mountains. It flows south through the rolling hills before emerging at the tidal area at the southern tip of Sonoma County. The creek flows through the tidal area

Looking back toward the park headquarters and seasonal Tolay Lake from the East Ridge Trail.

before discharging in San Pablo Bay, which is the northern half of San Francisco Bay (see Hike 40).

The hike through the park is diverse, passing through wetlands, ranchlands, and some oak woodlands and up grassy hills. The natural setting is lovely, and the vista from the park's highest point is fantastic. It should be noted that this is a relatively new park and that additional trails are planned. This hike tries to maximize the existing trails and combines them to form an excellent, scenic loop with a few side trips. Since the park is new, it is not open to the public at large. To hike here it is necessary to come for a short orientation and then receive a free permit. The orientation is only necessary once. Once the permit has been obtained, it enables hikers to return to the park repeatedly.

Starting at the ranch at the trailhead, head east on the Causeway Trail. This old ranch road cuts across the lower section of Tolay Lake. Even when the lake seems to have nearly dried up, the ground here is always marshy. After 0.25 mile the lake is left behind, and the road now runs parallel to a ranch fence. Cows are usually present on the other side. The level path makes a slight bend and then continues its level trajectory to the east, heading toward some high, rounded hills. Once past the lake, few trees grow in this part of the park, though some trees line the causeway. A few tall oaks at the far end of the valley offer the only shade. While this portion of the trail lacks trees, it does pass beside an attractive vineyard on the left. After nearly a mile, a gate crosses the trail. Always leave the gate in the same position that you find it: If it

Appropriately named Vista Pond.

is open, it may be that the rancher is planning to move the cattle, so it is best to leave it open; if the gate is closed, be certain to shut it.

Once through the gate, stay straight. This marks the beginning of the first side trip off of the loop. The route ultimately leads back to this point, at which the trail to the right continues the loop. Past the junction, the trail starts the climb, which is the only significant elevation gain of the hike. At a little more than 0.2 mile, the trail makes a sharp turn to the north. This section of the hike crosses private land so it is important to stay on the trail and not trespass. The views to the north and west open up, and the path rises above a sea of vineyards. The rounded massif to the north is Sonoma Mountain, the highest and largest peak in the Sonoma Mountains. Designated its own AVA, the mountain is home to a significant amount of Wine Country history. Its most famous denizen was prolific early twentieth-century author Jack London, whose ranch was on the mountain's eastern slopes.

After the trail has climbed above the vineyards, it makes another turn to the east, entering a narrow defile between the rounded humps of the hills above Tolay Lake. The trail soon enters a dense oak forest, which is the only significant forest cover on the hike. After climbing to the east, the trail leaves the woods and makes a turn to the south, passing through a peaceful vale as it continues to climb. While running along the park's boundary for a time, it cuts away from the fence line and heads toward a cluster of bald summits to the south. At the top the trail makes a small circuit around the highest point, culminating in the Three Bridges Vista. Here hikers can look out over San Pablo Bay and see much of eastern Marin County, including iconic Mount

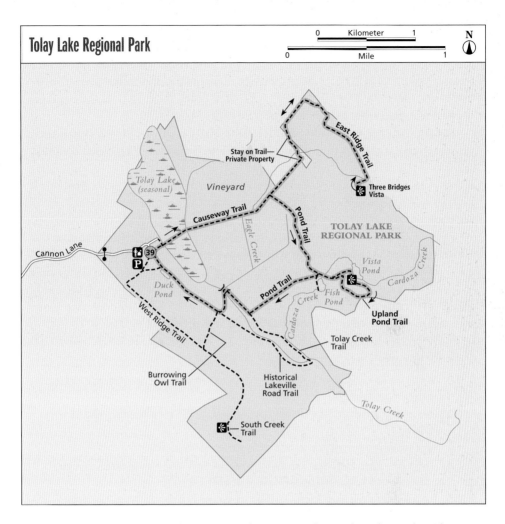

0   Kilometer   1

0   Mile   1

N

East Ridge Trail

Stay on Trail—
Private Property

Tolay Lake
(seasonal)

Vineyard

Three Bridges
Vista

Causeway Trail

Eagle Creek

Pond Trail

TOLAY LAKE
REGIONAL PARK

Cannon Lane

39
P

Duck
Pond

Vista
Pond

Cardoza Creek

Pond Trail

Cardoza Creek

Fish
Pond

Upland
Pond Trail

West Ridge Trail

Tolay Creek
Trail

Burrowing
Owl Trail

Historical
Lakeville
Road Trail

Tolay Creek

South Creek
Trail

Tamalpais. Parts of the Golden Gate Bridge, Bay Bridge, and Richmond Bridge are visible from this vantage. From here retrace your steps back to the gate.

As the trail approaches the gate, turn left and hike south on an old ranch road, which is referred to as the Pond Trail. The trail passes the foot of the hills just climbed, and within 0.2 mile it passes directly beneath the Three Bridges Vista. Views to the west and south are good as the trail undulates through the grassy mounds. In spring this area explodes in a profusion of bright yellow mustard. After crossing an old bridge, the trail curves through some hills before arriving at a second junction.

To easily complete the loop, turn right here, passing through another gate. However, for those looking to lengthen the trip by another mile and explore one of the prettiest corners of Tolay Lake Regional Park, head left and climb up the Upland Pond Trail toward Vista Pond. Stay left at a fork and climb a short distance to the edge of the small, scenic body of water. The view to the north from the south end of the pond is particularly inviting, taking in the rolling Tolay hills, vineyards, and the distant bulk of Sonoma Mountain. Continue on the trail, looping to the south around a grassy knob before heading back toward the fork below Vista Pond. Just before completing the loop, the path traverses rocky outcroppings and crosses a small, seep-fed stream. Once the loop is complete, head back down the trail to the gate and go through it. Again, leave the gate in whatever position you find it.

Past the gate, the trail—still called the Pond Trail—heads southwest for 0.5 mile before arriving at the junction with the Tolay Creek Trail. Hang a right and continue on a course parallel to the creek for another 0.25 mile. The trail turns left and crosses the creek on a large bridge. Continue a short distance before reaching a final junction. Staying straight climbs the hills to the west and follows the power lines back to the trailhead.

For a more direct route that avoids the obtrusive power lines, turn right onto the Historical Lakeville Road Trail. The road was once the main route between Lakevillle, 1.5 miles to the west on the Petaluma River, and the tidal flats that run all the way to Napa and Vallejo. The road, another old, unpaved ranch road, heads back north toward the trailhead, thus completing the loop. The trail passes through two more gates before coming to an end at the old ranch at the trailhead.

Miles and Directions

0.0 To start the hike, head past the big green barn and walk along the causeway that crosses seasonal Tolay Lake.

0.9 Pass through a gate and stay straight at a trail junction. This is the beginning of the East Ridge Trail.

1.2 Walk through another gate, entering a small section of private land.

1.4 A third gate marks entry back into the regional park. From here the trail enters a narrow, heavily wooded canyon and begins to climb steadily.

2.55 The trail ends at the Three Bridges Vista on the summit of a high hill. After enjoying the view, retrace your steps to the first of the three gates.

4.2 At the junction by the first gate, turn left and begin hiking on the Pond Trail.

4.8 Stay left to hike the pretty Upland Pond Trail.

5.7 Return to the beginning of the loop and turn left, passing through the gate.

6.25 Turn right onto the Tolay Creek Trail.

6.45 Turn left and cross over Tolay Creek.

6.65 Turn right onto the Historical Lakeville Road Trail.

7.25 Arrive back at the trailhead.

40 Lower Tubbs Island Trail

The hike to Lower Tubbs Island is an easy trail with surprisingly panoramic views despite the flat terrain. The highlight of the hike is the walk along a mile of Sonoma County's rarely seen shoreline on San Francisco Bay.

Total Distance: 7.8 miles out and back
Hiking Time: About 4 hours
Difficulty: Moderate
Elevation Gain: None
Season: All year
Canine Compatibility: Dogs are not permitted
Fees: None
Trail Contact: San Pablo Bay National Wildlife Refuge, 2100 CA 37, Petaluma, CA 94954; (707) 769-4200; www.fws.gov/refuge/san_pablo_bay/
Other: Some maps and descriptions of this trail show a loop at the end. A portion of the loop has collapsed into the marshes and is impassable. The bay shoreline is still accessible in its entirety, but the loop cannot be completed.

Finding the trailhead: From the intersections of CA 37 and CA 121, drive east on CA 37 for 0.8 mile. Turn right into the trailhead parking lot. Note that returning west from the trailhead requires driving all the way to the Mare Island turnoff 8.5 miles to the east. There you can turn around and travel on westbound CA 37. GPS: N38°09.18233' / W122°26.16783'

The Hike

It often comes as a surprise to many that Sonoma County is one of the nine counties that are included in the San Francisco Bay Area. With the county's population centers well to the north, the bay often seems a world away from the rugged mountains, vineyard-filled valleys, and windswept coastline. Yet the county has approximately 7 miles of shoreline on San Pablo Bay, the large, northern lobe of San Francisco Bay. With no towns or villages and only a handful of scattered farmhouses, this part of Sonoma County is almost entirely forgotten. Yet what is lost to the public consciousness is a hidden gem for hikers. The Lower Tubbs Island Trail in the San Pablo Bay National Wildlife Refuge is the ideal way to explore this underappreciated part of the Wine Country. With surprisingly excellent views, the level hike accesses a 1-mile section of wild, undeveloped bay coastline, a rarity in the heavily urbanized Bay Area. The trail is also a fantastic place to observe diverse wildlife, including an exasperating number of birds as well as seals.

The trailhead for the Lower Tubbs Island Trail is located next to a large tidal marsh that fills with water when the tide is in. Tolay Creek, which begins to the north in Tolay Lake Regional Park, flows through the marsh. Across the water, vineyards blanket low rolling hills. The tall mountains of Marin County loom along the horizon, capped by iconic Mount Tamalpais. From the trailhead, walk around a gate and follow

A seal rests on a rare, wild stretch of San Pablo Bay's shoreline at Tubbs Island.

the trail, an old road, to the south. It quickly turns to the right and arrives at a nice spot with a picnic table next to the tidal marsh 0.3 mile from the trailhead. This spot has an improved variation on the view from the trailhead.

From the point next to the tidal marsh, the trail turns south again and begins to run beside a levee that cuts off views to the west. Tolay Creek continues to flow along the trail, but it cannot be observed unless you climb up on the brushy levee. To the east, a vast expanse of farmland stretches out. This area was reclaimed from the bay by levees long ago. Above the fields, the southern end of the Mayacamas Mountains and the mountains above the city of Napa loom on the horizon.

The road continues to the south for another 2.25 miles, passing a pumping station at 1.8 miles. It finally arrives at a fork. There are some displays and interactive exhibits describing the birds in the area. Stay to the right and almost immediately come upon another fork marked by a kiosk with more information about the wildlife refuge. This fork once marked the beginning of a loop, but the upper section of the trail has collapsed and is no longer passable. Consequently, stay to the left at the fork and plan on returning that way as well.

Beyond the fork, the trail continues to the south for another 0.3 mile until it finally arrives at the edge of San Pablo Bay. The surprising beauty of this area is a revelation. The panoramic 360-degree views are unexpected, considering how flat the trail is, yet with no topography to obscure the vista, the surrounding landmarks are a magnificent spectacle. To the west, the mountains of Marin rise above the bay, with Mount Tamalpais making another appearance. The southern mountains of Sonoma

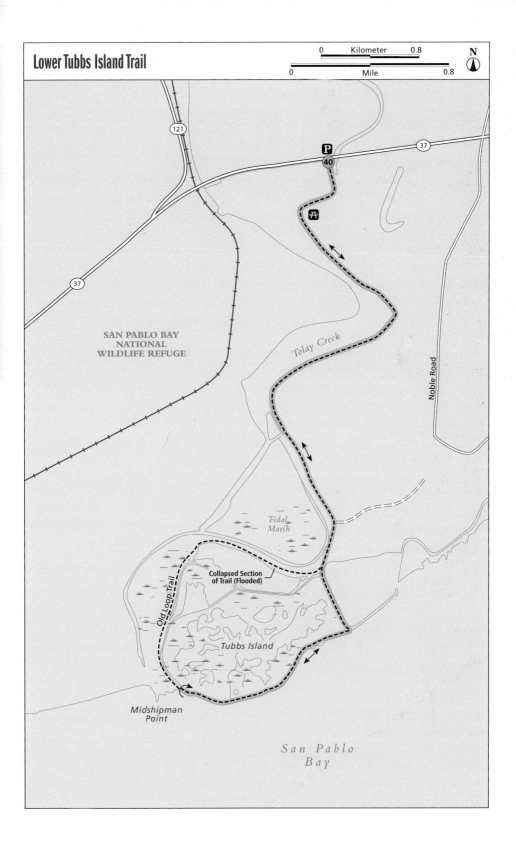

Lower Tubbs Island Trail

0   Kilometer   0.8

0   Mile   0.8

N

121

P
40

37

37

Noble Road

SAN PABLO BAY
NATIONAL
WILDLIFE REFUGE

Tolay Creek

Tidal
Marsh

Old Loop Trail

Collapsed Section
of Trail (Flooded)

Tubbs Island

Midshipman
Point

San Pablo
Bay

and Napa Counties, including Mount Veeder above the city of Sonoma and the peaks around the city of Napa, are all visible. Separating these peaks from the hills above the East Bay and towering Mount Diablo is the Carquinez Strait. It is hard to believe, standing here in southern Sonoma County, that the strait, that narrow gap in the mountains, is the point through which most of the water from the enormous Sierra Nevada and significant portions of Northern California (from as far away as Mount Shasta and the Modoc Plateau) flows into San Francisco Bay.

Turning right where the trail meets the edge of the bay, the trail continues to the west for an additonal 1 mile. Running along a seaside levee, the trail gradually narrows. It crosses over a pair of culverts where the seawater can be seen surging inland when the tide is coming in. The force of the water flowing through the culverts is impressive. Some sections of the shoreline are lined with riprap (rock used to armor land threatened with erosion). Other areas are essentially a wild edge of the land where the surf pounds against the unprotected earth. Topped with thick grass, it is a strange and beautiful sight. Watch for seals hopping out of the water and reclining on these grassy areas. At the end of the mile, the trail turns inland, continuing on to what used to be a loop. Here there is a wider beach with several large driftwood logs that make great benches. Sit and enjoy the view of nearby Midshipman Point, the large grassy area immediately west, backed by Mount Tamalpais as well as the rest of San Pablo Bay. When it is time to leave this tremendous place, retrace your steps back to the trailhead.

Miles and Directions

0.0 Walk around a gate and begin hiking to the south.

0.3 The trail passes a picnic table with nice views of the tidal marsh, vineyards, and Mount Tamalpais.

2.55 Stay right at a junction.

2.65 Stay left at a second junction.

2.95 Arrive at the edge of San Pablo Bay. The trail turns right and follows the shoreline.

3.9 The trail begins to veer away from the shoreline. Since the loop is no longer passable, this is the place to turn around and retrace your steps to the trailhead.

Section II.

Napa County

Home to the prestigious Napa Valley, Napa County is at the heart of the Wine Country. While the vineyards and wineries naturally receive the recognition, they are set in a beautiful landscape that is an essential part of their quality. The valley runs the length of the county, beginning at the foot of giant Mount Saint Helena and extending to the south where it ends at the tidal marshes at San Pablo Bay.

The sides of the valley are lined with tall peaks, deep canyons, and rugged cliffs and rock formations. These give the vineyards a dramatic backdrop that enhances their scenic beauty significantly. The eastern part of Napa County is a nearly forgotten region that is very sparsely populated and seemingly forgotten by time. Nonetheless, it is a productive grape-growing area with great natural beauty waiting to be discovered.

The trails in Napa County explore a number of different parts of both the Napa Valley and the vast, eastern part of the county. Hikes journey to the top of soaring mountains, ragged cliffs, bizarre rock formations, long ridges with awesome vineyard views, rolling hills, and tidal marshes. The public lands in Napa County are a patchwork of federal, state, county, and city parks, as well as a few other odds and ends added for good measure. The effort is underway by both county and city governments to add to and improve their park systems and to make new lands available so the public can enjoy the beautiful landscapes. At the federal level, the recently established Berryessa Snow Mountain National Monument promises to attract more attention to the eastern part of Napa County. Even now, though, the trails that are currently available present a fantastic opportunity to explore the premier wine-making area in California.

41 Alston Park

The hike through the city of Napa's Alston Park is a great introduction to the Napa Valley. With copious views of wineries and the southern half of the Napa Valley, this is a good place to get a sense of the area's beautiful terrain.

Total Distance: 2.7-mile loop
Hiking Time: About 1.5 hours
Difficulty: Easy
Elevation Gain: 200 feet
Season: All year
Canine Compatibility: Dogs are permitted
Fees: None

Trail Contact: Napa Parks and Recreation; 707-257-9529; www.cityofnapa.org/index .php?option=com_content&view=article&id=4 2&Itemid=63
Other: Alston Park is very dog friendly. There is a leash-free dog park and section of the park where dogs are welcomed on the trails without leashes.

Finding the trailhead: From CA 29 at the north end of Napa, turn left onto Trower Avenue and drive 1 mile. Turn right onto Dry Creek Road and immediately turn left into the parking area. GPS: N38°19.38150'/W122°19.96317'

The Hike

Located on the western fringe of the city of Napa, Alston Park is a bastion of a fairly wild 157 acres set between the urban development of the city and the vineyards. Occupying a series of low bluffs, the park is a great place to quickly escape into a more rural environment and enjoy a nice hike alongside beautiful vineyards and great views of the southern Napa Valley. One of the unique features of the park is its accommodation of dogs. A dog play area is near the parking lot, and in the southern third of the park, dogs are permitted to run free without being leashed. Though dogs must be on a leash in the rest of the park, it is still a great place to explore with a four-footed friend!

The trailhead is at the southern end of Alston Park, in the leash-free area. From the parking lot, follow the level, wide path past the trailhead sign and continue straight for a short distance to a large junction with trails splitting off in numerous directions. The trails are unsigned, and several unofficial trails course throughout the park so that it can be difficult at times to pick the right path. Fortunately all trails lead through pretty territory, so if the exact route described here is not followed, an enjoyable hike still lies ahead.

At the junction, take the wide path to the left, which heads south. It immediately crosses another wide trail before narrowing to single track. Stay on this path heading south. Soon side trails will branch off to the right. Hikers can either climb up these or stay on the path until it dead-ends into another trail. If taking the side routes, climb

Vineyards surround Alston Park.

up the low bluff and then take a left on the wide path at the top. Look for the water spigot at the top if you want to cool off. If taking the lower path, turn right when the trail dead-ends at the trail that parallels the park boundary. Climb the low bluffs here and then join the main trail at the top. Like much of the park, this level, grassy area has numerous trails crisscrossing it. The prettiest route is to follow the trail near-est the park boundary. Staying on this path means hiking alongside rows of vineyards and having good views to the south. The path makes a pair of right turns as it rounds the back end of the property before coming to a junction with a trail branching off to the left.

At the junction, a sign indicates that the trail is leaving the leash-free area and that dogs must now be put back on the leash. Turn left onto this trail and follow it in a northwesterly direction, passing more vineyards on the left. After 0.25 mile the trail arrives at another complex junction, this one marked by another water fountain. Take the leftmost path, a short single-track trail that quickly climbs onto a paved service road. Stay on the service road, which accesses some large water tanks, for only 0.1 mile. Enjoy the great views to the south, taking in numerous vineyards, the southern portion of Alston Park, and the southernmost section of the Napa Valley. Note the two summits of Mount Diablo, one of the Bay Area's signature mountains, poking up above the horizon.

Soon the service road reaches another fork. Stay right and follow the trail as it nears the edge of a little canyon and rounds the back end of the park. The trail comes

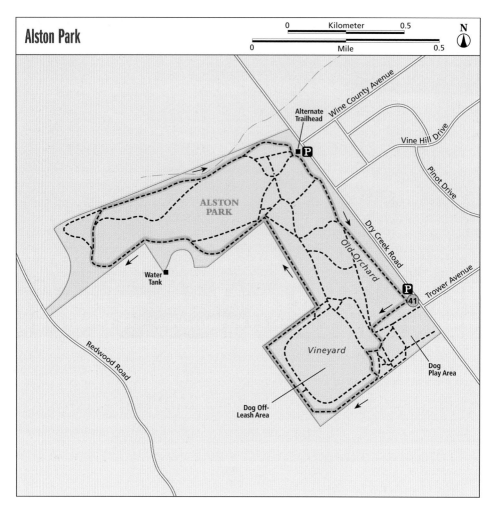

0   Kilometer   0.5

0   Mile   0.5

N

Wine County Avenue

Alternate
Trailhead

Vine Hill Drive

Pinot Drive

ALSTON
PARK

Dry Creek Road

Old Orchard

Trower Avenue

Water
Tank

41

Redwood Road

Vineyard

Dog
Play Area

Dog Off-
Leash Area

to another fork near some oak trees; both paths lead to the same place. To the right is the main trail, which is shorter, while veering left adds a little distance and passes another vineyard before rejoining the main trail. If taking the shorter route, stay left at a second junction where a trail splits off to the right and descends into the small canyon.

Once on the trail that parallels Alston Park's northern boundary, great views of Napa Valley open up to the north. The path begins to descend, steeply at times. It soon crosses the creek emerging from the small canyon. The creek may be dry during much of the summer. Once across the small creek, you will find that the trail now parallels it for a short distance before coming to yet another fork. Stay left, rounding the base of a small hill and staying close to vineyards on the edge of the park boundary. The trail shortly arrives at the park's small northern parking lot. Cross the service road and take the trail heading south. It immediately crosses a small bridge and makes a quick, steep ascent up a small knoll.

From there the trail continues south, running parallel to Dry Creek Road and the edge of Napa. The route passes two paths heading to the top of the bluffs before coming to another fork, this time with two paths heading to the south, about 0.25 mile from the north parking area. Stay to the left and cross another bridge while skirting the edge of an old orchard before arriving at the large trail junction that marked the beginning of the hike. Turn left and walk the short distance back to the trailhead.

Miles and Directions

0.0   From the trailhead, hike west on the wide main path, past the fenced dog play area.

0.1   At a junction with numerous trails, turn left onto a wide path. This trail instantly crossed another wide trail. Stay straight and then take the next left, climbing to the top of the hill.

0.2   At the main trail on top of the hill, turn left.

0.3   Near the fence, veer right to begin hiking the outer trail along the park's property line. Numerous side trails split off the outer main trail along the outer loop. Stay on the obvious trail and follow the park's perimeter.

0.8   Near the end of the fence, turn left and continue following the fence line.

1.05 At a junction with numerous trails, turn left, following the outermost trail. It soon merges with a service road and continues up a hill, alongside a vineyard.

1.2   Stay right, turning off the service road. Then stay left when another trail merges from the right.

1.6   At a junction, stay to the right. Another junction comes a short distance later. Stay right again.

2.1   Stay left on a trail that rounds a hillside and arrives at a second trailhead.

2.25 Cross the small trailhead parking lot, cross a small bridge, and continue hiking. Stay left at all of the falling forks in the trail.

2.7   Arrive back at the trailhead.

42 Westwood Hills Park

Napa's city park in the Westwood Hills is a nice little spot right at the edge of the urban area. With a mix of scenery that ranges from eucalyptus groves and bald hills to oak forests, enough variety is here to keep the trails interesting. Numerous trails, both official and unofficial, weave through the park, offering a number of possible trips. This hike stays around the perimeter and combines scenic forests with nice views.

Total Distance: 1.8-mile loop
Hiking Time: About 1 hour
Difficulty: Easy
Elevation Gain: 380 feet
Season: All year
Canine Compatibility: Dogs are permitted

Fees: None
Trail Contact: Napa Parks and Recreation; 707-257-9529; www.cityofnapa.org/index .php?option=com_content&view=article&id=4 2&Itemid=63

Finding the trailhead: From CA 29 in Napa, take the 1st Street exit and go west on 1st Street for 0.8 mile. Continue another 0.3 mile after 1st Street becomes Browns Valley Road. Turn left into the Westwood Hills parking area. GPS: N38°18.17083' / W122°19.16817'

The Hike

Westwood Hills Park is a small, 110-acre retreat on the west side of the city of Napa. Encompassing a group of small hills that rise out of the urban development, the park makes it easy to quickly escape the activity of Napa County's largest city. Offering hikers an opportunity to enjoy a variety of landscapes, Westwood Hills Park is a mix of oak forests, grassy hills, and a large grove of eucalyptus trees. The trail winds through canyons and over hills and boasts some great views of the Napa Valley. All of this is located just a short distance from the thriving bustle of downtown Napa. Though the park is not large, it is riddled with trails, both official and unofficial, that offer numerous possible hikes. This route stays near the perimeter of the park and samples the various types of terrain in the Westwood Hills.

Starting at the trailhead at the parking lot's east end, the trail immediately begins climbing up a canyon, passing a private residence on the left. Eucalyptus trees appear immediately. After passing a gate, make the first obvious left about 0.2 mile from the beginning of the hike. The trail climbs out of the canyon, leaving the eucalyptus behind and transitioning into a forest dominated by oak and bay. Avoid veering off the main trail onto the narrow unofficial trails that break away to climb up the hill.

When the forest recedes, the trail crosses hillsides carpeted with thick grass. Views of the city of Napa are good here. This section of the hike has a number of side trails, making navigation a bit frustrating. Don't take any trails downhill or any path that does not seem to receive a lot of use. At 0.45 mile an obvious wide path splits off to

The Napa Valley extends north from the Westwood Hills.

the right and climbs steeply uphill. Follow this for a short distance to another fork and take this to the left. The path traverses a hillside before coming to a level area where numerous trails converge. Turn left and follow the excessively wide path uphill, towards a cellphone tower disguised as a tree. At the top of the bare hill, a panoramic view is revealed. Numerous landmarks are visible from here, including the city of Napa, San Pablo Bay, Mount Diablo to the southeast, and much of the length of the Napa Valley to the north, including the rounded Haystack and the Stags Leap area.

To return to the trailhead, take the trail climbing down the west side of the hill along a fence. The trail momentarily passes a vineyard and then plunges back into the dark forest. It immediately comes to another fork. Stay to the right and follow the path along a steep slope where the trail is reinforced by large beams of wood. In a clearing at the bottom of the slope, stay left where more trails converge. Leave the woods behind again and climb steeply up a grass-covered knoll topped by oak trees. Look for the summit of Mount Tamalpais peeking out from behind low hills to the south. The oaks at the top of the knoll make a great place to climb a tree and enjoy a short break. Continuing the hike, head down the knoll's north slope and turn left when it merges with another trail at the bottom. Stay left at another fork on a bare slope before the trail enters the shady forest yet again. The well-constructed trail eventually becomes a confusing tangle of unofficial trails. A basic rule of thumb in this forest is to stay to the right and head to the east. Eventually the trails connect with the main trail coming up the canyon through eucalyptus trees. Go left on the wide path and follow it back to the trailhead.

Westwood Hills Park

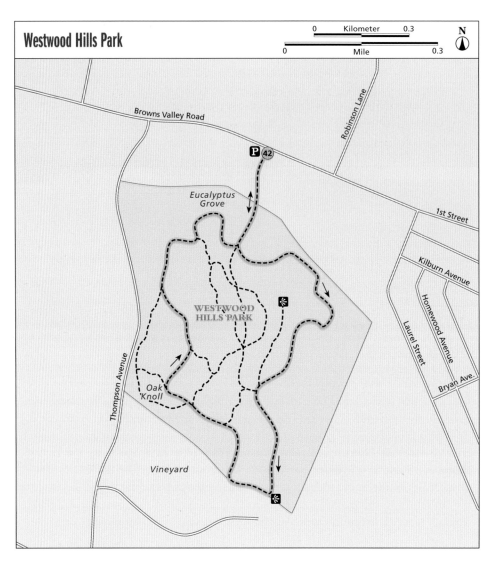

0   Kilometer   0.3

0   Mile   0.3

N

Miles and Directions

0.0   Hike down the road, past the parking area, going through a gate.

0.15   Turn left onto a well-established path that heads east. Stay on the main path, avoiding side trails.

0.45   At a nice view of the city of Napa, turn left and climb a steep, wide path. Climb 100 yards then turn left onto a path that traverses the hillside to the south.

0.7   Near the top of the hill, turn left on the very wide worn trail and continue to the south.

0.85   Arrive at the highest point in the park and enjoy the great view of the city of Napa and the Napa Valley. To continue the loop, turn right near the fence and begin descending the back side of the hill.

0.95 Turn right at a junction onto a trail that crosses a steep hillside. Turn left at the next junction.

1.15 Stay straight and cross over a wide trail. Climb to the top of the hill then turn right and hike down the north side. Stay left at the junction near the bottom.

1.4 Keep to the right at another fork and enter the woods. After 0.1 mile the trail splits into several different paths. Follow the largest, most obvious path.

1.7 Turn left back onto the main trail from the parking area.

1.8 Arrive back at the trailhead.

43 Timberhill Park

The modest Timberhill Park encompasses the right-of-way along an old abandoned road. The trail climbs through a short canyon before crossing bald slopes to the top of a hill where great views unfold.

Total Distance: 1.6 miles out and back
Hiking Time: About 1 hour
Difficulty: Easy
Elevation Gain: 370 feet
Season: All year
Canine Compatibility: Dogs are permitted

Fees: None
Trail Contact: Napa Parks and Recreation; 707-257-9529; www.cityofnapa.org/index .php?option=com_content&view=article&id=4 2&Itemid=63

Finding the trailhead: From CA 29 in Napa, take the 1st Street exit and go west on 1st Street for 0.8 mile. Continue 1.1 miles after 1st Street becomes Browns Valley Road. Make a slight left to stay on Browns Valley Road and proceed another 0.3 mile. Turn left onto Buhman Avenue, go 0.2 mile, then turn right onto Meadowbrook Drive. Continue 0.3 mile and turn left on Stonybrook Drive. Go 0.2 mile, then turn right on Timberhill Lane. The trailhead is at the end of the road. GPS: N38°18.20833'/W122°20.96950'

The Hike

Tucked away in an unassuming Napa neighborhood, the Timberhill Park is among the more unusual parklands in the Wine Country. The land that constitutes the park wraps around a high hill to the southwest of Napa and is centered on an old paved road that now serves as a hiking trail. Do not veer too far off of the road or you will cross onto private property. While it may have an odd shape and the trail is a bit unusual, Timberhill Park is still quite scenic and offers memorable views without expending a lot of effort.

The trailhead is at the end of a residential street. Pass through the gate marking the park's entrance and begin hiking up the paved road. After a couple hundred yards, pass through a second gate and continue climbing the old paved road. Note the small creek on the north side of the road, which often will have water in it during the spring. The road continues to climb beneath a canopy of oak and bay trees. After 0.3 mile, the road arrives at a washout where the creek has undermined the old roadbed and the pavement collapsed into the deep gully. A dirt trail now makes a short but steep climb up the side of the hill and traverses the edge of the washout. It quickly returns to the pavement immediately beyond the washed-out section of road.

Continuing to climb up the old road, the route soon emerges from beneath the forest cover where views of a small, grassy valley open up. Cattle may be grazing the

Iconic Mount Diablo and the bay can be seen from the end of the Timberhill Trail.

hillside opposite the trail. In the spring these hills are a vibrant green, while in the warmer parts of the year the grass turns gold.

The old road continues to climb up the east side of the small valley. After 0.5 mile the road finally makes a tight switchback and turns back toward the north, maintaining its moderate grade as it proceeds. Ahead lies a small peak cloaked with dense woods but with an exposed, grassy summit. To reach the summit the trail climbs another 0.1 mile to a fork. Stay to the right on the obvious path before the old road finally comes to an end 0.7 mile from the trailhead.

Beyond the pavement the trail becomes single track and it continues a short distance to the top of the grassy summit. A lone, bent bench, the park's sole amenity, marks the end of the hike. An unofficial trail continues beyond the bench but veers into private property and should be avoided. However, the summit makes a fine destination. Terrific views spread out below the hill, especially to the south and the southeast. Grassy slopes fall away from the top of the hill and give way to vineyards of the Carneros region. Farther to the south, the waters of the bay and much of its maritime industry are visible, especially the old Mare Island submarine base. Mount Diablo, one of the great Bay Area mountains, is prominently visible, towering high above the hills of the American Canyon area. After having enjoyed the view, retrace your steps the trailhead.

Timberhill Park

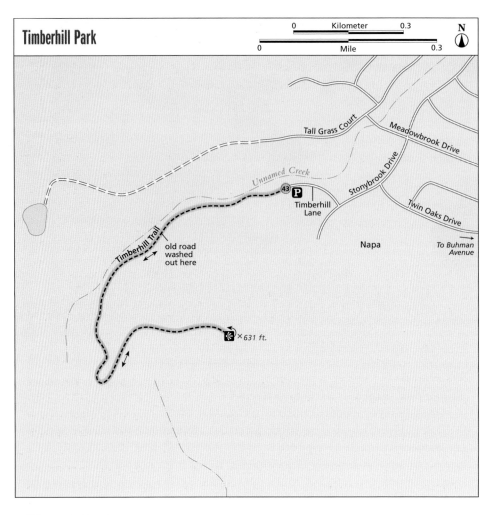

Miles and Directions

0.0 Pass through the gate at the beginning of the trail, which is an old, paved ranch road.

0.3 Skirt the edge of a washed-out section of the old road.

0.5 The trail makes a hairpin turn and continues to climb.

0.7 The old, paved road ends. A narrow path leads a little farther.

0.8 The trail ends near a broken bench with a fantastic view to the south. Retrace your steps back to the trailhead.

44 Napa River Trail: John F. Kennedy Memorial Park

The Napa River flows for nearly 55 miles through the entire length of the Napa Valley. The section of the Napa River Trail at JFK Park offers hikers the chance to view the river as it is nearing its mouth at San Pablo Bay.

Total Distance: 3.85-mile lollipop
Hiking Time: About 2 hours
Difficulty: Easy
Elevation Gain: None
Season: All year
Canine Compatibility: Dogs are permitted

Fees: None
Trail Contact: Napa Parks and Recreation; 707-257-9529; www.cityofnapa.org/index .php?option=com_content&view=article&id=4 2&Itemid=63

Finding the trailhead: From CA 29 in Napa, take the Imola Avenue exit. Drive east on Imola Avenue for 1.5 miles. Turn right onto CA 221. Drive south for 0.2 mile. Turn right onto Magnolia Drive. At the roundabout, veer right into a large parking lot. GPS: N38°16.71167'/W122°16.52983'

The Hike

The Napa River is the largest waterway in the Napa Valley. Though it is a diminutive stream in the northern part of the valley near Calistoga, by the time it arrives at the city of Napa, it is much larger and runs through the center of town. There has been an effort in Napa to construct a trail along the river as it flows through the city. Though it has not been completed, several unconnected sections have been constructed and make great hikes in the heart of the city. The best section, claiming the most natural setting and the best views of the southern end of Napa Valley, is the section that leads to JFK Park, just south of the city. While it is not in a wilderness area and there is a significant amount of development along the trail, it still gives hikers a chance to observe the river and the mountains that surround the city of Napa, all just minutes away from the downtown area.

There are a few trailheads for the Napa River Trail section through JFK Park. The trail itself is shaped like a lollipop, with a stem connecting to a loop. To take advantage of this arrangement, it's best to park just north of Napa Valley College, where a parking area provides access to the trail.

At the parking area, take the paved walkway west past the roundabout at Napa Valley College, cross a small stream, and then pass a cinder-block structure. Just after crossing the railroad tracks, turn left on the paved path. To the north a large bridge over the Napa River looms above the landscape. Heading south on the trail, the path passes several installations related to Napa Valley College, including baseball diamonds and a large field covered with solar panels. To the right is a large marsh with the Napa

The Napa River.

River flowing beside it. On the other side of the river is a housing development built around a series of canals that connect to the river. The area is flat and open with few trees, which allows for great views of the area. To the east the rounded dome of Sugarloaf, the highest point in the Skyline Wilderness Park, is visible. Beyond the river to the west, the southern tip of the Mayacamas Mountains, including the Mount Veeder area, rise above the city.

About 0.7 mile from the trailhead, the path veers from the development at Napa Valley College. A small, crushed-gravel trail branches off and runs parallel to the main path. A few benches are scattered along the gravel trail with views toward the river. Either route is fine as they stay close to each other and meet again after only 0.1 mile. When they do meet, the trail is on the outskirts of JFK Park. It first passes more baseball diamonds before going by another trailhead and a large grass area near playgrounds and picnic areas. Though the trail has not yet come close to the Napa River itself, a small tidal marsh is off to the right, which may be full of water when the tide is in. A short distance later a wide path splits off to the right and heads down to the river for the first time. Continuing a little farther, the trail arrives at circular driveway next to the main parking area for JFK Park. A wooden dock makes a great place from which to enjoy the river.

The trail continues south from the dock, passing the parking area. At the south end the trail splits. Stay to the right and follow the Napa River. Here are several places with great views of the river, and it feels a long way from the mountains and vineyards that surround this area. The river and the trail run alongside each other for more than

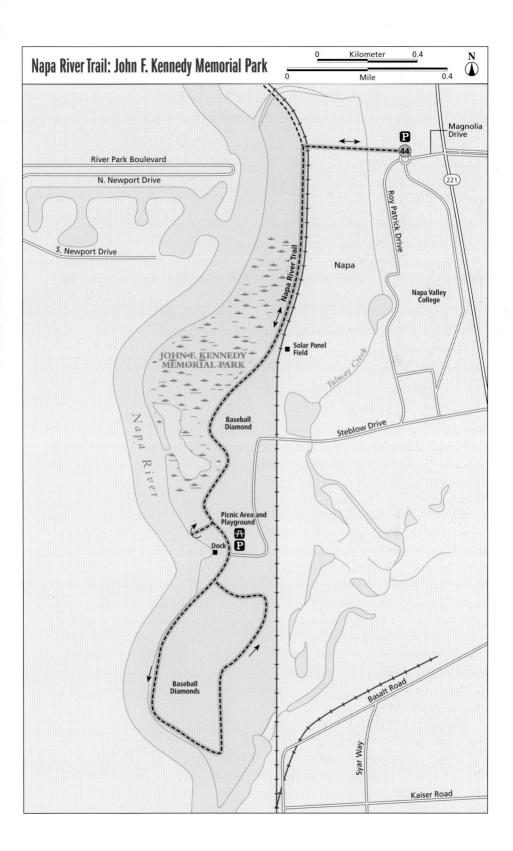

Napa River Trail: John F. Kennedy Memorial Park

0   Kilometer   0.4

0   Mile   0.4

N

River Park Boulevard

N. Newport Drive

S. Newport Drive

Magnolia Drive

P
44

221

Roy Patrick Drive

Napa

Napa Valley College

Napa River Trail

Solar Panel Field

Tulucay Creek

JOHN F. KENNEDY MEMORIAL PARK

Napa River

Baseball Diamond

Steblow Drive

Picnic Area and Playground

Dock

P

Baseball Diamonds

Basalt Road

Syar Way

Kaiser Road

0.5 mile. When they separate, the trail makes a sharp turn to the north while the river continues the rest of its trek down to San Francisco Bay.

Heading back toward the parking area at JFK Park, the path passes still more baseball diamonds before it climbs onto a levee around a marshy area where four tall radio towers stand. The trail then turns back to the west where it finally rejoins the trail near the main section of the park. From there retrace your steps back to the trailhead on the north side of Napa Valley College.

Miles and Directions

0.0   Leave the parking area by the roundabout and follow the paved path to the west.

0.25 After crossing the railroad tracks, turn left onto the Napa River Trail.

1.2   A spur trail leads to the river.

1.4   The trail arrives at the park's large parking lot. There is a little boat launch and other facilities. Cross the road and continue hiking.

1.5   Stay right at the fork and begin the loop while following alongside the Napa River.

2.5   Complete the loop and begin hiking back to the trailhead on the Napa River Trail.

3.85 Arrive back at the parking lot.

45 River to Ridge Trail

Connecting John F. Kennedy Memorial Park with the urban wilderness Skyline Wilderness Park, the River to Ridge Trail offers quick access to rugged terrain, views of Napa Valley, and isolation just a short distance from bustling Napa.

Total Distance: 3.6 miles out and back
Hiking Time: About 2.5 hours
Difficulty: Easy
Elevation Gain: 365
Season: All year
Canine Compatibility: Dogs are permitted
Fees: None

Trail Contact: Skyline Wilderness Park, 2201 Imola Ave., Napa, CA 94559; (707) 252-0481; www.skylinepark.org/
Other: This trail makes a good addition to the Skyline Wilderness Park's Lower Skyline Loop (Hike 46) or possibly the Rim Rock Loop (Hike 47).

Finding the trailhead: From CA 29 in Napa, take the Imola Avenue exit. Drive east on Imola Avenue for 1.5 miles. Turn right onto CA 221. Drive south for 0.7 mile. Turn right onto Streblow Drive and drive 0.2 mile. Turn left into the Formal Garden's parking lot. GPS: N38°16.16450' / W122°16.54350'

The Hike

The River to Ridge Trail is something of an odd duck when it comes to trails in the Wine Country. It does not have a clear destination, and it has some oddly out-of-place sections that run through fenced passages. However, it is still a scenic trail running nearly the entire length of the Napa Valley to the north, and it has some good views of the city of Napa. It also has the unique distinction of being one of the few trails that begins at sea level and climbs into the mountains, contrasting the diverse geography of the region. It also connects a pair of trail systems, allowing motivated hikers to create a variety of long trips utilizing the Napa River Trail at JFK Park and the extensive trail network in Skyline Wilderness Park. Whether you are looking for a convenient trail in the city or a longer trek with sections of wild terrain, the River to Ridge Trail is a good option.

The best place to begin is at the Formal Garden parking lot. Turn right onto the paved bike path and follow it to busy Napa Vallejo Highway (CA 221). Cross over the wide road carefully, waiting for the crossing signal to allow you to do so safely. A sign marks the beginning of the trail, which is flanked by a pair of chain-link fences. As you walk down the long, fenced passage, watch for metal silhouettes of native animals hanging on the left. On the other side of the fence is the Napa State Hospital, a psychiatric hospital founded in the late nineteenth century. The River to Ridge Trail runs along the hospital's property for its entire length. The wide path runs between the fences for 0.3 mile before finally emerging into an oak forest.

The city of Napa is not far from the River to Ridge Trail.

Once in the woods, the trail begins to climb up an easy grade. After another 0.3 mile of easy hiking, the woods recede and the views open up as the trail crosses grassy hillsides punctuated with numerous rocks and clumps of brush. Patches of rock run across the path, making the trail a little rugged in some section. Views to the west over the southern end of the Napa Valley and also to the north up the valley highlight this part of the hike. The quiet hillside gives little indication of the massive quarry that lies just to the south, where much of the hill has been excavated. The trail continues to climb as it swings around a shoulder of the hill. It passes a clearing on the left with an old, deteriorating, flat-topped building.

Having reached its apex near the old building, the River to Ridge Trail now begins to go downhill gently. A spur to the right leads to a large water tank above the trail. The trail makes a pair of switchbacks as it completes its descent and comes to a paved road. Cross the road and continue on the trail, which has leveled off. It turns into a wide gully that narrows quickly. Just before crossing a small, seasonal stream, the trail passes a large concrete structure that is being overtaken by the forests. The structure is the remnants of a quarry operation that once operated here. Chutes, once used for loading gravel in carts, line the side of the old building. This indicates that the area's quarrying activity began a long time ago. After crossing the small stream, the trail soon merges with a wide path. This is the Lower Skyline Trail, which is part of the trail system in Skyline Wilderness Park. This marks the end of the River to Ridge Trail. Turning left on this trail leads to Lake Marie Road in approximately 100 yards. This is the main trail artery for the park. From this point there are numerous options.

River to Ridge Trail

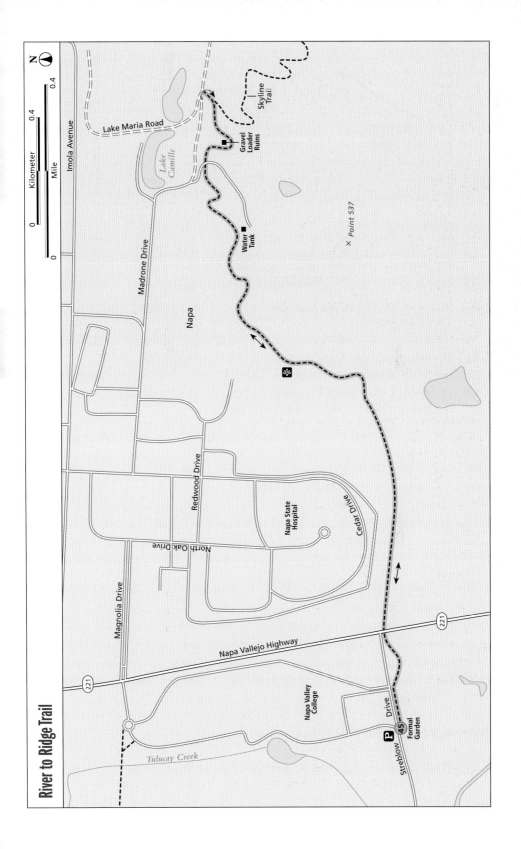

N

Kilometer
0   0.4   0.4

Mile
0

Imola Avenue

Lake Maria Road

Lake Camille

Gravel Loader Ruins

Skyline Trail

Madrone Drive

Water Tank

Napa

X *Point 537*

Magnolia Drive

Redwood Drive

North Oak Drive

Napa State Hospital

Cedar Drive

Napa Vallejo Highway

221

221

Napa Valley College

Tulucay Creek

Streblow Drive

P

45

Formal Garden

The Lower Skyline Loop would add 4.3 miles and explores the lower section of hills on both sides of Marie Creek's canyon.

For the ambitious, the Rim Rock Loop (Hike 47) adds 6.8 miles and some stiff climbing, but it is the prettiest hike in the Skyline Park and makes a great all-day addition to the River to Ridge Trail. The Lower Skyline Loop (Hike 46) is a less strenuous option for extending the hike. It is also possible to just hike up the canyon to Lake Marie, which has minimal elevation gain. The Lake Marie Road can also simply be the end of the hike. Whichever option you choose, retrace your steps along the River to Ridge Trail and back to the parking lot.

Miles and Directions

0.0 Begin the hike from the Formal Garden area's parking lot. Follow the paved River to Ridge Trail to the crossing at CA 221 (Napa Vallejo Highway).

0.2 Cross CA 221 and continue through the fenced section of the hike.

0.5 The trail continues beyond the fences, taking on a more natural appearance as it climbs onto a rocky hillside.

1.35 Stay on the main trail, avoiding side trails that lead up to a large water tank.

1.55 After descending a pair of switchbacks, the trail crosses a paved road.

1.65 Pass an old, dilapidated gravel loader.

1.8 Merge onto the Lower Skyline Trail. Either continue hiking one of the Skyline Wilderness Park trails or retrace your steps back to the trailhead.

46 Lower Skyline Loop

This loop in the lower section of Skyline Wilderness Park is a fantastic hike through rugged hills that starts right on the edge of the city of Napa. With isolated vistas overlooking San Pablo Bay and Marie Creek Canyon, the hike offers varied scenery and solitude just minutes from the downtown area.

Total Distance: 4.25-mile loop
Hiking Time: About 3 hours
Difficulty: Moderate
Elevation Gain: 700 feet
Season: All year
Canine Compatibility: Dogs are not permitted

Fees: $5 entrance fee
Trail Contact: Skyline Wilderness Park, 2201 Imola Ave., Napa, CA 94559; (707) 252-0481; www.skylinepark.org/
Other: Park hours change seasonally; check with the staff for current hours.

Finding the trailhead: From CA 29 in Napa, take the Imola Avenue exit and drive east on Imola Avenue for 2.9 miles. When the road turns left, look for the park entrance on the right. GPS: N38°16.72767' / W122°14.97917'

The Hike

Skyline Wilderness Park is the city of Napa's awesome backyard park. With 850 acres, it is one of the largest blocks of public land in the Napa Valley. The park consists of a cluster of high hills and canyons in the southeast corner of the city, hills that form the southern wall of the Napa Valley. Centered on the Marie Creek Canyon, the area is rugged and undeveloped. Most of the park is covered in forests, chaparral, and open hillsides. Occasional rocky outcrops highlight the walls of the canyon. Over 25 miles of trail wind through Skyline, giving hikers numerous options for hikes both long and short. One of the best routes links the lower half of the canyon's outer trails. The hike climbs onto some hills at the south end of the park, where there are fantastic views to the south. It then drops down into Marie Creek Canyon, crosses over the small stream, and loops around the canyon's north end.

The hike begins at the trailhead parking lot, which is just to the right of the entrance station. Head out on the path and immediately skirt the edge of a large native plant garden. Climbing up a set of stairs leads you to the park's campground. Turn right on the road and then turn left onto Lake Marie Road at the edge of the campground. The road is now flanked by fences as you pass through Napa State Hospital property. Through the fences you can see two small ponds formed by impounding Marie Creek. On the right is Lake Camille and on the left is Lake Louise. Once it passes beyond the fenced-off lakes, the route arrives at a fork, roughly 0.35 mile from the trailhead. Turn to the right and begin hiking on the Skyline Trail. Ignore the River to Ridge Trail that soon branches off to the right (Hike 45).

Rugged cliffs rise above Marie Creek.

After hiking 0.15 mile up the trail, a large unmarked path climbs uphill to the left. Turn uphill and begin climbing up the side of the hill in earnest. A series of switchbacks over the next 0.5 mile leads to the top of the hill. The first part of the climb crosses the hill's open flanks. The lack of forest cover gives you a chance to get a feel for the surrounding geography. The trail then enters a heavily wooded area as it finishes the climb to the top of the hill. Most of the elevation gain on the hike is now behind you.

At the top of the hill, stay right when the Lower Skyline Trail merges with the path you had been hiking. The trail quickly drops down the back side of the hill and enters a large field. A rock wall runs parallel to the path, and beyond it are great views to the south. A large quarry lies immediately below the hill. In the distance is San Pablo Bay, the great northern lobe of San Francisco Bay. The skyscrapers of San Francisco can be seen farther to the south. At the south end of the field, stay right at another junction. Even though you reenter the woods, the bay is still visible, especially at one point where the edge of the quarried hillside comes to within a few feet of the trail. The path soon turns to the east and arrives at a series of junctions. Turn left and follow the signs directing you to the Passini Road. This old ranch road makes one sweeping switchback and then ends at Lake Marie Road.

Turn left onto Lake Marie Road and follow it for only 100 yards before turning right and crossing over Marie Creek. On the far side of the creek, turn left and follow the signs for the Manzanita Trail. After following the creek for only 0.1 mile, begin to climb and then enter an expansive chaparral thicket that includes the trail's

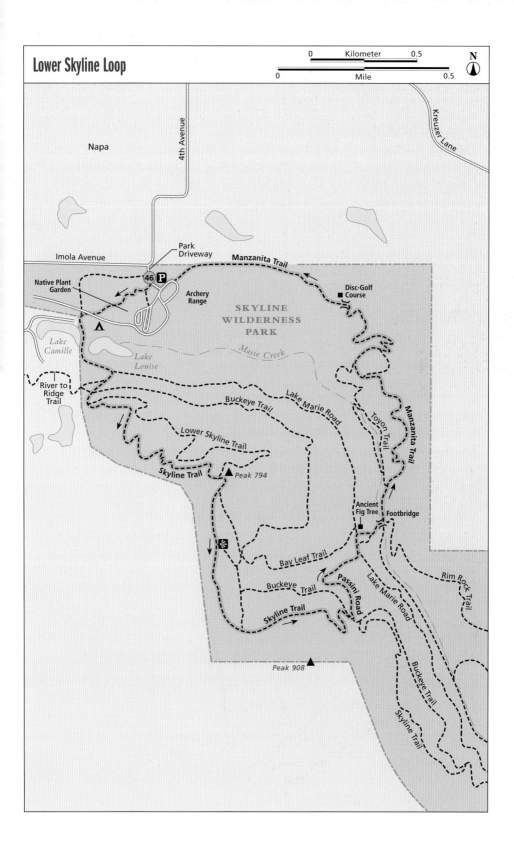

Lower Skyline Loop

Kilometer
0   0.5

Mile
0   0.5

N

Napa

4th Avenue

Kreuzer Lane

Imola Avenue

Park Driveway

Manzanita Trail

Native Plant Garden

46 P

Archery Range

SKYLINE WILDERNESS PARK

Disc-Golf Course

Lake Camille

Lake Louise

Marie Creek

River to Ridge Trail

Buckeye Trail

Lake Marie Road

Toyon Trail

Manzanita Trail

Lower Skyline Trail

Skyline Trail

Peak 794

Ancient Fig Tree

Footbridge

Bay Leaf Trail

Rim Rock Trail

Buckeye Trail

Passini Road

Lake Marie Road

Skyline Trail

Peak 908

Buckeye Trail

Skyline Trail

namesake brush. Stay to the right when the Toyon Trail branches off to the left. This path follows the creek rather than climbing high. By staying on the Manzanita Trail, you climb above the trees at the bottom of the canyon and enjoy views of Napa and the canyon. The arid terrain is embellished by old rock walls, making the route feel like it is passing through an old Western movie.

About 0.6 mile after crossing Marie Creek is a fork. Stay left. The route to the right is a bypass for mountain bikers. The Toyon Trail rejoins the Manzanita Trail as the path narrows and crosses a steep hillside. A few switchbacks finally lead down to the bottom of a small gully. Cross over the stream and pass by a large disc-golf course. From here it is 0.65 mile back to the trailhead. The path follows the stream while running parallel to parts of the disc-golf course. Recross the stream and climb over a low rise. You will emerge onto an open, grassy hill where an elaborate archery range spreads out to the left. Soon the path ends at the edge of a parking area. The trailhead lies just ahead, past the entrance station.

Miles and Directions

0.0   Leave the trailhead and pass by a native plant garden.

0.2   Turn left onto Lake Marie Road and pass between Lakes Camille and Louise.

0.4   Turn right onto the Skyline Trail. Stay on the main path, avoiding the River to Ridge Trail to the right and the Lower Skyline Trail to the left.

0.5   The Skyline Trail veers left off of the old road, which soon dead-ends. The path now begins a long series of switchbacks up the side of the hill.

1.2   Reach the top of the hill, finishing most of the hike's elevation gain. Stay right when the Lower Skyline Trail rejoins the Skyline Trail.

1.35 Great views of San Francisco Bay can be seen beyond a rock wall. Stay right again at a junction a little farther ahead.

1.55 There is another excellent view from the edge of the cliff above a quarry.

2.1   Turn left onto Passini Road.

2.4   Turn left again onto Lake Marie Road. Walk 100 yards down the road and turn right onto the trail signed for the Manzanita Trail and the Rim Rock Trail.

2.5   After crossing over Marie Creek, turn left onto the Manzanita Trail. A short distance later, stay right at the junction with the Toyon Trail.

3.1   Stay left when the mountain-bike bypass climbs up to the right. The Toyon Trail then rejoins the Manzanita Trail.

3.6   Cross over a small stream then turn left to stay on the Manzanita Trail. This marks the beginning of the disc-golf course.

3.8   Recross the stream, cross over a rise, and begin hiking alongside the archery range.

4.25 Arrive back at the trailhead, completing the loop.

47 Rim Rock Loop

The hike on Skyline Wilderness Park's Rim Rock Loop explores the highest section of the park, where there are panoramic views of the northern Bay Area. The trail climbs steadily up the side of the Marie Creek Canyon, crossing over rock outcroppings. After reaching the tallest point in the park, the trail descends back into the canyon while weaving through exposed volcanic strata. After passing Lake Marie, the hike follows Marie Creek through the beautiful inner canyon before returning to the trailhead.

Total Distance: 6.75-mile lollipop
Hiking Time: About 4.5 hours
Difficulty: Strenuous
Elevation Gain: 1,460 feet
Season: All year
Canine Compatibility: Dogs are not permitted

Fees: $5 entrance fee
Trail Contact: Skyline Wilderness Park, 2201 Imola Ave., Napa, CA 94559; (707) 252-0481; www.skylinepark.org/
Other: Park hours change seasonally; check with the staff for current hours.

Finding the trailhead: From CA 29 in Napa, take the Imola Avenue exit and drive east on Imola Avenue for 2.9 miles. When the road turns left, look for the park entrance on the right. GPS: N38°16.72767'/W122°14.97917'

The Hike

Even though the Skyline Wilderness Park begins right at the edge of the city of Napa, it lives up to its name. The upper reaches of the park—the parts that form the city's eastern skyline—are indeed wild. The centerpiece of the park is Marie Creek's long canyon, which extends more than 2 miles into the hills at the southern end of Napa Valley. The highest point in the park, a hill known as Sugarloaf, a forest-capped dome that stands 800 feet over the floor of the canyon, looms large. It is a dramatic landscape that seems far removed from the thriving city just a few miles away. Perhaps the best way to explore Skyline Wilderness Park is to hike the Rim Rock Trail. After heading into the canyon on the Lake Marie Road, the Rim Rock Trail climbs up the north side of the canyon. As it crosses over craggy rock outcroppings, great views of Marie Creek's drainage open up. Nearer to the summit of Sugarloaf are excellent vistas of southern Napa County. From the summit, the trail descends back to the canyon floor through layers of volcanic rock. The return route passes scenic Lake Marie and follows Marie Creek.

The hike into Skyline Wilderness Park begins at the main trailhead parking lot. Head south, pass the native plant garden, and climb a flight of stairs to reach the park's campground. Turn right, pass the west end of the campground, then turn left onto Lake Marie Road. The road is initially flanked by fences as it passes between a pair of ponds: Lake Camille is on the right and Lake Louise is on the left. Just past the lakes, the fences end, and the road arrives at a junction. The Skyline Trail departs to the right. Stay straight and continue on Lake Marie Road.

The road climbs gradually as it heads farther into the canyon. As it climbs, nice views of the Napa Valley unfold to the north. The large peak above Stags Leap, a famous wine appellation, rises prominently on the east side of the valley. After hiking up the road for 1 mile, a signed trail that turns off Lake Marie Road is on the left. Follow this path and cross over Marie Creek. Just before the turnoff of Lake Marie Road, look for a footpath that disappears into a tunnel of brush. This enters a fascinating brush-enclosed cave formed by the branches of an ancient fig tree. Pass through the little tunnel; inside is plenty of room to stand up and walk around under the tree's canopy.

Immediately after crossing Marie Creek, you arrive at a junction. Turn right onto the Rim Rock Trail. The trail begins to climb right away, and its grade does not level off until you have reached the top of Sugarloaf. A few switchbacks help lessen the grade initially, but the trail then begins a long traverse up the side of the canyon. For the most part, the trail is out in the open, and views up and down the canyon help make the climb a little less miserable. It crosses over a few large rock outcroppings, adding a little more interest to the ascent. After crossing the rocky areas, the route enters a side canyon that feeds into Marie Creek.

After a few short switchbacks, the path makes another long traverse that brings the trail to the top of the side canyon. Now only the towering dome of Sugarloaf looms overhead. To get to the top, the trail makes a series of long, sweeping switchbacks up the bare, grassy slopes. The open terrain yields magnificent views to the south, overlooking southern Napa County, San Pablo Bay, San Francisco, Mount Tamalpais in Marin County, and much of the East Bay. Just as the last switchback comes to an end, the trail levels off as you cross the rounded, forested summit of Sugarloaf, 1.6 miles after crossing Marie Creek. After the trail evens out is a single clear patch near the top providing good views to the north. This is a rugged part of the Napa city area that is rarely viewed.

The trail travels near the true summit of Sugarloaf, but the oak forest at the top means that there are no good summit views. When it is time to resume hiking, continue on the trail to the east side of the summit area. When the trail begins to descend, it is steep and covered in loose gravel in some areas. After 0.2 mile of climbing down beneath the tree cover, the path comes onto open hillsides. You can clearly see the east end of Marie Creek Canyon. Short switchbacks soon lessen the steepness as the trail winds through Technicolor bands of exposed volcanic rock: Orange and pink sections are interspersed with tans and whites. It is a very scenic stretch of trail. Finally, after hiking down the back side of Sugarloaf for 0.65 mile, the trail levels off as it arrives at a junction. Going left here leads to the Tuteur Loop, which explores the headwaters of Marie Creek in a remote salient on the Napa–Solano County line.

The Rimrock Trail has great views of the wild area just north of the park.

While that is a worthy hike, it is best to turn right at the junction and begin hiking on the Skyline Trail.

After the junction, the trail runs parallel to Marie Creek, though it stays well above the little stream. You soon reach another junction, staying right on the Chaparral Trail. Rather than dropping down to the little reservoir when it comes into sight, the trail climbs a bit higher and crosses chaparral-covered slopes with good views down to the water. At the far end of the lake, a trail finally drops down to the small dam. From there it connects with Lake Marie Road. While this is an option to get back to the trailhead, it is more scenic to press on past the lake for 0.2 mile and take the Lower Marie Creek Trail down to the creek's edge. From there the trail runs alongside the small stream through a beautiful, forest-shrouded canyon. This lovely riparian area seems a world away from the tall, grassy switchbacks near the summit of Sugarloaf. After following the creek for 0.7 mile, the trail finally arrives back at the beginning of the Rim Rock Trail, beside the crossing of Marie Creek. Walk back over the bridge and turn right onto Lake Marie Road. From there retrace your steps back to the trailhead.

Miles and Directions

0.0   Leave the trailhead and pass by a native plant garden.

0.2   Turn left onto Lake Marie Road and pass between Lakes Camille and Louise.

0.4   Stay straight on Lake Marie Road when the Skyline Trail veers off to the right.

Rim Rock Loop

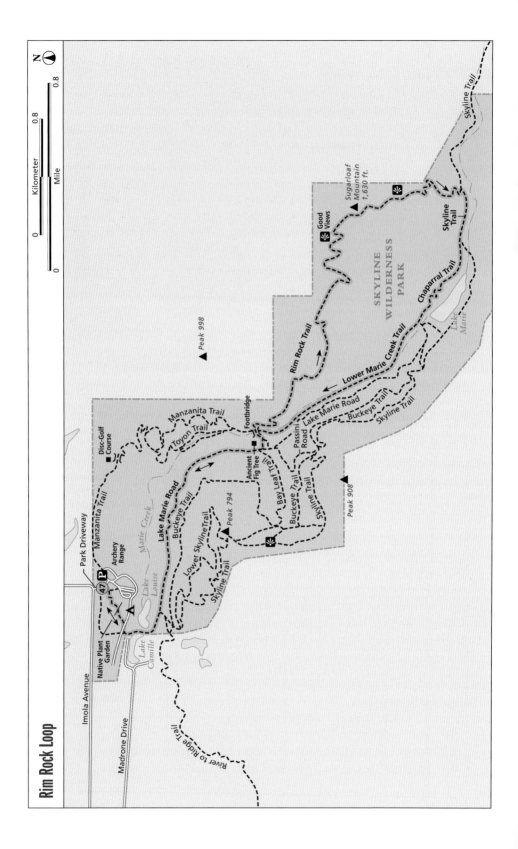

N

0   0.8   0.8
Kilometer
0   Mile

Imola Avenue

Madrone Drive

Park Driveway

47 P

Native Plant Garden

Archery Range

Lake Camille

Lake Louise

Marie Creek

River to Ridge Trail

Disc Golf Course

Manzanita Trail

Toyon Trail

Manzanita Trail

Lake Marie Road

Buckeye Trail

Lower Skyline Trail

Skyline Trail

Peak 794

Ancient Fig Tree

Footbridge

Bay Leaf Trail

Buckeye Trail

Skyline Trail

Passini Road

Lake Marie Road

Lower Marie Creek Trail

Buckeye Trail

Skyline Trail

Peak 908

Peak 998

Rim Rock Trail

SKYLINE WILDERNESS PARK

Lake Marie

Chaparral Trail

Lower Marie Creek Trail

Skyline Trail

Skyline Trail

Skyline Trail

Good Views

Sugarloaf Mountain 1,630 ft.

1.35 Turn left onto a signed trail and cross the footbridge over Marie Creek. Immediately turn onto the Rim Rock Trail.

2.5 Long switchbacks make the final march up to the summit of Sugarloaf. Views along this part of the trail are excellent.

2.9 The path levels off as it crosses Sugarloaf's broad summit area.

3.25 Begin the descent down the back side of Sugarloaf.

3.85 At the bottom of the canyon, turn right onto the Skyline Trail.

4.05 Stay right, proceeding on the Chaparral Trail.

4.55 After passing the Lake Marie dam, turn left onto the Lower Marie Creek Trail.

5.35 Turn left at the junction and cross back over Marie Creek. Turn right onto Lake Marie Road. From here retrace your steps back to the trailhead.

6.75 Arrive back at the trailhead.

48 Napa River and Bay Trail

Combining vineyards and tidal marshes, this hike is an easy trip along the last stretch of the Napa River before it empties into San Pablo Bay.

Total Distance: 5.6-mile reverse lollipop
Hiking Time: About 3 hours
Difficulty: Easy
Elevation Gain: None
Season: All year
Canine Compatibility: Dogs are permitted

Fees: None
Trail Contact: American Canyon Parks and Recreation, 100 Benton Way, American Canyon, CA; (707) 648-7275; www.cityofamericancanyon.org/things-to-do/trails-and-open-space

Finding the trailhead: Starting at the junction of CA 121 and CA 29, drive south on CA 29 for 4.1 miles. Turn right on Napa Junction Road and continue 0.1 mile. Turn left onto Theresa Avenue and drive 0.3 mile. Turn right onto Eucalyptus Drive and follow it for 0.9 mile to the parking area just before a gate. GPS: N38°10.84167'/W122°16.36500'

The Hike

The Napa River runs the entire length of Napa Valley, from the lower flanks of Mount Saint Helena north of Calistoga all the way to the former naval base at Mare Island, where the river empties into San Pablo Bay, which is the northern lobe of San Francisco Bay. For much of its journey down the valley, it is a small stream winding through bucolic vineyards. By the time it flows south of the city of Napa, it has widened considerably and becomes a large tidal estuary. This part of the river is strikingly different from the small, winding river that weaves its way through one of the world's greatest wine-growing regions. Although the area seems to have more in common with the maritime regions around San Francisco Bay, a surprising number of classic Wine Country elements are still present here. One of the best ways to explore this less-traveled part of the Napa area is on the Napa River and Bay Trail in American Canyon. Reclaimed from a variety of industrial lands, this trail is surprisingly scenic despite its commercial history.

The trail begins at the large parking area on Eucalyptus Drive. Just past the parking area, a gate blocks cars from the road. Walk around the gate and proceed west down the road. After 0.2 mile, turn right onto a wide, paved trail. Tall eucalyptus trees line the trail on the right. On the left, marshy wetlands spread out to the west. The trail soon turns west by a pond and then quickly turns north again, arriving at a fork in the road. Stay to the left and then immediately stay to the right at a second fork, maintaining a course on the paved trail. Pass a few more wetland ponds before crossing a wide bridge, about 0.75 mile from the beginning of the hike.

The railroad lift bridge is an interesting sight at the end of the trail.

Once you cross the bridge, the trail comes to another fork. Turn right and head north. This begins the main part of the hike. The trail extends north for 1.7 miles. The entire length of this section of the hike is flanked by a large tidal marsh that was once a complex of salt evaporation ponds. The area is being restored to a natural state, and it is difficult to discern the remnants of the old salt-evaporating areas. Although the Napa River is still more than a mile to the west, the restored tidal marshes fill with brackish water when the tide is in.

Heading north on the trail, vineyards soon appear on the right and remain alongside the path for 0.7 mile. Views of the mountains around the southern end of the Napa Valley are prominently visible to the east and north. The mountains above the town of Sonoma in Sonoma County, including the high, rounded summit of Sonoma Mountain, are also visible. Once past the vineyards, the trail loses some of its appeal, but it continues to the northwest for another 0.8 mile. Aside from the views of the surrounding mountains, the most interesting feature is the old railroad lift bridge spanning the Napa River. The bridge is an impressive remnant of a bygone age. At the end of the trail is a staging area where hikers could be dropped off. There are no parking facilities here, so few use this as a trailhead.

However far one chooses to hike this section of trail, one must return to the bridge. Cross back over it and turn to the right, heading south for 0.3 mile beside an old drainage channel. Turn right at the junction and hike another 0.3 mile out to a riverside vantage of the Napa River. The trail passes a surprising group of large agave plants. Return back to the last junction and continue straight. A short distance

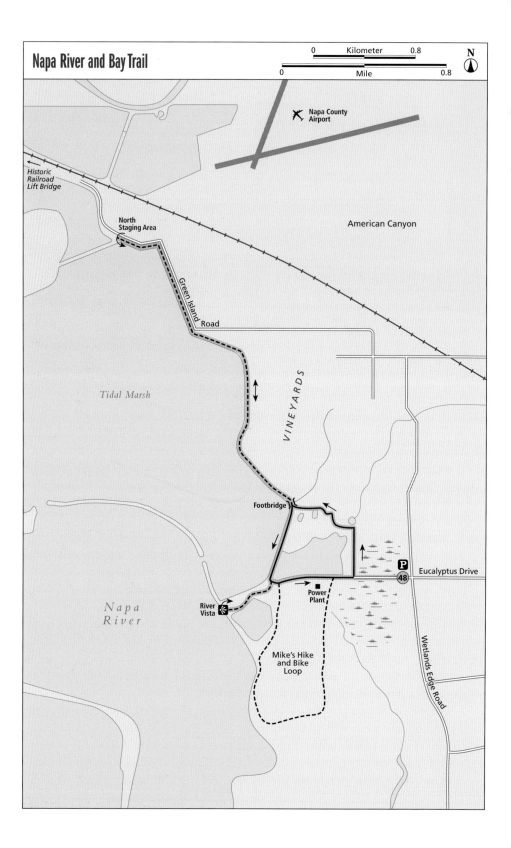

Napa River and Bay Trail

0   Kilometer   0.8

0   Mile   0.8

N

Napa County
Airport

American Canyon

Historic
Railroad
Lift Bridge

North
Staging Area

Green Island Road

Tidal Marsh

V I N E Y A R D S

Footbridge

P
48

Eucalyptus Drive

Napa
River

River
Vista

Power
Plant

Wetlands Edge Road

Mike's Hike
and Bike
Loop

later the trail arrives at another junction at the base of a large grassy mound. Once a landfill, the mound has now sealed in the trash. Pipes coming from within the mound transport the methane produced by the rotting garbage to a small power plant where the gas is used for generating electricity. A long trail encircles the mound but does not add much in the way of scenery and can be skipped. Continue straight toward the power plant, after which the trail reverts back to Eucalyptus Drive. Follow it back to the trailhead.

Miles and Directions

0.0 To begin the hike, go around the gate on Eucalyptus Drive and walk down the paved road.

0.2 Turn right onto the wide trail.

0.75 Cross a bridge and turn right onto the wide trail.

2.45 After passing vineyards and tidal marshes, the trail arrives at the north staging area. Turn around here and return to the bridge.

4.1 Cross the bridge and turn to the right.

4.45 At the fork, go right on the long spur out to the Napa River.

5.0 Return to the junction and go straight, avoiding any turns on the way back to the trailhead.

5.6 Arrive back at the parking area.

49 Newell Open Space Preserve

This is a beautiful hike through a former ranch, the Newell Preserve, with its bald hills, small canyons, and great views. The highlight of the hike is the traverse of the ridge that forms the boundary between Napa and Solano Counties. It has awesome views to both the east and west.

Total Distance: 5.3-mile lollipop
Hiking Time: About 3 hours
Difficulty: Moderate
Elevation Gain: 800
Season: All year
Canine Compatibility: Dogs are not permitted

Fees: None
Trail Contact: American Canyon Parks and Recreation, 100 Benton Way, American Canyon, CA; (707) 648-7275; www.cityofamericancanyon.org/things-to-do/trails-and-open-space

Finding the trailhead: Starting at the junction of CA 121 and CA 29, drive south on CA 29 for 5.1 miles. Turn left onto Donaldson Way and go 0.7 mile. Turn left on Newell Drive, then quickly turn left into the trailhead parking lot. GPS: N38°10.54367'/W122°14.53717'

The Hike

The city of American Canyon at the southern end of Napa County is one of the fastest-growing parts of the Wine Country. Numerous housing developments have filled in the level strip of land between the Napa River and some of the southernmost hills of the enormous North Coast Range. The Newell Preserve was donated to the city to help hem in the growing sprawl and keep it from encroaching on the hills to the east of the city. It prevented growth on the hills, but for a long time the preserve was cut off from the community because there were no roads affording public access to the park. Fortunately that was remedied when a new trail was built that connected a parking area near one of the housing developments to the network of old ranch roads that wind through the preserve. Hikers now have free and open access to the beautiful hills that boast awesome views and quiet seclusion amid canyons and wind-swept ridgelines.

There are two options for hiking in the Newell Preserve. One is a lower loop that explores the interior of some canyons at the east end of the property. The other option climbs higher and connects to an awesome ridge-top trail in the Lynch Canyon Open Space Park, just across the county line in neighboring Solano County. Although the upper loop is the more scenic, Lynch Canyon is only open on certain days, in which case it is better to take the lower loop. It is important to note that cattle are still run on parts of the Newell Preserve. Where the trail passes through gates, pay extra attention to keeping them closed after passing through.

The bay trees on the ridge above the Newell Preserve are shaped by fierce winds.

The trail starts at a low-key dirt parking lot behind a housing development. Passing through a gate, it skirts the edge of a pasture. Dense brush hugs the right side of the trail, blocking access to a small, seasonal creek. The trail follows the pasture for 0.4 mile before passing through a rickety wire gate in a barbed-wire fence. The trail continues north along the other side of the fence for 0.2 mile before arriving at what used to be the old trailhead. An old kiosk and protective enclosure for a now-removed outhouse mark the spot. Before the construction of the new trailhead, it was necessary to get a key from the city to open a gate and drive a private road to this trailhead. Though it adds a bit of distance, the new option is much more convenient. From the old trailhead, the path comes alongside the creek, and they parallel each other while climbing moderately up a small canyon for 0.5 mile before arriving at a junction.

Stay right at the junction and cross the creek. On the other side are several picnic tables in a clearing above the creek. Go past and begin climbing in earnest the side of the open, grass-carpeted hillsides. Pass through a gate and go under some power lines, climbing to another junction. Here you must decide whether to keep climbing up to the Lynch Canyon Open Space Park or take the loop that stays within the Newell Preserve. The latter option, known as the Newell Preserve Loop, scallops through the interior of the canyon. It passes some seeps by a large, impressive rock outcropping. To take this loop, go left at the fork. The trail, a decommissioned ranch road, cuts across the top of the canyon, just below some large rocks. The seeps along this section of the trail can keep the grass green longer than drier grasses in the surrounding

Newell Open Space Preserve

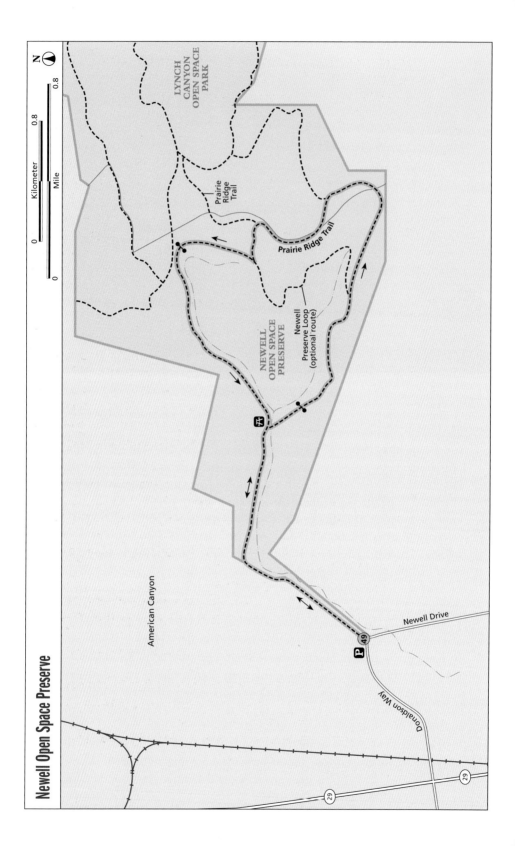

N

Kilometer
0   0.8

Mile
0   0.8

LYNCH CANYON OPEN SPACE PARK

Prairie Ridge Trail

Prairie Ridge Trail

NEWELL OPEN SPACE PRESERVE

Newell Preserve Loop (optional route)

American Canyon

Newell Drive

Donaldson Way

P 49

29

29

area. The path soon arcs around a knob, where there is a good vista of San Pablo Bay and Marin County. The trail turns to the east and passes beneath a power line. At the intersection with the trail returning from the Lynch Canyon Open Space Park, turn left to complete the loop and return to the Newell Open Space Preserve trailhead.

To continue on the longer, more scenic loop, continue climbing. As it rounds a shoulder, the path reveals awesome views to the west, where the peaks of Marin County and the Sonoma Mountains rise above San Pablo Bay and the Napa River. The trail turns back to the east, following the power lines to a junction with the trail coming over the ridge from the Lynch Canyon preserve. On days when the Lynch Canyon preserve is open, take this route and climb past the junction to the top of the ridge. Veer left onto the Prairie Ridge Trail, which is a narrow single-track path. Follow this along the ridge, passing groves of stunted, oddly shaped bay trees. The unusual growth pattern of these trees is caused by the powerful winds whipping over the ridge from the bay. The vistas from this trail are tremendous and offer one of the few glimpses of California's great interior region from a Wine Country trail. Follow the ridge for 0.7 mile before turning left at a junction and dropping down the ridge to rejoin the shorter Newell Preserve Loop.

Once the trails have converged, follow the old ranch road north through a small vale. At another junction where two drainages meet, pass through a gate and turn left. Here the trail enters a narrow canyon and begins to descend toward the beginning of the loop. As the canyon widens, the views to the west improve. The trail passes through a small grove of eucalyptus trees before arriving at the end of the loop by the picnic area. From here retrace your steps down the canyon and back to the trailhead.

Miles and Directions

0.0 At the trailhead go around the fence and follow the path to the northeast.

0.6 Open the barbed-wire gate and go through. After a few more yards, arrive at the old trailhead. Turn right and follow the road.

1.15 At a fork in the trail, turn right and cross over the creek. On the opposite side is a picnic area. Hike past it as the grade begins to steepen.

1.24 Go through the gate and continue climbing the hill.

1.85 If the Lynch Canyon Open Space Park is open, stay right at the fork and continue climbing. If not open, go left and traverse the upper reaches of the canyon via the Newell Preserve Loop.

2.25 The trail reaches the top of the ridge. Turn left and hike the narrow Prairie Ridge Trail. The views from the trail are great.

2.9 Turn left at a junction and descend a hill, reentering the Newell Open Space Preserve.

3.05 Near some large power lines, turn left at a junction and head through a small valley.

3.4 Go through a gate and turn left, entering a narrow canyon.

4.25 At the first fork near the picnic area, rejoin the main trail and retrace your steps back to the trailhead.

5.3 Arrive back at the trailhead.

50 Napa River Ecological Reserve

The short hike in the Napa River Ecological Reserve is the only trail access to the Napa River north of the city of Napa. The river is not very wide and not extremely swift moving, but it is a wild waterway, and there is beauty in the free-flowing water.

Total Distance: 1.2-mile lollipop
Hiking Time: About 1 hour
Difficulty: Easy
Elevation Gain: None
Season: All year
Canine Compatibility: Dogs are not permitted
Fees: None

Trail Contact: California Department of Fish and Game, Bay Delta Region Napa Office; (707) 944-5500; www.wildlife.ca.gov/Lands/Places-to-Visit/Napa-River-ER
Other: The hike's main loop requires a ford across the Napa River; if the water level is high, this should not be attempted.

Finding the trailhead: From CA 29 in Yountville, turn right onto Madison Street. Go 0.1 mile, then turn onto Washington Street. Go another 0.1 mile and turn left onto Starkey. Drive 0.1 mile and turn left onto Yount Street. Turn right onto Yountville Cross Road. Continue for 0.9 mile, then turn left into a parking lot just before a bridge over the Napa River. GPS: N38°25.05967'/W122°21.19033'

The Hike

The Napa River runs through the entire length of the Napa Valley, a long, sinuous thread weaving through vineyards and low hills. The river's setting in the valley is incredibly scenic, highlighted by rows of grapevines and elegant wineries overshadowed by rugged mountains. Unfortunately, most of the river passes through private land, rendering the scenic waterway inaccessible. Sections of the river in the city of Napa and farther south are fronted by trails, but for the majority of the river that flows through the heart of the Napa Valley, there is only one publicly accessible section.

The Napa River Ecological Reserve is a small nature preserve near Yountville. It contains a section of the Napa River and its confluence with Conn Creek, one of the river's largest tributaries. A short trail loops through the preserve, giving hikers unique access to the Napa River. Though the trail is not long, it is a welcome natural oasis amid the beautiful expanse of viticulture.

The trail begins at a small parking lot. Hike north along the wide path leading out of the parking area. Just beyond the trailhead, a short loop trail branches off from the main path and winds through a native plant garden where signs indicate the species. Returning to the main trail, it soon climbs onto a levee. Trails branch off in three directions. For the main loop, go straight. Climb down the opposite side of the levee into the Napa River's overflow channel. The river is somewhat obscured by thick

Fall colors along the Napa River.

vegetation. If you are only looking for a quiet spot from which to enjoy the river, a good one is off to the right.

To continue on the loop, stay straight in a northerly direction for a few yards, passing through riparian brush until reaching the edge of the water. It is necessary to cross over the river. Unfortunately, there is no longer a bridge so you must ford the river. When the rain runoff is high, this may not be possible. When the water is low, cross over to the other side. Look for concrete foundations and the ruins of the bridge that once stood here.

The loop begins right away. Stay to the left and follow along the edge of the Napa River. There are some nice spots to gaze down on the water. The trail heads north, passing through thick brush. As the trail turns to the east, the path becomes overgrown, though the route is still discernable. Watch out for thorny plants. These will overtake the trail if they are not cut back soon. After crossing a gully, the trail heads south, running between Conn Creek and a small meadow. As the path rounds the south end of the meadow, it reaches the end of the loop and returns to the Napa River. Some sections in this area can be hard to follow but the path is usually apparent.

Cross back over the river at the same point. To add a little more distance to the short hike, head north along the river and follow a series of use trails that run parallel to the water. These paths eventually merge with the main trail on the top of the levee.

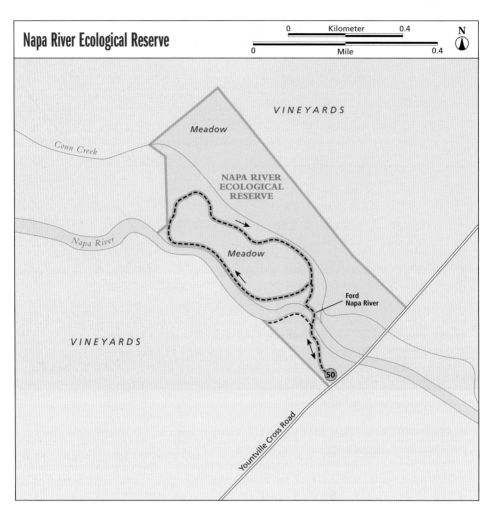

Napa River Ecological Reserve

This continues north a little bit before coming to an end at the edge of a vineyard. To return, head back along the levee to the first three-way junction. Turn right and head back to the trailhead on the main path.

Miles and Directions

0.0 Start the hike by walking past the large sign and across an open field.

0.1   Climb up the levee and drop down to the river.

0.2 After fording the river the trail splits. Stay to the left and begin the loop.

0.75 The trail crosses a gully and travels between Conn Creek and a small meadow.

1.0 Return to the fork in the trail, completing the loop. Stay to the left and ford the river to return to the trailhead.

1.2 Arrive back at the trailhead.

51 Rector Reservoir Wildlife Area

This severely underappreciated hike climbs steeply to the top of a ridge on the east side of Napa Valley. It then traverses the top of the ridge, leading to a rock outcropping near famed Stags Leap, a series of volcanic crags and cliffs. Incredible views, stretching from downtown San Francisco in the south to towering Mount Saint Helena at the north end of the Napa Valley, are constant along the hike's entire length. In terms of grand views of classic Wine Country terrain, this trail is tough to beat.

Total Distance: 3.7 miles out and back
Hiking Time: About 3 hours
Difficulty: Strenuous
Elevation Gain: 900 feet
Season: All year
Canine Compatibility: Dogs are not permitted

Fees: None
Trail Contact: California Department of Fish and Game, Bay Delta Region Napa Office; (707) 944-5500; www.wildlife.ca.gov/Lands/ Places-to-Visit/Rector-Reservoir-WA

Finding the trailhead: From CA 29 in Yountville, turn right onto Madison Street. Go 0.1 mile, then turn onto Washington Street. Go another 0.1 mile and turn left onto Starkey. Drive 0.1 mile and turn left onto Yount Street. Turn right onto Yountville Cross Road. Continue for 1.9 miles, then turn left onto Silverado Trail. Drive north 0.8 mile and turn right into an unmarked pullout next to a chain-link fence. GPS: N38°26.21267'/W122°20.95133'

The Hike

The Rector Reservoir Wildlife Area is an oddly shaped tract of land that is owned by the Department of Veterans Affairs but is administered by the California Department of Fish and Game. The trail climbs a ridge leading to Stags Leap, a massive volcanic formation much like the Palisades at the north end of the Napa Valley near Calistoga, with spectacular views of the Napa Valley and much of the northern San Francisco Bay Area.

The trail begins next to a Yountville maintenance facility. Look for the narrow path along the fence on the north side of the facility. Follow the trail around the fence and begin to climb. The path is narrow and cuts through tall grass amid scattered oak trees. This is obviously a no-frills trail; little maintenance is done, and it is routed directly up the hillside with no thought to the grade. Still, the increasingly excellent views compensate for the hard work.

After climbing for 0.4 mile, the trail descends into a gully and climbs out the far side; a few steps later, arrive at a fork. The main trail continues to the left and continues to climb the steep hillside. The path to the right leads to a briefly level section of trail and a nice vista overlooking the Yountville area. From the vista the trail then climbs back to the main route. Though still going uphill, this slight detour moderates the grade somewhat and provides a nice place to take a rest.

The trail has great views of the Napa Valley.

Once back on the main trail, the route continues to climb the hill for another 0.1 mile before arriving at a second trail junction. This time the main trail stays to the right. Turning left leads to the top of the hill, a couple hundred feet away. The climb is steep but short. From the top of the hill is a vantage point where hikers can peer down to the Rector Reservoir, which is nestled into a deep, steep-walled canyon. Note the vineyards amid the chaparral above the lake on the far side of the canyon. After taking in the view, hikers can descend the way they came back to the main trail or follow a well-established use trail that leads back to the main path but makes heading downhill unnecessary and saves hikers from climbing another 50 feet.

As you continue on the trail, the route finally levels off. It does so moderately at first but eventually levels off considerably as the path reaches the top of the ridge. Having climbed 800 feet in a mile, the worst is now thankfully over. The reward for the grueling climb is a fantastic view in every direction, taking in much of the Napa Valley, especially the Yountville, Stags Leap, and Oak Knoll districts. A patchwork of vineyards covers most of the valley floor. It is broken up by the wooded Yountville Hills and the town of Yountville, which lie just to the south. To the east are the rounded bulk of Haystack peak and some attractive vineyards situated precariously on the edge of cliffs high above the Rector Reservoir. After reaching the top of the ridge, the trail undulates along its crest to the south. Occasional rock outcroppings provide some distraction to the awesome views.

The trail proceeds south along the ridge for another mile before arriving at the top of a large crag. En route, the views get increasingly grand. Not only is the

Rector Reservoir Wildlife Area

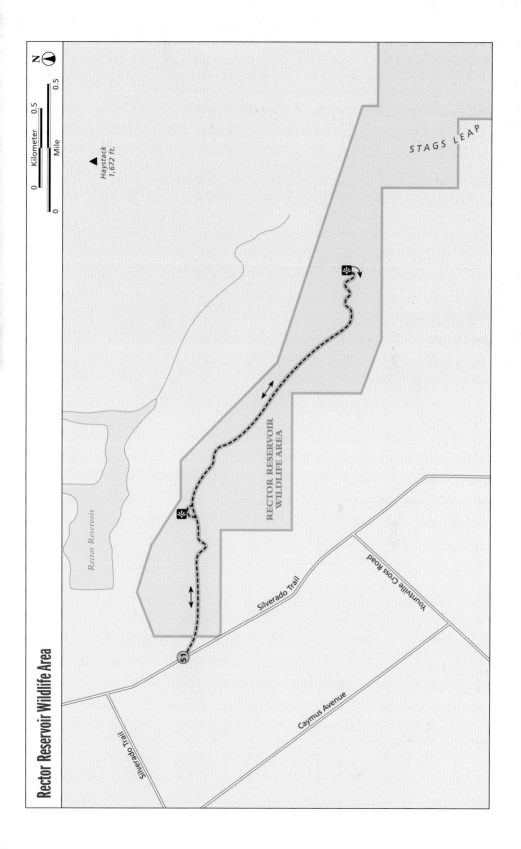

immediate vicinity of the Napa Valley visible but also the high peaks of Mount Saint Helena and Cobb Mountain far to the north, and spectacular views of the city of Napa, the Carneros region, San Pablo Bay, and the Point Richmond area; even the skyscrapers of downtown San Francisco are noticeably visible from the trail. When the path finally arrives at the prominent rocky crag, the scene is spectacular. In addition to the previous elements of the view, the tall cliffs of Stags Leap loom a short distance away; here is a great opportunity to peer down at the Stags' Leap vineyards, one of the most historic winemakers in Napa Valley. It is a stunning sight and a great place to enjoy a picnic lunch.

From the large crag, the trail continues to the south, but it is much less distinct and is hard to follow at times. It descends to a broad saddle before disappearing into the brush. The adventurous can attempt to follow it through the dense chaparral, but the views don't get better, and there is no clear destination. It is better to simply turn around at the crag and enjoy the views again while hiking back to the trailhead.

Miles and Directions

0.0 The trail begins next to the fence. Follow it to the corner at the south end of the parking area. From there the path turns east and begins climbing toward the top of the ridge.

0.6 After climbing steeply, a spur branches off to the left. Follow this up to an overlook above the Rector Reservoir. From there either return to the main trail or follow an obvious use trail to the left, which soon reconnects to the primary path.

1.0 The trail reaches the top of the ridge and finally levels off. There are awesome views in all directions from the top. The path continues to the south, undulating across the ridgeline.

1.85 After hiking south with consistently excellent vistas of the Napa Valley, the trail arrives at a large rock outcropping. To the south looms the tall crag of Stags Leap. The view from here is epic. Even though a narrow path continues south from here, this is the best place to turn around and retrace your steps back to the beginning.

52 Lake Hennessey

Tucked away in a secluded valley just east of the Napa Valley, Lake Hennessey is a scenic reservoir that provides water for the city of Napa. The lands on the east side of the lake have been incorporated into Moore Creek Park and offer hiking next to creeks, over high, open ridges with panoramic views, and along Lake Hennessey's beautiful shoreline.

Total Distance: 7.1-mile lollipop
Hiking Time: About 4 hours
Difficulty: Moderate
Elevation Gain: 500 feet
Season: All year

Canine Compatibility: Dogs are permitted
Fees: None
Trail Contact: Napa County Regional Park and Open Space District; www.napaoutdoors.org

Finding the trailhead: *Moore Creek Park trailhead:* Starting at the junction of Silverado Trail and Highway 128 in Napa Valley, drive east on Highway 128 for 3.8 miles. Make a slight left on Chiles Pope Valley Road and continue for 1.3 miles. Turn left into Moore Creek Park and proceed to the large parking area. GPS: N38°30.59117'/W122°21.32833'

Conn Valley Road trailhead: Starting at the junction of Silverado Trail and Highway 128 in Napa Valley, drive north on Silverado Trail for 3.3 miles. Turn right onto Howell Mountain Road. After 1.2 miles, stay straight on Conn Valley Road. Continue for 4.1 miles to the end of the road. Park on the edge of the road.

The Hike

Lake Hennessey was built in 1948 to provide water for the city of Napa. Located at the confluence of Conn, Chiles, and Moore Creeks, the lake is impounded by the Conn Dam. Conn Creek continues below the dam before joining the Napa River near Yountville. The lake is set in a scenic basin fed by several canyons, separate from the rest of Napa Valley by a low ridge. It is surrounded by low peaks where vineyards have been established amid the chaparral-lined slopes. Although a significant amount of the land around the lake is publicly owned, there has been little development of the property for recreation. Locals hungry for hiking opportunities frequented public roads that lined the eastern and western shorelines. The eastern shore of Lake Hennessey had a lot of potential because it was long, filled with views, travelled next to the water, and was backed by hundreds of acres of public land. Nonetheless, no improvements were made and this beautiful slice of the Napa region remained neglected. That changed when the Moore Creek Park was established. A nearby ranch was bought by the county and converted into a large public park. This property was connected to the public lands on the east side of the lake and the potential for an even larger, more diverse park was recognized. Now the two blocks of public land have

Trail view of Lake Hennessey and the Napa Valley.

been joined into one contiguous block of public land, and trails have been built connecting the main Moore Creek Park trailhead to a loop through the public lands that incorporates the old east shore road and paths meandering through the hills above the water. With trail along creeks, high views of Lake Hennessey and the Napa Valley, remote forests, and miles of trail along the lakeshore, the new loop trail is destined to be one of Napa Valley's classic hikes.

For hikers looking for a somewhat shorter option, it is possible to park at the access point for the east shore trail at the end of Conn Valley Road. Starting here allows hikers the option of doing the 5.2-mile-loop without having to hike the 1.8 miles that connect the route to the Moore Creek Park trailhead. This is definitely a good option if time is a little short, but with no constraints, the section along Moore and Chiles Creeks is worth the time. It is easy and offers the opportunity to hike near the running water.

Begin the hike at the southern end of the large Moore Creek Park trailhead parking lot. Walk along the road for a few yards, passing the Valentine's Vista Trail that sets out on the left. The actual trail begins on the right and drops down off the road near a thicket of blackberry vines. A large gap in the vines leads to a crossing of Moore Creek. There is no log or bridge so a high-water crossing can be tricky. Once on the other side, the trail climbs a little and then follows the contours of the hillside above the creek. Though it is not visible from the trail, a short distance from the crossing, Moore Creek joins larger Chiles Creek. Eventually the trail descends some switchbacks and passes a gate as it joins an old dirt road. Follow the road a few hundred more yards to a fork. Stay to the right.

From the fork the old road begins to climb steeply through a forest of oak and buckeye. A few switchbacks help to moderate the grade but it is still a somewhat steep climb. About 0.5 mile from the fork, the path reaches its first view just after some switchbacks. The trees recede from the trail near a power line and the panorama of Lake Hennessey and the western wall of the Napa Valley unfolds. It is a great place to stop and take a break. Continuing on from this point, the trail climbs a little more before finally clearing the trees and emerging on a long, open ridge. Views to the south, west, and north are great. Particularly notable is an improved view of Lake Hennessey and the wall the forms the western edge of the Napa Valley. It is a dramatic vista. As you move west along the ridge, the trail begins to descend as it enters a wide, shallow drainage. The seasonal creek flows through a gully cut into open, grassy slopes that are dotted with occasional oak trees. As the trail continues to lose elevation, it finally arrives at a fork, 2.2 miles after beginning the climb near Chiles Creek. Going right here provides swift access to the Conn Creek Road trailhead. Instead, stay left, hiking down the Ken's Cutoff Trail. In short order the trail ends at a junction with the Lake Hennessey Shoreline Fire Road, the original route utilized by hikers on the east side of the lake. Turn left here.

The old fire road is an easy, level path that follows along the edge of the lake. The path travels a narrow bench between the grassy hills above the lake and the reed-choked shoreline. Few trees stand along the trails and the views out over the water are great. The pleasant scenery and level path make travel easy along this section of the hike. Nearly 0.75 mile from the junction of Ken's Cutoff Trail and the shoreline road, the path crosses over a large wooden bridge. The seasonal creek flowing beneath drains all the hills east of the lake. Beyond the bridge the trail continues to parallel the east shore of the lake for another 0.6 mile before it begins to turn to the east and skirt the eastern arm of the lake. This area was once part of Chiles Creek. As you move east, the terrain steepens and soon the trail is slung on a slope high above the waters. Watch for the kayak put-in on the far side of the lake. For a long time this was the only significant recreational improvement in the area. The route eventually begins to turn to the north, still following the lake along the Chiles Creek drainage. It is another 0.65 mile along the edge of the lake before reaching the first trail junction and completing the loop. From here retrace your steps 0.9 mile back to the trailhead.

Miles and Directions

0.0   Start the hike at the large Moore Creek Park trailhead parking area. Walk south along the road and then follow the trail down to the crossing over Moore Creek. Proceed along the trail through the hills.

0.9   Just after merging with an old ranch road, the trail comes to a fork. Stay right and begin climbing high above the creek.

1.5   The first excellent views open up when the route passes a large power line.

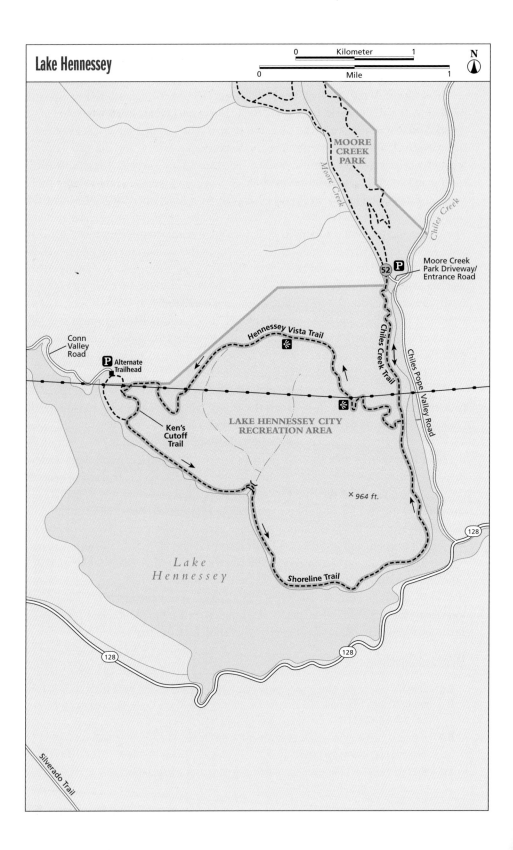

Lake Hennessey

0 Kilometer 1

0 Mile 1

N

MOORE CREEK PARK

Moore Creek

Chiles Creek

52 P Moore Creek
Park Driveway/
Entrance Road

Conn
Valley
Road

P Alternate
Trailhead

Hennessey Vista Trail

Chiles Creek Trail

Chiles Pope Valley Road

LAKE HENNESSEY CITY
RECREATION AREA

Ken's
Cutoff
Trail

× 964 ft.

128

*Lake
Hennessey*

Shoreline Trail

128

128

Silverado Trail

2.1 The trail reaches the highest point on the hike as it crosses a large, open ridge with panoramic views.

3.2 At the fork, stay left and hike down the Ken's Cutoff Trail.

3.4 Turn left onto the shoreline road that parallels the east side of Lake Hennessey.

4.15 Cross the bridge over the large, unnamed creek.

4.75 Begin following along the Chiles Creek arm of the lake.

5.5 The trail turns north and continues along Chiles Creek.

6.2 Stay right at the junction and begin hiking on the footpath back toward the trailhead.

7.1 Arrive back at the Moore Creek Park trailhead.

53 Moore Creek Park

The hike along Moore Creek is a journey into the deep recesses of a secluded canyon. The trail first climbs high on the canyon wall and enjoys sweeping vistas before descending to the creek. It then follows the stream through the narrow gulch, crossing the water several times. The trail ends at a small gorge, where water races through a series of chutes and pools in the bedrock.

Total Distance: 7.6-mile reverse lollipop
Hiking Time: About 4 hours
Difficulty: Moderate
Elevation Gain: 900 feet
Season: All year
Canine Compatibility: Dogs are permitted
Fees: None

Trail Contact: Napa County Regional Park and Open Space District; www.napaoutdoors.org
Other: The upstream portion of the hike has many creek crossings. If the water level is high, it is best to avoid this part of the trail. The loop section can still be hiked during periods of high water.

Finding the trailhead: Starting at the junction of Silverado Trail and CA 128 in Napa Valley, drive east on CA 128 for 3.8 miles. Make a slight left on Chiles Pope Valley Road and continue for 1.3 miles. Turn left into Moore Creek Park and proceed to the large parking area. GPS: N38°30.59117'/W122°21.32833'

The Hike

Moore Creek drains a large canyon to the east of the Napa Valley. Beginning high on Howell Mountain, the creek flows through Los Posadas State Forest before entering a deep, narrow canyon. South of the canyon the river flows into Lake Hennessey. The heart of Moore Creek Canyon is now a part of Moore Creek Park, one of the newest natural preserves in Napa County. The park includes approximately 3 miles of the creek as well as the steep walls of the canyon and surrounding hills. One of the park's highlights is a great hike along the creek that leads to the Moore Creek Pools, where you will find some small cascades and a nice little swimming hole. A new section of trail climbs high up on the flanks of the canyon with great views to the north and south, following much of Moore Creek's watershed. The new trail forms a reverse lollipop, climbing high on the first part of the hike and then returning to the trailhead along the creek. A long hike through remote country, the Moore Creek Trail is destined to become a Napa County classic.

At the large trailhead are two options to begin the hike. If you want the easier and direct route up Moore Creek, follow the road north for 1 mile to where it joins the new Valentine Vista Trail just before reaching the ranger's residence. Even though this route follows the creek, it stays well above the water, with few water views. It is not

The trail ends at a series of small swimming holes on Moore Creek.

nearly as scenic as the upper trail and is more enjoyable as a means of quick return to the trailhead at the end of the hike.

To take the upper, more interesting route, go to the south end of the parking lot to find the start of the trail. It immediately begins to climb, though the grade is easy and the ascent is moderated by two series of switchbacks. Shortly after the first set of switchbacks, the trail passes massive boulders before making a long traverse of the hillside. It then climbs through the second set of switchbacks before leveling off a bit when the trail begins heading north, about 0.75 mile from the beginning of the hike. From here the path undulates across the side of the canyon, gradually gaining elevation. Though the slopes are marked by oak trees and an occasional gray pine, it is generally open, grassy country. Views are constant and good.

To the north you can look along much of Moore Creek Canyon, where the second half of the trail explores the canyon bottom. To the south the rest of the creek's journey can be seen all the way to its inlet at Lake Hennessey. Above the finger of the lake rises Pritchard Hill, with vineyards clinging to its steep sides amid a sea of discouragingly thick chaparral. Finally, 2 miles from the parking lot, the path reaches its highest point. It then makes a 1-mile, switchback-laden descent to the Moore Creek Trail. There are great vistas for much of the way down.

Once at the Moore Creek Trail, turn right and hike up the road. In short order the road splits. To the left is a driveway that leads down to a ranch house, which is the ranger's residence. Stay right on the old road. It quickly narrows as a dark forest

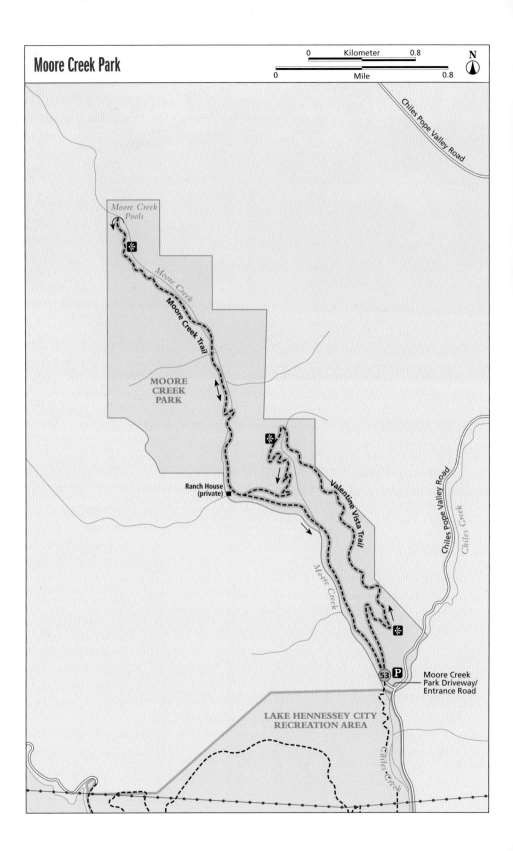

Moore Creek Park

0   Kilometer   0.8

0   Mile   0.8

N

Chiles Pope Valley Road

Moore Creek Pools

Moore Creek

Moore Creek Trail

MOORE CREEK PARK

Ranch House (private)

Valentine Vista Trail

Moore Creek

Chiles Pope Valley Road

Chiles Creek

53 P

Moore Creek Park Driveway/ Entrance Road

LAKE HENNESSEY CITY RECREATION AREA

Chiles Creek

closes in. The trail makes several crossings back and forth across the creek. Long beams have been placed across the creek and secured by cables. At one point the old road has been washed away, and the trail makes a brief climb on a narrow but well-constructed trail to get around the washed-out area. This entire section of the hike is fairly level and is easy, pleasant hiking. Moore Creek is a perennial stream, and even if no water is flowing past the trailhead, there is usually a decent flow in the upper canyon above the ranger's residence.

The trail crosses the creek for the last time about 1 mile north of the ranger's residence. Now on the west side of Moore Creek, the route climbs above the creek on the old road. After you cross a small stream that feeds Moore Creek, a spur branches off to the right. This leads to a nice bench and a great vista south from this remote section of the canyon.

Back on the main trail, it begins to go downhill. Follow the signs pointing the way to the Moore Creek Pools. The path finally reaches the bottom of the canyon next to the creek. Large bedrock outcroppings break up Moore Creek, causing the water to flow over little cascades and through small chutes. Go downstream, hopping on rocks and crossing the creek when necessary. After about 60 yards, the narrow gorge widens. Moore Creek falls over a tiny waterfall into a lovely pool that is just large and deep enough to take a dip. After enjoying this beautiful and refreshing spot, retrace your steps 2 miles south to the junction with the Valentine Vista Trail. Stay right on the main road. From there it is 1 easy mile back to the trailhead.

Miles and Directions

0.0 At the south end of the parking lot, begin hiking up Valentine Vista Trail.

0.75 Reach the top of a long series of switchbacks.

2.0 After traversing the side of the canyon, begin descending toward Moore Creek.

3.0 Turn right at the junction with the Moore Creek Trail and begin hiking into the interior of the canyon.

4.0 After several creek crossings, the trail makes one final crossing to the west side of Moore Creek. It then begins to climb high above the water.

4.55 A spur trail to the right leads to a nice vantage point looking south, down the length of the canyon.

4.75 Arrive at the Moore Creek Pools. Enjoy the small pools and little cataracts. When it is time to return, retrace your steps to the junction of the Valentine Vista Trail and the Moore Creek Trail.

6.55 Stay right at the junction with the Valentine Vista Trail.

7.6 Arrive back at the trailhead.

54 Las Posadas State Forest

The loop through Los Posadas State Forest combines narrow trails, old fire roads, and a few sections of well-used service roads. It travels through an amazing number of habitats as it circles the headwaters of Moore Creek, including a rare Wine Country ponderosa pine forest, redwood groves, and arid chaparral.

Total Distance: 4.1-mile lollipop
Hiking Time: About 2.5 hours
Difficulty: Moderate
Elevation Gain: 570 feet
Season: All year
Canine Compatibility: Dogs are permitted

Fees: None
Trail Contact: None
Other: A 4-H camp is located along the trail; please be respectful if activities are taking place.

Finding the trailhead: Starting at CA 29 at the north end of Saint Helena, drive north on CA 29 for 0.8 mile. Turn right on Deer Park Road. Drive 4.7 miles, crossing Silverado Trail and climbing the east side of Napa Valley. On the outskirts of the town of Angwin, turn right onto Cold Springs Road. After 0.2 mile, continue straight onto Las Posadas Road. Drive 0.8 mile. The trailhead is located where the road makes a sharp right-hand turn. GPS: N38°34.15250'/W122°25.41833'

The Hike

Las Posadas State Forest is a small block of public land hidden away in the Howell Mountain area on the east side of the Napa Valley. Howell Mountain—a high, broad plateau—is home to the community of Angwin and Pacific Union College, a small university. Due to its high elevation and volcanic soils, Howell Mountain is also a distinct wine-making region, separate from the Napa Valley to the west and the Pope and Chiles Valleys to the east. Las Posadas is just east of Pacific Union College. The state forest was once a private ranch but it was donated to the state early in the twentieth century. The park contains the headwaters of Moore Creek, a tributary of Conn Creek, which in turn feeds into the Napa River. The most striking feature of the trails through Las Posadas State Forest is the impressive diversity of the landscape. Ranging from a rare ponderosa pine forest and the typical mixed forest of the Mayacamas Mountains to arid chaparral and gorgeous redwood groves, this is one of the most diverse hikes in the Wine Country.

The hike begins at a ninety-degree bend in the road leading from Angwin. Across the road are large, scenic vineyards that are part of the Howell Mountain appellation. Adjacent to the small pullout that serves as a parking area for Las Posadas State Forest is another small parking area that serves a private trail network running through the undeveloped land belonging to Pacific Union College. Most of the trails in Las Posadas were either roads at one time or are roads that are still in use. Many of these

Boulders and pine trees are found along the trail.

have faded and are nearly indistinguishable from a normal trail; others are wide, dusty paths.

To start the hike, head through the gate and immediately turn right onto a wide dirt path. Though separated by a fence, the trail initially runs parallel to the road but soon veers away and weaves through a forest of tall ponderosa pines. These trees are uncommon in the Wine Country but are one of the most common trees in the higher mountains around California. At 0.2 mile stay left at a fork. Watch for a narrow trail branching off to the right. It leads through an attractive cluster of large boulders before rejoining the main trail. About 0.6 mile from the beginning of the hike, the trail arrives at a four-way intersection. Stay to the far left, heading up what is known as Roosevelt Road.

The old road climbs slightly before passing beside a fence that separates the state forest from lands owned by Pacific Union College. Here the trail enters a small redwood grove. Though the trees here are small, this is the beginning of a fairly extensive grove that contains some large trees. It descends the hill from here toward the headwaters of Moore Creek. The end of the loop through Las Posadas travels through the lower, larger section of the redwood grove. The trail continues through the redwoods and then begins to switchback down the side of the hill, finally merging with a fire road 1.25 miles from the trailhead.

The fire road is wide and dusty and one of the least attractive hiking surfaces. Despite this, there are interesting views to the south as the road descends 0.35 mile through mixed forest before arriving at another junction. Though either road leads to the same spot, turn right onto Serpentine Road for the most direct route. The road continues to lose elevation as it passes through an arid landscape with abundant chaparral and gray pines. A dilapidated baseball diamond on the left indicates that the trail is approaching a few side roads that lead down to a 4-H camp. Stay on the main road and cross the bridge over fledgling Moore Creek after hiking on Serpentine Road for 0.55 mile. Moore Creek is a perennial stream, although its flow may be small late in the summer.

Once across the creek, turn right and begin to climb a wide road. About 0.2 mile from the creek, a historical marker identifies the short side trail that leads up to a small pioneer cemetery. Continuing on the road, stay left right after the trail to the pioneer cemetery. The road to the right leads down to the 4-H camp. Proceed up the road for another 0.15 mile before turning left onto a narrow hiking trail. Several trails are listed on the sign, including the Full Moon Rock Trail, which is the best route to complete the loop and return to the trailhead.

The trail soon passes through large redwood trees and shortly arrives at another junction. Stay to the left and continue climbing through the trees. The path soon levels off and begins to cut across the side of a long ridge. Some of the redwoods are quite large. Their presence here in the Howell Mountain area puts to rest the oft-repeated fallacy that the redwood grove at nearby Bothe–Napa Valley State Park is the easternmost example of these spectacular trees.

After traversing the side of the ridge for a while, a few trails split off, but white signs marking the hike lead the way back down to the main camp road. Following the road uphill, it soon passes large but somewhat unimpressive Full Moon Rock. A short distance from the rock, the road make a sharp hairpin turn to the west, nearly doubling back on itself. Two narrow trails continue to the east. Take the right-hand trail and pass through the woods before entering a large boulder field. A short, well-made path breaks away to the right and drops down to Moore Creek. When water is flowing through this part of the creek, the spur trail ends next to some nice cataracts. The main trail continues to climb through the boulders before leveling off and crossing Moore Creek. This uppermost part of the creek may be dry even when water is flowing farther downstream. Beyond the creek the trail climbs to a wide fire road. Turn left and walk a short distance back to the first four-way junction. Proceed straight throughout and rejoin the initial section of trail that heads back to the trailhead through the ponderosa pines.

Miles and Directions

- **0.0** Note the two sets of gates at the trailhead. Enter the right-hand gate by the larger parking area. This enters Los Posadas State Forest. The other accesses Pacific Union College land. After passing through the gate, turn right and follow the trail that runs parallel to the fence.
- **0.25** Stay left at a fork and then pass a rock garden filled with large boulders.
- **0.6** At a four-way junction, turn left and follow the canyon uphill through a wide gully.

Las Posadas State Forest

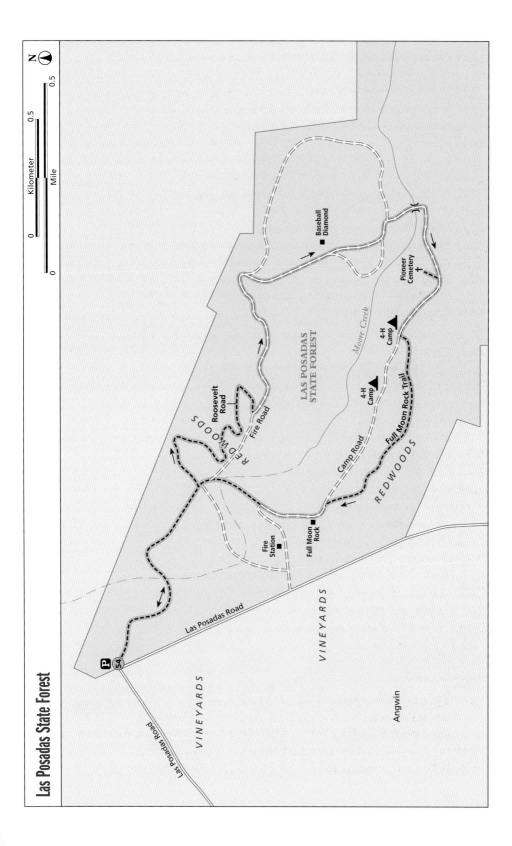

N

Kilometer
0   0.5   0.5

Mile
0   0.5

REDWOODS

Roosevelt
Road

Fire Road

LAS POSADAS
STATE FOREST

Moore Creek

4-H
Camp

4-H
Camp

Full Moon Rock Trail

Baseball
Diamond

Pioneer
Cemetery

REDWOODS

Camp Road

Fire
Station

Full Moon
Rock

Las Posadas Road

VINEYARDS

VINEYARDS

Angwin

Las Posadas Road

P

54

0.75 Hike past a gate entering Pacific Union College. The trail now enters a cluster of small, young redwood trees.

1.25 Turn left onto a wide service road.

1.6 Turn right at a junction and follow the wide road downhill to an arid, chaparral-covered valley that contains a dilapidated baseball diamond. Stay on the main road when smaller roads branch off.

2.15 Cross Moore Creek and turn right onto another service road.

2.35 Turn right onto the short spur to visit the pioneer cemetery.

2.6 Turn left onto the signed hiking trail. Immediately after beginning the climb, continue straight when it crosses an overgrown road.

3.2 The trail merges back onto the service road.

3.4 At a hairpin turn in the road, two trails continue to the east. Take the one on the right. As you follow it, look for a wide spur leading down to Moore Creek.

3.5 After crossing Moore Creek, turn left onto the service road. Quickly arrive at the first four-way junction. Continue straight and retrace your steps back to the trailhead.

4.1 Arrive back at the trailhead.

55 Bale Grist Mill History Trail

The short hike from Bothe–Napa Valley State Park to the historic Bale Grist Mill is a great hike for history lovers. The hike starts near the pioneer cemetery then climbs over a low hill and descends to the impressive remains of the mill's diversion pond. It then connects to the impressive gristmill, a fascinating glimpse of a bygone era.

Total Distance: 2.2 miles out and back
Hiking Time: About 1 hour
Difficulty: Easy
Elevation Gain: 280 feet
Season: All year
Canine Compatibility: Dogs are not permitted

Fees: $8 entrance fee
Trail Contact: Napa County Regional Park and Open Space District; www.napaoutdoors.org
Other: Tours of the historic gristmill require a separate fee. The mill is only operated on weekends.

Finding the trailhead: *From the north end of Saint Helena:* Drive north on CA 29 for 4.2 miles. Turn left into the main entrance for Bothe-Napa Valley State Park. Drive 0.3 mile to a fork, passing the entrance station on the way into the park. Stay left at the fork and drive 0.4 mile to the trailhead at the end of the road. Note that driving from Saint Helena passes the regular entrance to the gristmill. Continue past this to the entrance of Bothe-Napa Valley State Park. GPS: N38°32.98383' / W122°30.85517'

From the intersection of CA 20 and CA 128 on the west side of downtown Calistoga: Drive south on CA 29 for 3.4 miles. Turn right into the main entrance for Bothe-Napa Valley State Park. Drive 0.3 mile to a fork, passing the entrance station on the way into the park. Stay left at the fork and drive 0.4 mile to the trailhead at the end of the road.

The Hike

The Bale Grist Mill is a fantastic slice of old California history. Built in 1846, the mill processed Napa Valley grain into flour or meal and functioned as a gathering place for many of the valley's residents in the nineteenth century. Today the mill has been restored and is a great opportunity to witness what life was like in that era. It also offers a fascinating glimpse of the impressive engineering employed by people in the nineteenth century.

Though the gristmill is easily accessible by car and is located just off of CA 29, the trail connecting the Bale Grist Mill State Historic Park to adjacent Bothe–Napa Valley State Park is a great alternative to driving to the park. In addition to making a nice walk to the mill, it also passes an old pioneer cemetery and the ruins of the old mill pond that stored the water for the mill.

From the loop parking lot, pass the trailhead marker and follow the wide path to the south. Busy CA 29 is only a few yards away to the left. Ignore the sound of traffic and follow the trail for 100 yards to a right-hand turn that enters a grassy clearing. The pioneer cemetery is on the left. Some headstones stand inside a white picket

The historic Bale Grist Mill.

fence while others are scattered about the grassy area. Those who are interested can walk among the headstones and read the inscriptions. Beyond the cemetery, the trail reenters the forest and begins to climb at a moderately steep grade. After climbing through oak, fir, and bay for nearly 0.5 mile, gaining 280 feet, the trail finally crests unassumingly in the midst of the forest and begins a gradual descent.

While heading downhill, the trail briefly leaves the dense forest and passes through a drier area with a lot of manzanita. The edge of a nearby vineyard is visible through the brush as the trail continues heading south. The trail reenters the forest and continues downhill. It soon crosses a seasonal creek, which is a tributary of perennial and appropriately named Mill Creek. Shortly after the crossing, the path comes to a fork. Staying right leads directly to the gristmill. Instead, go left and follow the creek. Note how the gully soon widens, marking the beginning of the old mill pond, which stored water for the mill's use during the drier summer months. At the far end of the pond are the ruins of the breached dam that impounded the creek. After passing the dam, the trail rejoins the main trail and shortly comes to the developed gristmill area. The path soon runs alongside shady Mill Creek and then arrives at the mill itself. Though it now flows with water piped to the top, the flume is still an impressive sight, as is the waterwheel. It is amazing how little water is actually necessary to move the wheel and operate the mill. Enjoy the creek and the old mill, which has a couple of picnic areas around it, before turning around and returning to the trailhead.

Bale Grist Mill History Trail; Bothe–Napa Valley State Park

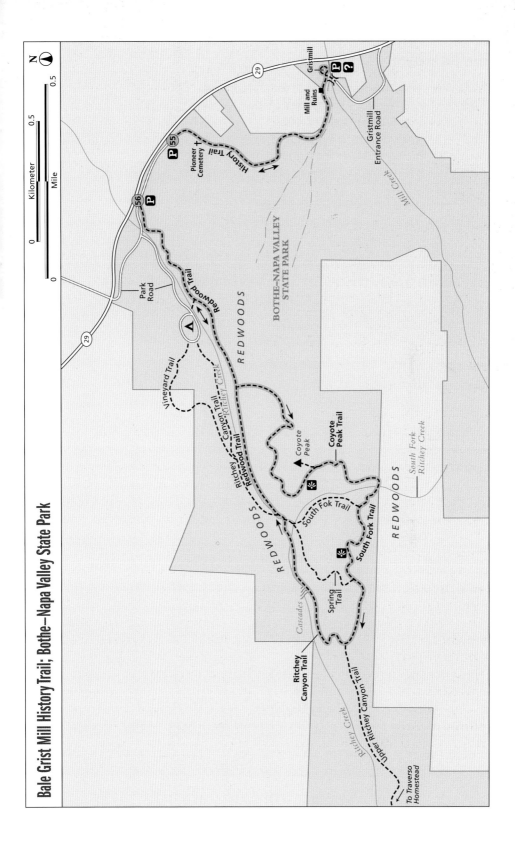

Miles and Directions

0.0   Begin hiking to the south, passing through a shady forest.

0.1   The pioneer cemetery is to the left of the trail as it crosses a clearing. On the far side of the open area, the trail begins to climb.

0.8   At a fork, the trail splits. To the left, the path leads through the remains of the old diversion pond then regains the trail. This is the more interesting option.

1.1   Arrive at the gristmill. Explore the historic area then retrace your steps back to the trailhead.

2.2   Arrive back at the trailhead to finish the hike.

56 Bothe-Napa Valley State Park

This hike features rough terrain in a wild canyon, a beautiful, perennial creek, and an excellent grove of large redwood trees.

See map for Hike 55.
Total Distance: 5.2-mile lollipop
Hiking Time: About 3.5 hours
Difficulty: Moderate
Elevation Gain: 810 feet

Season: All year
Canine Compatibility: Dogs are not permitted
Fees: $8 entrance fee
Trail Contact: Napa County Regional Park and Open Space District; www.napaoutdoors.org

Finding the trailhead: *From the north end of Saint Helena:* Drive north on CA 29 for 4.2 miles. Turn left into the main entrance for Bothe-Napa Valley State Park. Drive 0.3 mile to a fork, passing the entrance station on the way into the park. Stay left at the fork and drive 0.1 mile to the trailhead on the right side of the road. GPS: N38°33.10383' / W122°31.13417'
From the intersection of CA 20 and CA 128 on the west side of downtown Calistoga: Drive south on CA 29 for 3.4 miles. Turn right into the main entrance for Bothe-Napa Valley State Park. Drive 0.3 mile to a fork, passing the entrance station on the way into the park. Stay left at the fork and drive 0.1 mile to the trailhead on the right side of the road.

The Hike

Bothe–Napa Valley State Park is located at the northern end of Napa Valley roughly between Calistoga and Saint Helena. The roots of the park are traced to its founding as a resort property by Reinhold Bothe, an early Napa Valley entrepreneur. The property eventually came under the jurisdiction of the state and was opened as a state park in 1960. The centerpiece of the property is Ritchey Creek and its canyon. About 3 miles long and more than 700 feet deep in places, it is a scenic stretch of the rugged Mayacamas Mountains. Within the canyon is a large and magnificent grove of redwoods. Farther inland than the majority of old groves, this is one of the few examples of redwoods on the east side of the Mayacamas crest. Spring-fed Ritchey Creek is a perennial stream, and its path through towering redwoods is an especially welcoming sight.

The park has a well-developed trail system that allows for a number of possible loop options. For a satisfying hike that explores a few of the park's different kinds of environments, set out from the trailhead and follow the level Redwood Trail through the woods a short distance to a road crossing. On the far side of the road, the trail bends to the left, skirting the edge of a group campground. The trail soon comes alongside Ritchey Creek and parallels it for a while. The redwoods rise high above the creek; however, the grove is not a single, cohesive unit, and the trail often passes out of the redwoods and into a mixed forest of oak and other common types of trees.

Redwood trees line Ritchey Creek.

The trail climbs very moderately, and the going is easy for the first stretch of the hike. At 0.85 mile from the trailhead, stay left at a fork and begin the steep climb up the Coyote Peak Trail. For those looking for an easier and more relaxing outing, simply continue along the creek on the Redwood Trail for a while. Continuing on the Coyote Peak Trail, the path climbs through the forest for another 0.35 mile until it makes a single switchback at a seasonal stream. This marks the beginning of a traverse around the base of heavily wooded Coyote Peak. The climbing is steady as the trail rounds the north side of the peak.

As the path rounds the west side of the peak, the forest thins and awesome views of the upper section of the canyon emerge. The dense forest and a few rocky crags seem to be far removed from the cultivated serenity of nearby Napa Valley. Here the canyon is rugged, wild, and remote. Finally, 0.85 mile of steady climbing after leaving the Redwood Trail and Ritchey Creek, the trail arrives at another junction. To the left the rocky trail climbs to the wooded summit of Coyote Peak. After making the short jaunt to the top, resume hiking on the main trail through some chaparral with views of the far side of the Napa Valley to the east.

The trail now has an easy downhill grade as it reenters the forest. It soon passes through another lovely redwood grove that is centered on the small south fork of Ritchey Creek. Water is usually found in the creek, even in dry years, and the sound of cool water comes as a relief after the hot climb up to Coyote Peak.

After crossing the creek, the trail briefly runs parallel to its increasingly deep, redwood-tree-lined canyon. The trail then veers away from the edge and soon encounters a junction with the South Fork Trail. This path follows the south fork of Ritchey

Creek down to the main branch. This is a good option for a shorter loop. Continuing the longer hike, the trail begins to climb again, but the ascent is brief and culminates at another fork in the trail. To the right a short path climbs quickly to a vista point. Unfortunately, the forest is slowly encroaching on the view, and the vista of the distant Palisades, on the east side of the Napa Valley, is not what it once was. Nonetheless, it is worth the short climb to get to the vantage point, which is the highest spot on the loop.

Once back on the main trail, the path continues a short distance until it encounters a rarely used dirt road in another redwood grove. The road, now referred to as the Spring Trail, heads down toward the canyon bottom and joins the main trail through Ritchey Creek Canyon at the same place as the South Fork Trail. Instead of hiking down the road, turn left and follow the road uphill until it comes to an end on a small landing and a single-track trail continues deeper into the canyon. Eventually the path emerges from the forest cover and enters a drier environment dominated by chaparral.

Here the trail comes to yet another fork. Hanging a left heads even deeper into the canyon and to the old Traverso homestead. However, this is the time to finally begin the descent down Ritchey Creek Canyon and back to the trailhead. Turn right and immediately begin going downhill while reentering the forest, which is dominated by oak, madrone, and bay. Soon, however, the path again passes into a beautiful redwood grove and does not leave the majestic trees again until near the end of the hike. The sounds of Ritchey Creek are soon audible as the trail traverses the steep canyon wall. Just before the trail reaches the bottom of the canyon, it crosses a small tributary of Ritchey Creek as it tumbles down a beautiful cascade.

Miles and Directions

0.0 The Redwood Trail departs the parking area and quickly crosses over a road.

0.25 The path begins to run parallel to Ritchey Creek. Redwoods begin to appear in greater numbers as the trail heads upstream.

0.85 Turn left onto the Coyote Peak Trail and begin to climb the side of the canyon.

1.75 The short spur to the summit of Coyote Peak branches off to the left.

2.15 In a cluster of redwood trees, stay left at the junction with the South Fork Trail.

2.5 A short side trail climbs to the highest point on the hike, where there is a view of the east side of the Napa Valley.

2.6 Stay left at the junction with the Spring Trail and continue to the left on an old dirt road. The road soon ends as the trail continues as a narrow footpath.

3.0 In a large patch of chaparral, turn right onto the Ritchey Canyon Trail and begin to descend back toward the creek.

3.25 Arrive back beside the creek near a scenic cascade. The trail crosses the creek and runs parallel to it on the north side.

3.7 Cross back over the creek and continue to follow it on its south side.

4.4 Reach the junction with the Coyote Peak Trail. Stay straight and follow the creek back to the trailhead.

5.2 Arrive back at the trailhead, completing the hike.

57 Mount Saint Helena

The hike to the summit of Mount Saint Helena is a classic Wine Country hike. On the way to the summit, it passes the historic location of author Robert Louis Stevenson's cabin, a pair of popular rock-climbing crags, and sweeping vistas of the Napa Valley and the rugged mountains of eastern Napa County. The panoramic vista from the summit is one of the best in the Wine Country.

Total Distance: 10 miles out and back to the main summit, 11 miles out and back including the ascent of the east summit
Hiking Time: About 6 hours
Difficulty: Strenuous
Elevation Gain: 2,100 feet
Season: All year
Canine Compatibility: Dogs are not permitted
Fees: None

Trail Contact: Robert Louis Stevenson State Park, 3801 Saint Helena Hwy., Calistoga, CA 94515; (707) 942-4575; www.parks.ca .gov/?page_id=472
Other: Even though this trail can be hiked in the winter, Mount Saint Helena is one of the few places in the Wine Country that is high enough to receive substantial winter snow. Be sure to check conditions prior to hiking.

Finding the trailhead: Starting at the intersection of CA 29 and Silverado Trail near downtown Calistoga, drive north on CA 29 for 7.5 miles. At the summit of the long grade, turn right into the trailhead parking lot. GPS: N38°39.15917'/W122°35.98217'

The Hike

Mount Saint Helena is without doubt the most dominant landmark in the Wine Country. No other physical feature makes its presence felt the way the mountain does. A ubiquitous landmark for Sonoma and Napa Counties, it is visible from many corners of the three regions. Whether on top of peaks along the coast, at the southern end of the Mayacamas Mountains, or on remote hilltops near Lake Berryessa, the imposing mountain dominates the horizon. Even the valleys in both counties witness the mountain brooding above the landscape. Given the size and prominence of Mount Saint Helena, it is easy to guess that the mountain is an old volcano. Historically this was assumed to be the case. However, while Mount Saint Helena is composed of volcanic rock resulting from lava flows emerging from vents rather than volcanoes, the mountain is actually evidence of a fault block, the same phenomenon that created the mighty Sierra Nevada.

Whatever the forces that created the peak, there is no denying the mountain's stature and central position in the Wine Country. Such a feature will naturally draw the interest of hikers, and Mount Saint Helena does not disappoint. Befitting a mountain of its stature, the trail to the summit of Mount Saint Helena is among the longest hikes, with the most elevation gain, in the Wine Country. The route, located in

Looking down on the north end of the Napa Valley from Mount Saint Helena.

Robert Louis Stevenson State Park, is diverse and passes through several different plant communities, including a surprising cluster of sugar pines, just below the summit. Historic sites and popular rock-climbing crags line the trail. The view from the top is one of the finest in the region.

Busy CA 29 separates the parking area from the trailhead. Carefully cross the highway and begin climbing the trail. A forest of bay and fir envelops the trail immediately. After climbing steadily, the trail begins a series of seven switchbacks. The trail is well constructed with an easy grade, but tracks have been worn into the hillsides by people cutting off the switchbacks. This causes erosion both on the hillside and also on the main trail. Avoid these tracks and stay on the main trail.

After the seventh and last switchback, the trail rounds a small shoulder and arrives in a small grotto, 0.7 mile from the beginning of the hike. It was here in this grotto that Robert Louis Stevenson, author of famed works including *Treasure Island*, honeymooned with his wife. The cabin has long since fallen apart, but a memorial marks the place near where it stood. Some exploration among the rocks and cliffs of the grotto reveal old mines. The exteriors are worth checking out, but do not venture inside.

To climb out of the grotto, follow the trail over the roots of a large tree and up the increasingly rocky path. The forest begins to thin, and some filtered views appear to the south by a cluster of boulders. From here the trail ascends steep, rutted hardscrabble to emerge onto a fire road, 0.85 mile from the trailhead. Turn left on the fire road and continue hiking. The road has an easy grade, and progress is quick. There are views to the south, but they are partially obstructed by the short trees growing alongside the route.

Another 0.63 mile from the junction of the trail and the fire road, a switchback is marked by a large rocky cliff. This rock, known as the Bubble, is a popular spot with rock climbers. A little farther up the trail, be sure to look up at an even taller, larger cliff. This is known as the Bear, and it one of the best climbing destinations in Sonoma County. While the view of the climbing crags is interesting, they do not compare to the view to the south and east from the trail. The vegetation along the road has receded a bit, and the views are awesome and unobstructed. To the south is a great view of the length of the Napa Valley. To the east is the tangled knot of peaks and ridges that makes up the wild backcountry behind the superb band of cliffs known as the Palisades.

As the trail maintains its steady ascent, chaparral becomes increasingly common. The trail rounds a broad shoulder of Mount Saint Helena to reveal views to the north. From here the Collayomi Valley, home to the town of Middletown, extends northward to the hills that form the rim of the Clear Lake Basin. Another switchback cuts off this view as the trail heads back to the south. A few rocky pinnacles along the road are reminders of the volcanic forces that shaped the mountain.

A third switchback finally turns the route back to the north, and the trail climbs steadily beneath the towering heights of Mount Saint Helena's east summit. Eventually the trail reaches a high saddle where it crosses into a large central valley between the mountain's four peaks. The peaks get progressively higher moving toward the west. The highest is Mount Saint Helena's 4,343-foot west summit. Just past the saddle, a road branches off to the left and climbs 0.4 mile up to the 4,003-foot east summit, one of the tallest peaks in Napa County. The highest point in the county is just east of Mount Saint Helena's summit, which lies in Sonoma County. For those looking for the tallest peak in Sonoma County, that distinction belongs to a point on nearby Cobb Mountain, which lies a few miles away to the northwest. If you make the side trip to the top of the 4,003-foot eastern peak on Mount Saint Helena there are a jumble of radio towers, some brush-choked picnic tables and interpretive displays, and a staggering view down the length of the Napa Valley, punctuated by Mount Diablo, 65 miles distant. Only 3.8 miles from the trailhead, this makes a good place to turn around for hikers looking for a shorter journey.

Back on the main road, it is still another 1.6 miles to the summit of Mount Saint Helena. To get there, continue on the main road through the heart of the valley between the summits. Views to the south down the length of Yellowjacket Creek's canyon are great. The road makes a single switchback and then climbs to the north. Rounding a high shoulder of the mountain, the road begins to pass large sugar pine trees. These are common in mountain ranges like the Sierra Nevada, Coast Range, and Klamath Mountains, but they are unusual in the generally lower elevation counties like Sonoma County.

Mount Saint Helena

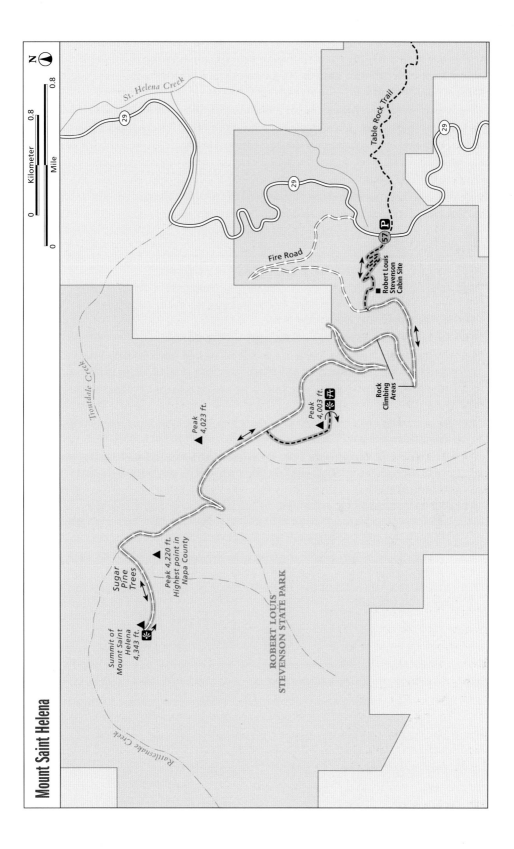

St. Helena Creek

29

Troutdale Creek

29

Fire Road

29

Table Rock Trail

Robert Louis
Stevenson
Cabin Site

57 P

Rock
Climbing
Areas

Peak ▲ 4,023 ft.

Peak ▲ 4,003 ft.

Peak 4,220 ft.
Highest point in
Napa County ▲

Sugar
Pine
Trees

Summit of
Mount Saint
Helena
4,343 ft. ▲

Rattlesnake Creek

ROBERT LOUIS
STEVENSON STATE PARK

N

0   Kilometer   0.8

0   Mile   0.8

Past the sugar pines, continue through a saddle before making the final ascent of Mount Saint Helena's west summit. At the top there are more radio towers. Ignore these necessary but unsightly towers and enjoy the spectacular 360-degree view. Most of the Wine Country is visible from here, including famed wine-making areas such as the Napa Valley, Pope Valley, Knights Valley, Alexander Valley, Russian River Valley, and Dry Creek Valley. The high peaks of the Mayacamas Mountains all vie to be seen from this incredible view. At the summit, which is a mound of hexagonal andesite columns, is a replica of the original plaque left by the Russian explorers who were the first Europeans to climb the mountain. The original plaque was removed to a museum in San Francisco, where it was destroyed in the 1906 earthquake.

Miles and Directions

0.0 Cross over CA 29 and begin hiking up a long series of switchbacks.

0.75 At the top of the switchbacks, the trail enters a rocky grotto. This was the site of Robert Louis Stevenson's honeymoon cabin. Past the grotto the trail climbs a little farther and then ascends a steep, rocky section of trail.

0.9 The trail ends at a fire road. Turn left and begin hiking up the road.

1.5 At a hairpin turn in the road, a large rock rises above the road. This is the Bubble, a popular rock-climbing spot. Great views of the Napa Valley open up a little farther up the road.

2.2 The road makes another hairpin turn. Views to the east get better along this part of the trail.

2.6 The road makes a final hairpin turn as it nears a large saddle between two of Mount Saint Helena's lower peaks.

3.4 At the saddle, the road arrives at a fork. To reach the main summit of Mount Saint Helena, stay right. The road to the left climbs 0.45 mile to a thicket of radio towers and a picnic area with great views.

4.0 After staying straight at the junction with the east summit spur and hiking through a hidden valley near the summit of the mountain, the trail makes another hairpin turn and begins the final ascent to the top of Mount Saint Helena.

4.5 Round one of the mountain's broad shoulders and pass by a grove of sugar pines that line the trail.

5.0 Arrive at the summit of Mount Saint Helena and take in the incredible view. Retrace your steps to the trailhead.

58 Table Rock Trail

Towering over 1,500 feet above the Napa Valley, the Palisades are an awesome series of volcanic cliffs. At the north end of the formation is rugged Table Rock, one of the most unusual and beautiful landmarks in the Wine Country. The trail to the top of Table Rock travels through wild, rugged canyons, lofty ridges, and the bizarre landscape of Table Rock itself, where twisted crags and weird rock formations are coupled with awesome views of the vineyards far below.

Total Distance: 4.6 miles out and back
Hiking Time: About 3.5 hours
Difficulty: Moderate
Elevation Gain: 1,100 feet
Season: All year
Canine Compatibility: Dogs are not permitted
Fees: None
Trail Contact: Robert Louis Stevenson State Park, 3801 Saint Helena Hwy., Calistoga,
CA 94515; (707) 942-4575; www.parks.ca .gov/?page_id=472
Other: The trail to Table Rock is also utilized as part of a shuttle that links the Table Rock Trail, the Palisades Trail (Hike 59), and Oat Hill Mine Road (Hike 60). This trip maximizes the scenery while avoiding the long climb back to the trailhead.

Finding the trailhead: Starting at the intersection of CA 29 and Silverado Trail near downtown Calistoga, drive north on CA 29 for 7.5 miles. At the summit of the long grade, turn right into the trailhead parking lot. GPS: N38°39.15917'/W122°35.98217'

The Hike

The Table Rock Trail is 2.3 miles from the trailhead to the summit of Table Rock. The trail begins climbing immediately through a typical Northern California hardwood forest. Trees include oak, bay, madrone, fir, and an occasional pine. The trail climbs moderately and follows an old roadbed. The first opportunity for views comes about 0.25 mile from the trailhead, where the trees clear and a rocky outcropping provides an excellent vista of Mount Saint Helena to the west and the southern end of the Collayomi Valley, which is home to the nearby community of Middletown. Far to the north, the Snow Mountain massif lines the horizon. If hiking in winter, Snow Mountain is likely blanketed in its white winter mantle, giving the view a far-reaching, almost alpine feel despite the relatively low elevation. Shortly after this vista the trail forks at a signpost. Stay to the right, climbing a series of short switchbacks. Following the trail to the left leads to a large set of crags and another view, similar to the first.

After the switchbacks the trail steepens and finally tops out on a ridge, a little more than a mile from the trailhead. A signpost marks the distance to Table Rock as being 1.3 miles from this point. Views to the east open up, and Bear Valley spreads out

Mount Saint Helena rises above the moonscape on top of Table Rock.

beneath the ridge. A few yards farther down the trail is a craggy outcropping with large rocks to scramble on and more great views. This is the Table Rock Trail's high point. When conditions are right, particularly in winter, one can look east and see the high peaks of the Desolation Wilderness in the Sierra Nevada in the distance.

After the crags the trail begins to descend steeply, passing rocky gullies filled with volcanic rubble. At the bottom of the descent path is a rock garden. Hikers have stacked and organized the stones into towers and designs throughout the area. The centerpiece of the rock garden is a large stone spiral. Snow Mountain is again visible to the north, beyond the rock garden. Departing the garden, the trail is swallowed up by knobcone pine and manzanita. It continues to descend, but now swings to the south. The forest soon recedes from the trail, and bizarre crags protrude from the ground around the route, hinting that Table Rock lies near. If hiking the trail in the winter or spring, one can often hear rushing water near the crags. Exiting the trail to the right, below the first large crag, one can follow the clearing to the top of an attractive 20-foot waterfall.

Continuing past the crags, the trail resumes its descent as it enters Garnett Creek Canyon. The trail began its descent into the canyon at the rock garden, but that is only apparent now, as the canyon narrows. There is a brief glimpse of the dark mass of Table Rock brooding above the far side of the canyon. Beside the trail, one may notice a surprisingly out-of-place telephone line. Until recently, there was a telephone box located there. It is uncertain how or why this was placed at this spot because there are no buildings anywhere nearby.

Table Rock Trail

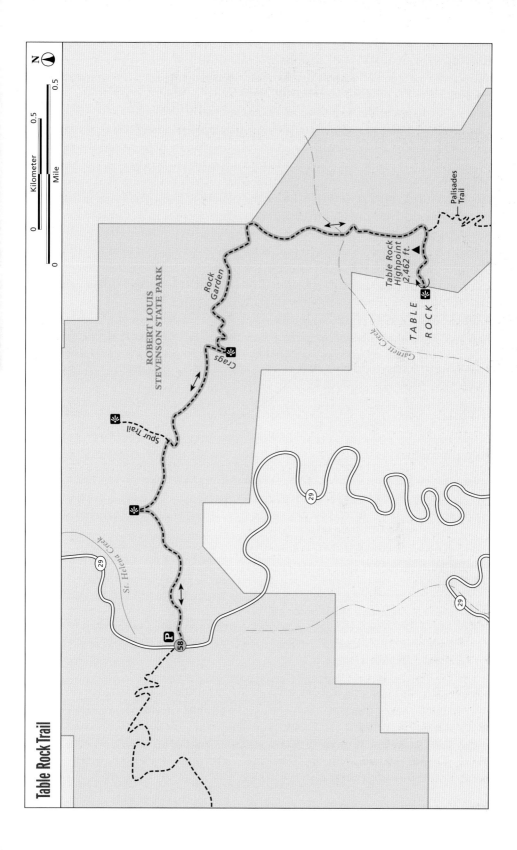

Continue along the trail to the bottom of Garnett Creek Canyon. Cross the creek, which often has a good flow into summer, and begin climbing again. The forest canopy is thick, being on the sheltered north slope of the canyon. The lush hardwoods are a stark contrast to the south side of the canyon where manzanita and knobcone pine dominate. The trail eventually crosses and then parallels a small, seasonal stream that begins on one of the Palisades high points, towering high above. On the right side of the trail, the rock that composes Table Rock begins to be exposed.

The path finally reaches a rocky plateau where a sign marks the beginning of the Palisades Trail. No formal trail exists on the summit of Table Rock, but it is easy to pick a route across the bizarre, rocky moonscape. Strange rock formations and unusual stones imbue the summit with a lunar feeling. Mount Saint Helena towers majestically to the west, while the north end of the Napa Valley spreads out to the south. The ordered squares of the vineyards are particularly attractive from the summit. Use extreme caution on the summit of Table Rock: The precipice is one of the most precarious to be found anywhere in the Wine Country.

From this point there are two options. The first is simply to retrace your steps back to the trailhead. A better option is to continue on the Palisades Trail. This route continues the spectacular views and includes more excellent rock formations and interesting trail engineering. The route can be taken as far as desired before returning to the Table Rock trailhead. The best option, however, is to arrange a car shuttle and take the Palisades Trail all the way to Oat Hill Mine Road (Hike 60), which lands at the outskirts of downtown Calistoga.

Miles and Directions

0.0 Start the hike at the south end of the parking lot at Robert Louis Stevenson State Park. The trail begins by climbing a short series of switchbacks.

0.45 A short side trail leads to a great overlook above the Collayomi Valley. Mount Saint Helena and distant Snow Mountain are also visible.

0.7 At a fork, stay to the right. The path to the left leads to a large rock outcropping and another vantage point.

1.1 At the highest point on the trail, climb a cluster of rocks for sweeping views of the north end of the Napa Valley and nearby Knights Valley in Sonoma County. From here the trail descends steeply on a heavily eroded trail.

1.4 Hike through a rock garden with numerous stone mazes and balanced rocks. There is a good view of Snow Mountain to the north. Just beyond the garden, the trail begins to descend down into a canyon.

1.85 Cross over Garnett Creek and begin climbing the far side of the canyon.

2.1 Arrive at the junction with the Palisades Trail. Turn right and scramble over the rocks to reach the edge of Table Rock. If you are doing the shuttle hike, this is the place to begin that trip.

2.3 Reach the precipice at the end of Table Rock. If you are returning to the trailhead, retrace your steps from here.

59 Palisades Trail

In terms of the sheer volume of wild, rugged terrain, impressive rock formations, staggering Wine Country views, and breathtaking trail, the Palisades Trail is tough to beat. It is also the hardest trail to access in the Wine Country. It is necessary to hike this trail with either the Table Rock Trail (Hike 58) or the Oat Hill Mine Road (Hike 60). The best option is to arrange a shuttle and hike all three trails together, beginning at top of the grade in Robert Louis Stevenson State Park and descending all three trails, ending on the outskirts of Calistoga.

Total Distance: 3.75 miles one way, 10.5 miles as shuttle with Hikes 58 and 60
Hiking Time: About 6 hours
Difficulty: Strenuous (due to lengthy access hike)
Elevation Gain: 700 feet
Season: All year
Canine Compatibility: Dogs are not permitted
Fees: None

Trail Contact: Robert Louis Stevenson State Park, 3801 Saint Helena Hwy., Calistoga, CA 94515; (707) 942-4575; www.parks.ca .gov/?page_id=472
Other: There is no road access to the Palisades Trail. It is necessary to hike either the Table Rock Trail or the Oat Hill Mine Road in order to reach the Palisades Trail.

Finding the trailhead: *Table Rock Trail:* Starting at the intersection of CA 29 and Silverado Trail near downtown Calistoga, drive north on CA 29 for 7.5 miles. At the summit of the long grade, turn right into the trailhead parking lot. GPS: N38°38.55567' / W122°34.78033'
Oat Hill Mine Road: The trailhead for the Oat Hill Mine Road is in Calistoga at the intersection of CA 29, Silverado Trail, and Lake Street. At the three-way intersection, drive south on Lake Street and immediately turn left into the dirt parking area. Cross over CA 29 to get to the trailhead.

The Hike

Simply put, the Palisades Trail is one of the most spectacular trails in the Wine Country. With magnificent views along the entire length of the trail complemented by wonderfully wild cliffs and rock formations, the trail is a long highlight reel of one of the most dramatic landscapes in the region. The awesome scenery is made all the better by the isolated nature of the trail, despite its presence above one of the most popular parts of the Napa Valley.

Slung on cliffs over 1,500 feet above the city of Calistoga, the Palisades Trail travels rough, remote country that is not immediately accessible by car but must be reached by either the Table Rock Trail or the Oat Hill Mine Road. Consequently, the Palisades Trail is not often hiked. Although it can be done in conjunction with either of these options, they are demanding and require long climbs. Instead, the best way to hike the Palisades Trail is to arrange a shuttle: Park one car at the Oat Hill Mine Road trailhead and drive the other car to the Mount Saint Helena/Table Rock

A trail view of the Palisades.

trailhead. This way the entire 10.5-mile network of trail can be enjoyed while most of the journey is downhill. The entire shuttle-hike is easily one of the best hikes around.

Table Rock Trail

The hike to Table Rock begins at the Robert Louis Stevenson State Park trailhead. Begin hiking up an old ridge that has occasional views to the north into Lake County. At the top of the ridge is a collection of rocks that you can scramble on to look down on the hills and vineyards far below. From there the trail descends into Garnett Creek canyon, passing increasingly rugged crags. Once across the creek, the trail climbs up the other side of the canyon to the base of Table Rock, where it joins the Palisades Trail. It is worth the time to hike 0.2 mile to the west, to the edge of Table Rock.

Palisades Trail

From the signed junction of the Table Rock and Palisades Trails, the trail makes a short climb up a shoulder of one of the Palisades' highpoints. The climb is moderate, and in short order the route begins to descend the south-facing ridge that connects the Palisades and Table Rock. Even though it is in need of maintenance, the trail is well engineered and the grade is gentle. At the switchbacks, large rocks have been placed to create stairs. In spite of the great quality trail, its narrow gauge and thick mat of forest debris indicate it receives little use.

After several switchbacks, the path levels out and soon passes a marker indicating the boundary of Robert Louis Stevenson State Park. The Palisades Trail is now on

Lasky family property. Looking back to the west, the nose of Table Rock and Mount Saint Helena are visible. The trail soon rounds a shoulder and reveals the first view of the Palisades. The band of dark rock undulates along the ridgetop, with numerous spires and high cliffs. A monument at the vista bears a plaque thanking the family of Moses Lasky for the right-of-way across their land. It states that Lasky was a lifelong climber who scaled the crags of the Palisades and even participated in pioneering a new route up Grand Teton in 1980.

Lasky Point marks the beginning of the Palisades Trail's journey through three cliff-ringed amphitheaters. As the trail enters the first amphitheater, it reenters Robert Louis Stevenson State Park. The vegetation alternates between chaparral, oak-dotted grassland and dense glades of fir and hardwood. At times the trail passes along the base of the Palisades cliffs, while at other times it is slung on precariously steep cliffs. Numerous gullies drain creases in the cliffs. At the east end of the first amphitheater, the route passes through a particularly thick glade watered by a small creek. It then rounds a shoulder and passes into the second amphitheater.

Once the trail has entered the second amphitheater, it enters an entirely new view shed. The cliffs of the Palisades get higher and are more vertical and jagged. Nonetheless, the trail retains similar features from the first amphitheater. The grade is generally level, with small, short ascents and descents. Views down into the Napa Valley and Calistoga are excellent, and Mount Saint Helena is often visible. This section of trail passes a few more small creeks that usually are flowing in the spring. The wall forming the east end of the second amphitheater protrudes far out from the main band of cliffs. Consequently the trail passes farther from the base of the cliffs. Views of the Napa Valley far below to the south are fantastic and are contrasted by the looming bulk of Mount Saint Helena, which is once again visible.

Soon the shoulder is traversed, and the Palisades Trail enters the third and final amphitheater. This is the most breathtaking of the three. A sawtooth-like wall climbs above the trail to join the main band of cliffs, which are a towering and tangled knot of walls and spires. The eastern high point of the Palisades is visible, but the awesome columnar basalt formation at the summit is not yet as visible as it is from Oat Hill Mine Road.

The trail passes through several rock outcroppings and arrives at a small, grassy canyon drained by a seasonal stream. Just below the trail, water pours off the lip of a basalt rim and plunges 30 feet into a narrow grotto. Sit on the edge of the rim and enjoy staggering, unobstructed views of the Napa Valley. Innumerable rows of grapevines cover the valley floor, their reach interrupted by the town of Calistoga, various wineries, and small wooded hills. This is one of the most beautiful spots in the entire Wine Country.

After crossing the creek just above the small seasonal waterfall, the trail climbs out of the little canyon and rounds a grassy shoulder. From here the Palisades Trail begins to climb a short series of switchbacks. It is necessary for the trail to gain elevation to reach the pass where it meets the Oat Hill Mine Road.

Palisades Trail

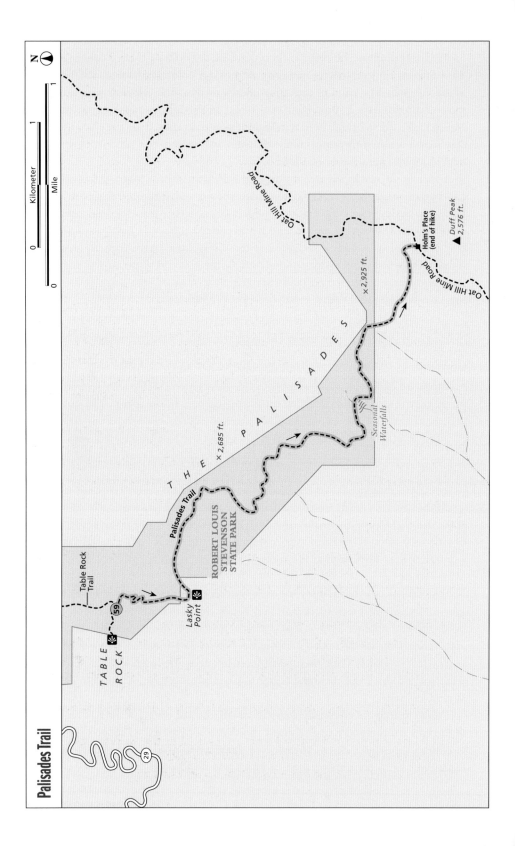

Once the trail reaches the top of the grade, it is directly beneath the final set of the Palisades' cliffs. As the path runs along the base of the cliffs, look for a large shelf above a fern-lined section of the trail. A pile of rocks on the left leads to the top; here the rock at the base of the Palisades is broad and flat. In the spring a tall waterfall crashes against the shaded bench. It is another of the trail's best locations. After the small waterfall, the trail follows the cliffs a little farther and then makes a swift descent to Holm's Place. The path grows faint here, but it is not difficult to follow it down to the ruins and the junction with the Oat Hill Mine Road. At the homestead, large hand-hewn stones are stacked, forming old walls and foundations. The presence of a big stone hearth is particularly interesting. Just past the ruins, the Palisades Trail ends at the signed intersection with Oat Hill Mine Road.

Oat Hill Mine Road

Starting at the ruins, it is only a few yards farther to the historic Oat Hill Mine Road. The road was constructed to access an old mine beyond the homestead. Wagon ruts worn into the volcanic stone are still visible in the highest section of the trail. The upper portions of Oat Hill Mine Road pass along the western flank of a rounded dome named Duff. Below the peak, a long ridgeline descends southward toward the city of Calistoga. Below Duff, the ridge begins to lose its craggy appearance and there is less exposed rock. The views of the Palisades from this section of trail are magnificent.

Mount Saint Helena broods to the west beyond the long rampart of the Palisades. Near the south end of Duff, the trail crosses from the west side of the ridge to the east and views of the Napa Valley open up, capped by distant Mount Saint Helena. The old road soon passes Bald Hill, where there is one last look at the Palisades, before making the final 3-mile descent down to Calistoga.

Miles and Directions

0.0 The Palisades Trail begins at the junction with the Table Rock Trail. It climbs a low ridge and begins a descent down a series of tight switchbacks.

0.6 Lasky Point has the first good view of the Palisades. This marks the beginning of the first amphitheater.

1.5 The trail curves around a broad shoulder and enters the second amphitheater.

2.4 After curving around another shoulder, the Palisades Trail enters the third amphitheater.

2.6 Cross over a seasonal creek. Just downstream from the crossing, the creek plunges over a cliff, forming a scenic waterfall. This area is the most picturesque section of the Palisades Trail.

2.7 As the trail winds through rock outcroppings and boulders, it begins to climb the steepest section of the Palisades Trail.

3.35 The trail finishes the last climb and arrives at the base of the cliffs. Watch for a flat-topped rock above the trail where there is often a tall seasonal waterfall.

3.75 Arrive at Holm's Place and the junction with the Oat Hill Mine Road.

60 Oat Hill Mine Road

Few trails bear the scars of history as well as Oat Hill Mine Road. Once an old wagon road, the ruts of nineteenth-century wheels are still evident in the rocky surface. Today the old road is a popular hiking and mountain-biking trail. It climbs from the outskirts of Calistoga over the mountains to a trailhead near Aetna Springs in Pope Valley. The section from Calistoga to an old homestead at the base of the Palisades is the most popular section and makes a good hike. One great option for this hike is to add it as the conclusion of a shuttle hike that combines the Table Rock Trail (Hike 58) and the Palisades Trail (Hike 59).

Total Distance: 9.0 miles out and back
Hiking Time: About 5 hours
Difficulty: Strenuous
Elevation Gain: 1,860 feet
Season: All year
Canine Compatibility: Dogs are not permitted

Fees: None
Trail Contact: Napa County Regional Park and Open Space District; www.napaoutdoors.org
Other: Oat Hill Mine Road also makes part of a fantastic shuttle that includes the Table Rock Trail and the Palisades Trail.

Finding the trailhead: The trailhead for the Oat Hill Mine Road is in Calistoga at the intersection of CA 29, Silverado Trail, and Lake Street. At the three-way intersection, drive south on Lake Street and immediately turn left into the dirt parking area. Cross over CA 29 to get to the trailhead. GPS: N38°35.36117'/W122°34.64083'

The Hike

Before wine making was big business in Napa County, mining in the mountains above the valley was a common source of work for many residents. This is especially true of the northern part of the county where there were numerous cinnabar mines, which is the ore from which mercury is extracted. The mines were in remote, rough country, and it was difficult to transport the ore down to Napa Valley. To meet this need, the Oat Hill Mine Road was constructed in the nineteenth century. It led from Calistoga up into the mountains where numerous mines were worked northwest of Aetna Springs. It is an impressive engineering feat. The road's grade is amazingly constant even though it passes through difficult, rocky terrain. It is still hard to imagine how miserable and dangerous driving wagons up the road must have been. When the mines were played out, the road was abandoned. It was eventually rediscovered as a hiking and mountain-biking trail, and it remains popular with both groups.

A hike up the Oat Hill Mine Road is a fairly easy hike despite its constant uphill climb. The latter half of the trail takes hikers through a gnarled, rocky landscape with spectacular views of the Napa Valley as well as the awesome cliffs of the Palisades

Hikers on Oat Hill Mine Road are blessed with great views of the Napa Valley and distant Mount Diablo.

leading toward the grand tower of Mount Saint Helena. The hike connects Calistoga with Holm's Place, a ruined homestead at the base of the Palisades.

Walk to the trailhead from the parking area by crossing over CA 29. The trail begins by the trailhead kiosk. It begins climbing immediately, but the even, moderate grade is quickly established and will not change for the rest of the hike to Holm's Place. Initially running parallel to CA 29, the old road makes a hairpin turn and swings around to the east. This trajectory lasts briefly before beginning a long northward ascent of a ridge running up to the base of the Palisades. After crossing some open slopes covered in grass and occasional oak trees, the trail plunges into a thick forest from which it will not emerge until halfway up the trail. Views along this section of the hike are sporadic, but looking down into Simmons Canyon below the trail confirms that the trail is indeed climbing high above Calistoga.

After climbing the side of the long ridge for 2.4 miles, the Oat Hill Mine Road suddenly breaks out of the woods to an awesome view down the length of the Napa Valley. Vineyards and small hills fill the valley floor. Tall mountains loom above both sides of the valley, while the twin peaks of distant Mount Diablo seem to float above the landscape. This view persists along the trail, the perspective changing subtly with each step. After the trail rounds a shoulder, the old road passes beneath Bald Hill, a high, grassy knoll topped by a cluster of volcanic rocks. This point marks a transition for the trail. The forest having faded away, so too will the grassy slopes be left behind in favor of bare rock and chaparral. With views of Napa Valley still present, the trail

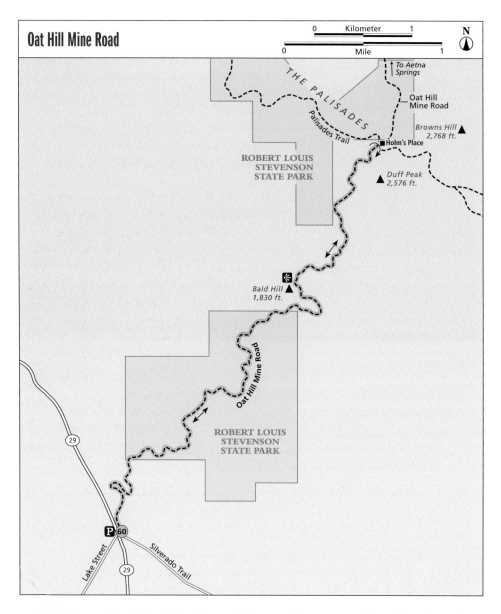

climbs for another 0.5 mile before reaching a saddle on top of the ridge. Here the route bids farewell to the Napa Valley and crosses over to the other side of the ridge, where a magnificent view of the Palisades and Mount Saint Helena await.

The Palisades are a long band of volcanic cliffs that run south from Mount Saint Helena for 2.5 miles. They are easily among the most impressive landmarks in the Wine Country. Forming an impressive skyline above the town of Calistoga, they seem wild and inaccessible from the valley floor. From the high vantage point on the Oat Hill Mine Road, they lose none of their imposing and wild appearance.

The cliffs undulate along the crest of the mountains, sprouting a tangled knot of spires and crags. The high point at the east end of the formation is notably crowned by a wall of columnar basalt, the same type of formation as the famed Devils Postpile in the Sierra Nevada. From the saddle the old road climbs 0.75 mile through increasingly stark and beautiful terrain. The towering Palisades and the striking bulk of Mount Saint Helena are constantly in view. The trail becomes increasingly rocky and eventually passes over long sheets of volcanic rock that still have wagon-wheel ruts worn into it. Finally, the Oat Hill Mine Road enters a glade of trees and arrives at the junction with the Palisades Trail, where the ruined Holm's Place homestead lies a few yards down the trail.

For those looking to extend the hike, the Palisades Trail has great scenery as it skirts the base of the namesake cliffs. However, the trail soon makes a descent into a canyon, which necessitates a long 650-foot climb back to the junction with the Oat Hill Mine Road. The trail actually continues past the junction for another 4 miles. It continues to pass through wild, remote country en route to a trailhead near Aetna Springs. The trail yields more bizarre rock formations and views down deep Swartz Canyon toward Pope Valley. Whether you attempt one of these extensions to the hike or enjoy the views of the Napa Valley from just below Holm's Place, return to the Oat Hill Mine Road and retrace your steps back to the trailhead.

Miles and Directions

0.0 Cross over CA 29 and begin the long, steady climb to Holm's Place.

0.45 After making a long hairpin turn, the trail rounds a shoulder and starts climbing the east side of a ridge leading to the base of the Palisades. The trail will stay on the east side for most of the hike.

2.1 The forest that has covered the trail for most of the hike until this point finally opens up, and views of the Napa Valley to the south begin to improve.

3.35 The grassy knoll above the trail is Bald Hill. Capped by volcanic rocks and boasting good views of the Palisades, it is the first indication of the rugged terrain that lies ahead.

3.8 The trail goes through a saddle and crosses over to the west side of the ridge, revealing the first opportunity to see the Palisades from the trail. The perspective on the awesome band of cliffs continues to change but improves as you climb.

4.5 Arrive at the junction with the Palisades Trail. The ruins of Holm's Place are a short distance on the left. From here retrace your steps down the Oat Hill Mine Road to the trailhead.

61 Oat Hill Mine Road: Aetna Springs Trailhead

The northern half of the historic Oat Hill Mine Road sees little use. Most activity on the trail begins at the Calistoga trailhead and climbs up to Holm's Place and the Palisades Trail junction. For those willing to make the drive to the trailhead near Aetna Springs, they can enjoy an equally rugged section of the Oat Hill Mine Road without the long uphill grade of the southern section. Sweeping views, bizarre rock formations, and the sense of deep isolation in the midst of rugged country are all highlights of this seldom-used section of trail.

Total Distance: 7.5 miles out and back
Hiking Time: About 4.5 hours
Difficulty: Moderate
Elevation Gain: 600 feet
Season: All year
Canine Compatibility: Dogs are not permitted
Fees: None

Trail Contact: Napa County Regional Park and Open Space District; www.napaoutdoors.org
Other: The last part of the drive to the trailhead is steep and slick and may be impassable when wet. Low-clearance vehicles are advised to park about 0.25 mile before the trailhead to avoid the final stretch of rocky road.

Finding the trailhead: Starting at CA 29 at the north end of Saint Helena, drive north on CA 29 for 0.8 mile. Turn right on Deer Park Road. Drive 4.7 miles, crossing Silverado Trail and climbing the east side of Napa Valley. On the outskirts of the town of Angwin, continue onto Howell Mountain Road. Drive for 5.9 miles and turn left onto Pope Valley Road. Continue for 3.7 miles. Turn left onto Aetna Springs Road. Drive 4.7 miles to the trailhead, where the road is blocked by a gate. The last 2.5 miles are on a dirt road and the final 0.25 mile may be impassable. Park low-clearance vehicles and walk the last bit of road. Trailhead parking is limited. Try to leave as much clearance along the road as possible. GPS: N38°38.82700'/W122°31.57333'

The Hike

Although Napa Valley is the largest and most famous of the wine-growing regions in Napa County, there are a few other valleys scattered around the sparsely populated eastern half of the county where wine growing is an important part of life. Among the largest and most important is Pope Valley. Located northeast of Napa Valley, Pope Valley settlement dates back to the nineteenth century, when it was dominated by ranching. The Aetna Springs resort, founded by Len Owens in the 1870s, was the hub of activity. It drew the famous and fashionable from San Francisco and the film industry (in part because Owens's daughter, Frances Marion, who was the first person to win two Oscars, was prominent in Hollywood circles). In contrast to the social activity taking place in the resort, the mountains directly behind Aetna Springs were the site of back-breaking mining work. The mines were established to extract large mercury-bearing cinnabar deposits. To access the mines from the Napa Valley and expedite the mineral's shipment, the Oat Hill Mine Road was constructed.

Strange rock formations line Oat Hill Mine Road.

Connecting Calistoga to Aetna Springs and the mines, the road was frighteningly bumpy and rugged. When the mines played out, the road fell into disuse. However, Napa County maintained ownership of it, and it slowly came to the attention of hikers and mountain bikers. Today the road is a well-maintained trail that penetrates deep into the primitive backcountry beyond the Napa Valley. While most use of the Oat Hill Mine Road begins in Calistoga and climbs to the craggy Palisades, the eastern half accessed from Aetna Springs is an exceptionally scenic and lonely trail waiting to be explored. Passing bizarre rock formations and great views, the eastern half of the trail is one of the least used routes in the Napa region.

At the trailhead, walk around the gate and head west on the wide, rough road. This section of the hike is still used by property owners to access their homes, so be respectful and stay on the road. The dense forest quickly gives way, and the road turns to the north, moving over rough white stone, indicative of the unusual geology that waits farther down the trail. The road soon passes fields sometimes used as shooting ranges before finally coming to a fork 0.25 mile from the trailhead. Signs point the way to the left, which is the beginning of the original section of Oat Hill Mine Road. The trail now begins to climb moderately through chaparral and knobcone pines. Look through the trees for a band of white rock that leads toward the eastern summit of the Twin Peaks, one of the taller mountains in this area. As the road climbs, it emerges from the chaparral, and the first good views of the unusual volcanic rock formations make the climbing easier. Soon the route begins to wind through the rocks as the path reaches the top of a small canyon and passes through a narrow gap in the rocks.

Beyond the gap the trail continues to climb moderately while it maintains a southwesterly course. Watch for small, stringy-barked Sargent cypress trees, a species endemic to California that is most highly concentrated in the mountains of the Wine Country. This is the same tree that constitutes the unusual pygmy forest on the north side of Sonoma County's Hood Mountain (see Hike 10). This section of the road is wide and straight, and the ruts cut into the volcanic stone by stout nineteenth-century wagon wheels are dramatic. Pause and consider the fortitude of the people who worked in this harsh environment.

Resuming the hike, continue the climb a little farther to an obvious crest on the trail. Near the top a wide road branches off to the left. Stay straight on the obvious main path and begin an easy descent through a tunnel of oak, bay, and fir trees. About 0.15 mile after the trail's crest, it makes a sharp, horseshoe bend to the right. Views of fantastic rock formations across the canyon are striking. While rounding the bend, notice the broad, hulking mass of Mount Saint Helena, the most dominant mountain in the Wine Country. The giant peak is 5.5 miles to the west.

From the horseshoe bend, the trail continues its moderate descent, moving over hard pink stone beneath a ridge topped by a thick stand of knobcone pines. Scattered about the area are dark volcanic boulders that have an appearance not unlike glacial erratics found in heavily glaciated mountains like the Sierra Nevada. As the trail rounds the head of the canyon, it crosses a seasonal creek and passes through a large cluster of Sargent cypress. The path soon begins to climb again and moves along the bottom of bizarre, heavily striated volcanic rock. This is the same kind of rock that creates the moonscape-like environment on nearby Table Rock (Hike 58). While climbing, a signpost notes that the trail is crossing onto private property. Be sure to stay on the trail and not trespass, especially when the old road passes beneath a cave-like grotto that is home to lush green grass. As interesting as the small cave is, climbing in it is not worth the possible loss of right-of-way across the private property the trespassing could provoke.

Beyond the rocks the trail makes another bend to the west as it comes to the edge of the Swartz Creek's deep canyon. It may not be the deepest mountain canyon in the Wine Country, but at more than 800-feet deep, it is still impressive, and the presence of large rocky protrusions greatly enhances its scenic qualities. Pope Valley and the distant Blue Ridge, which marks the easternmost part of the North Coast Range, are prominently visible beyond the canyon. For the next 1.5 miles, Oat Hill Mine Road winds through a series of small drainages that form the head of Swartz Canyon. The trail undulates a bit but generally maintains a fairly level grade. As the trail reaches the end of the canyon, it turns to the south and works through a series of small tributary drainages while passing through forest cover. The old road eventually straightens out a bit and passes through a grassy clearing where a few old fruit trees are visible. This marks the arrival to the old Holm's Place homestead. Here pioneer Karl Gustav

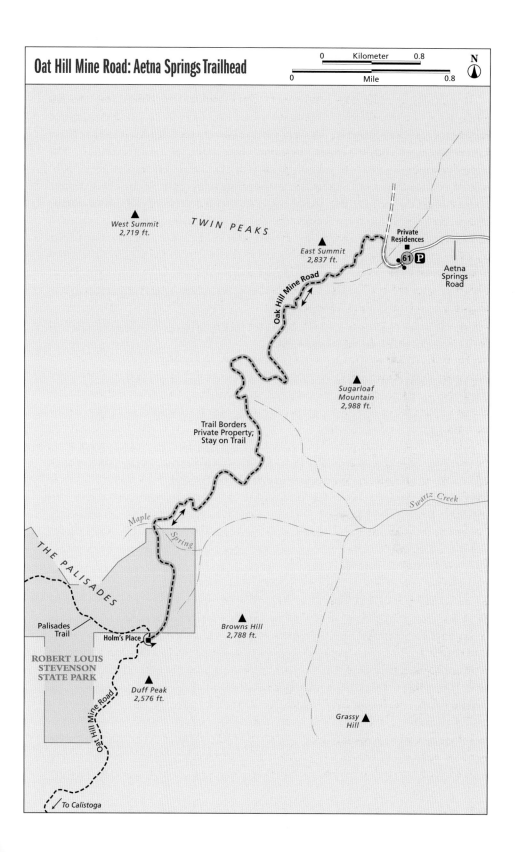

Oat Hill Mine Road: Aetna Springs Trailhead

Kilometer
0   0.8
0   Mile   0.8

N

West Summit
2,719 ft.

TWIN PEAKS

East Summit
2,837 ft.

Private
Residences

61 P

Aetna
Springs
Road

Oak Hill Mine Road

Sugarloaf
Mountain
2,988 ft.

Trail Borders
Private Property;
Stay on Trail

Swartz Creek

Maple

Spring

THE PALISADES

Palisades
Trail

Browns Hill
2,788 ft.

Holm's Place

ROBERT LOUIS
STEVENSON
STATE PARK

Duff Peak
2,576 ft.

Grassy
Hill

Oat Hill Mine Road

To Calistoga

Holms established a homestead in 1893. The ruins of several buildings can be found in a clearing a little farther down the trail, near the junction with the Palisades Trail.

If the historic homestead does not make an exciting enough conclusion to this scenic hike, walk another 0.2 mile down rutted Oat Hill Mine Road. As the trail begins to angle once again to the west, great views of the Palisades open up. These incredibly craggy cliffs are topped by some small columnar basalt formations. The entire formation is a result of volcanic activity. Views to the west are also great, highlighted by small Knight's Valley, which is the prime wine-growing area between the north end of the Napa Valley and the Alexander Valley, one of Sonoma County's premier grape-growing areas. Rocky jumbles along the trail make great places to sit and enjoy the sights. When it is time to return, retrace the route back to the trailhead.

Miles and Directions

0.0 Begin the hike by going around the gate and following the road. Be aware of private residences along the first part of the trail.

0.25 Turn left onto the historic section of the Oat Hill Mine Road and begin climbing through sporadic forest cover and unusual rocks.

1.2 Pass through a notch between rocks as the trail begins to descend.

1.35 At a hairpin turn, get the first good views of the large, unusual volcanic cliffs.

2.1 Pass an interesting grotto (on private property) next to the trail.

2.4 As the trail curves around a bend, great views down the Swartz Canyon to Pope Valley appear.

3.75 The trail arrives at the junction with the Palisades Trail. Holm's Place is just up the trail to the right. For some good views, continue down the Oat Hill Mine Road for another 0.2 mile. When it is time to return, retrace your steps to the trailhead.

62 Smittle Creek Trail

The serpentine Smittle Creek Trail is the only maintained trail on Lake Berryessa. The path weaves in and out of the lake's narrow coves as it crosses open, grass-covered hillsides dotted with oak trees. Nice views of the mountains across the lake are continuous along the entire trail. The hike ends at the Coyote Knolls picnic area.

Total Distance: 5.0 miles out and back
Hiking Time: About 2.5 hours
Difficulty: Easy
Elevation Gain: 300 feet
Season: All year
Canine Compatibility: Dogs are permitted

Fees: None
Trail Contact: Bureau of Reclamation Lake Berryessa Recreation Division, 5520 Knoxville Rd., Napa, CA 94558; (707) 966-2111; www .usbr.gov/mp/ccao/berryessa/visitors/index .html

Finding the trailhead: *From Rutherford:* From the intersection of CA 29 and CA 128 in Rutherford, drive 2.8 miles north to the intersection with Silverado Trail. Turn right on Silverado Trail and go 0.1 mile, then turn left onto CA 128. Continue 11.2 miles, then turn left on Berryessa Knoxville Road. Drive north for 8.5 miles, then turn right into the Smittle Creek trailhead. GPS: N38°34.15650'/W122°14.67600'

From Napa: At the intersection of Silverado Trail and Monticello Road/CA 121 at the north end of Napa, drive east on CA 121 for 12.3 miles. Turn left onto CA 128 and continue for 4.8 miles. Turn right onto Berryessa Knoxville Road and continue for 8.5 miles. Turn right into the Smittle Creek trailhead.

The Hike

Lake Berryessa was a rich agricultural region in the late nineteenth century and first half of the twentieth century. Originally a Spanish land grant, the old rancho was eventually broken up and sold off in smaller parcels. Farms once covered the broad valley. Located near the center of the valley, the town of Monticello was the hub of commercial activity. However, the decision was eventually made to impound Putah Creek and flood the valley. The residents sold their land, moved away, and, by 1963, Lake Berryessa was filled. Today the lake is a recreational magnet, particularly popular with boaters.

The Smittle Creek Trail is the only engineered and maintained hiking trail on Lake Berryessa. The path is low-key and gives hikers some intimate exposure to the lake. It connects two developed recreation areas, both of which offer further exploration of the numerous coves and peninsulas that form the lakeshore.

The snakelike trail curves around the lake's irregular shoreline, passing beautiful stands of oak trees and gray pines. The views from the trail are great, and they offer hikers a chance to observe some of the more interesting geography around Lake Berryessa. In particular, there are views of Big Island and Small Island—grassy, oak-dotted

Approaching Lake Berryessa on the Smittle Creek Trail.

hills that became islands when the Berryessa Valley was inundated. The trail can be hiked from either direction, but the Coyote Knolls picnic area at the south end has more exploration potential, so it may work better as a destination to the hike.

Starting at the north end of the trail, at the Smittle Creek trailhead, the first 0.7 mile of the hike is a nature trail. Be sure to grab one of the brochures that explain the numbered posts situated along the trail. From the trailhead descend the hillside to a bridge over a gully and then head east, running parallel to a long finger of the lake. A short distance out in the lake, the low slope of oak-covered Small Island rises out of the lake. In the distance the high Blue Ridge lines the horizon.

After the initial stretch leading away from the trailhead, the Smittle Creek Trail turns to the south and begins a series of four scallops through long, narrow coves. At the end of each scallop, wooden bridges cross small gullies. These gullies are usually dry most of the year, but in the spring they often have water flowing through them. About 0.9 mile from the trailhead, a marked side trail climbs up the grassy slope and leads to a restroom. Staying on the main trail, the path curves around the nose of a long peninsula and turns into another long cove. Another marked side trail branches off to the right and heads up to the same restroom. The end of the long cove marks the halfway point on the trail.

After crossing the small bridge, the trail heads back toward the main body of the lake. However, the majority of the lake is no longer visible but is obscured by a long, narrow peninsula protruding northward from the Coyote Knolls area. As the trail heads back out of the long cove, another marker indicates a trail leading to a second restroom. Past the side trail the path rounds a large knoll, and the picnic facilities at

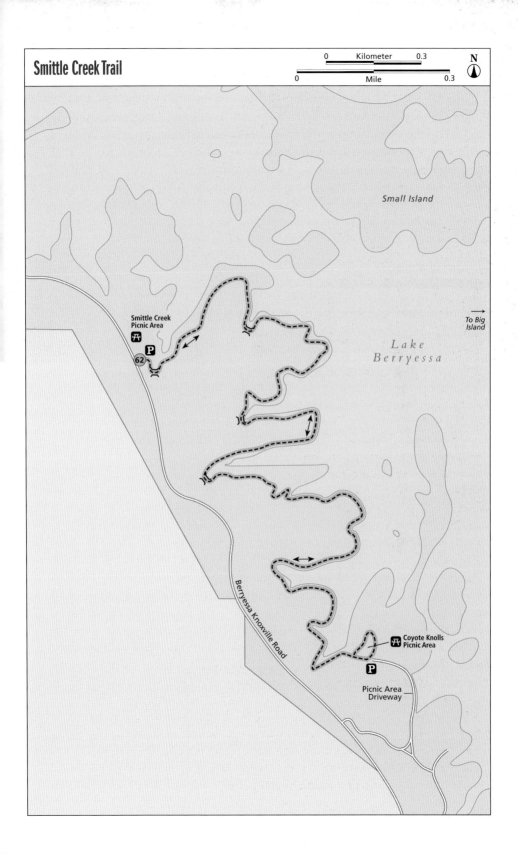

Smittle Creek Trail

Kilometer
0   0.3

Mile
0   0.3

N

Small Island

To Big Island

Lake
Berryessa

Smittle Creek
Picnic Area

62

Berryessa Knoxville Road

Coyote Knolls
Picnic Area

Picnic Area
Driveway

the Coyote Knolls become visible. Amazingly, even though they are only a short distance across water, the trail must scallop its way through two more coves and another 0.6 mile before reaching the end of the trail.

After rounding the large knoll, the trail heads west, passing another marked trail that leads to the second restroom. It then enters a relatively flat, grassy area at the far end of one of the many inlets. It then turns east and rounds another smaller knoll before scalloping into the final cove. The Coyote Knolls area lies just ahead. The trail climbs a short rise and ends at a parking lot. Numerous covered picnic areas and tables are scattered around the hills here, and there is plenty of room for exploring. Unofficial trails course through the area and provide access to the water in numerous places. When it is time to return, follow the trail back to the trailhead.

Miles and Directions

0.0 From the trailhead descend toward the water's edge.

0.6 The trail has a good perspective on Small Island and Big Island, just offshore.

0.95 A spur trail to the right leads up to a restroom.

1.6 Another side trail leads to a second restroom.

1.8 The trail comes within sight of the Coyote Knolls area.

2.5 Arrive at the Coyote Knolls picnic area. Retrace your steps from here back to the trailhead.

63 Barton Hill

The short walk out to Barton Hill is all that remains of a large trail network that once followed the northern shore of Lake Berryessa. This lonely stretch of trail is short, but it has great access to Lake Berryessa and a fantastic view of Berryessa Peak towering above the east side of the lake.

Total Distance: 1.0 mile out and back
Hiking Time: About 1 hour
Difficulty: Easy
Elevation Gain: 50 feet
Season: All year
Canine Compatibility: Dogs are permitted

Fees: None
Trail Contact: Bureau of Reclamation Lake Berryessa Recreation Division, 5520 Knoxville Rd., Napa, CA 94558; (707) 966-2111; www .usbr.gov/mp/ccao/berryessa/visitors/index .html

Finding the trailhead: *From the south end of Lake Berryessa:* Starting at the intersection of CA 128 and Berryessa Knoxville Road, drive north on the Berryessa Knoxville Road for 16.1 miles, then turn right into the small pullout for the Gibson Flat trailhead. GPS: N38°39.45467'/W122°16.71600'

From Angwin: Beginning in central Angwin near Pacific Union College, drive north on Howell Mountain Road for 4.1 miles. Merge onto Chiles Valley Road and continue for 0.8 mile. Turn left on Pope Valley Cross Road and proceed for 1.0 mile. Turn left onto Pope Canyon Road and go 8.4 miles. Turn left onto Berryessa Knoxville Road, drive 3.2 miles, and turn right into the small pullout for the Gibson Flat trailhead.

The Hike

The north end of Lake Berryessa once had an extensive trail system that stretched along the west side of the lake from Putah Creek's inlet almost all the way to the point where Eticuera Creek flows into the lake. Much like the Smittle Creek Trail (Hike 62), the path made a circuitous route around the numerous coves and peninsulas that form Lake Berryessa's shoreline. The trail was constructed decades ago, employing unsustainable trail-building methods. The bridges were not designed for long-term use and rotted away. The decision was made eventually to condemn the entire trail.

Though hikers continued to use it, nature has slowly reclaimed much of the old trail. The most prominent features still visible are the numerous gateways that mark the trailheads along the Berryessa Knoxville Road. Sections of the old trail lead through the gateways and descend as far as the lakeshore, only to disappear.

The only section of the once extensive trail network that remains is a short section of the trail on the north side of Barton Hill, a small, round, grass- and oak-covered knoll that protrudes into the lake. This was once encircled by a trail, but the path now extends only around the north side. The faint remnants of the old trail continue beyond where the established path fades away and can be used by hikers

Berryessa Peak forms a dramatic backdrop above Lake Berryessa.

looking to add a little distance and a different perspective to the short hike. Though the hike is short, it is highlighted by a fantastic view of Berryessa Peak looming dramatically, high above the lake.

To begin the hike, pass through the hiker's access gate at the Gibson Flat trailhead. The trail makes a mild descent of about 50 feet through a grassy field. After crossing through a small band of rocks, the trail swings close to the lake's high-water mark and begins to run parallel to the lake. When the lake is full, the water is only feet from the trail. If the lake is drawn down, there may be a wide, grassy area between the water and the path. After 0.2 mile, the trail arrives at a small flat with some large driftwood logs and a fantastic view of Berryessa Peak. Only 4.5 miles away, the peak is capped by an impressive escarpment, which adds drama to the mountain.

Though the trail fades significantly at the vista by the driftwood logs, it is possible to continue to hike the remnants of the old trail around to the south side of Barton Hill. It is not much more than a deer trail, but the narrow path arcs around the knoll, at times coming within feet of the lake's high-water mark. Once on the south side, the faint path crosses a shallow gully and heads due south to a point populated by a few oak trees, where expansive views of the lake to south open up. It makes a nice place to sit and relax.

The path once continued west to the old Barton Hill trailhead, but that route has been overtaken by encroaching grass. It is possible to find the remains of the trail and form a little loop around the hill. However, it is much more pleasant to retrace the

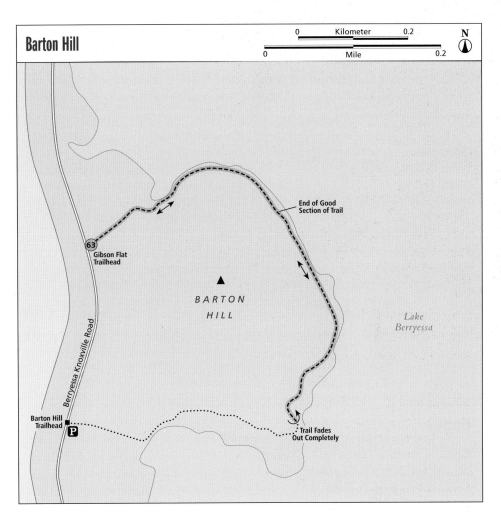

0   Kilometer   0.2   **N**

0   Mile   0.2

End of Good
Section of Trail

63
Gibson Flat
Trailhead

BARTON
HILL

Lake
Berryessa

Berryessa Knoxville Road

Barton Hill
Trailhead

Trail Fades
Out Completely

route back to the Gibson Flat trailhead, enjoying the views of Berryessa Peak on the way back.

Miles and Directions

0.0   Walk through the pass-through in the fence at the trailhead and descend down the hill toward the lake.

0.25   The obvious trail becomes hard to see by the time you reach a collection of large logs. Though faint, the trail continues to curve around Barton Hill.

0.5   The trail fades out completely. Either retrace your steps to the trailhead or continue to bushwhack all the way up to the Barton Hill trailhead.

64 Pope Creek Canyon

Following an old, historic roadbed through Pope Creek Canyon, this hike highlights rugged terrain and seasonally large Pope Creek before reaching a lonely corner of Lake Berryessa.

Total Distance: 2.8 miles out and back
Hiking Time: About 2 hours
Difficulty: Easy
Elevation Gain: 200 feet
Season: All year
Canine Compatibility: Dogs are permitted

Fees: None
Trail Contact: Bureau of Reclamation Lake Berryessa Recreation Division, 5520 Knoxville Rd., Napa, CA 94558; (707) 966-2111; www .usbr.gov/mp/ccao/berryessa/visitors/index .html

Finding the trailhead: *From Angwin:* Beginning in central Angwin near Pacific Union College, drive north on Howell Mountain Road for 4.1 miles. Merge onto Chiles Valley Road and continue for 0.8 mile. Turn left on Pope Valley Cross Road and proceed for 1.0 mile. Turn left onto Pope Canyon Road and go 6.2 miles. Turn left into the unsigned pullout next to a brown gate. GPS: N38°37.46650'/W122°19.38633'

From the south end of Lake Berryessa: Starting at the intersection of CA 128 and Berryessa Knoxville Road, drive north on the Berryessa Knoxville Road for 13 miles, then turn left onto Pope Canyon Road. Drive 2.2 miles and turn left into the unsigned pullout next to a brown gate.

The Hike

Pope Creek drains the grape-growing Pope Valley and contributes its waters to large Lake Berryessa. For most of its journey, the creek runs through private property and is off-limits to hikers. However, Pope Creek's last few miles are within Bureau of Reclamation land surrounding Lake Berryessa. The trail offers great views of the creek's deep canyon and rushing water as well as rugged rock formations.

The trail follows the route of the original road that once connected Pope Valley to the now submerged town of Monticello in the Berryessa Valley. Little has been done to improve the path, but the route is obvious and easy to follow. The path follows the creek for its entire length, eventually disappearing beneath the water of Lake Berryessa (when the lake is full). Other sections of the old road exist downstream near Lake Berryessa, and plans exist to build new sections of trail to link the Pope Canyon Trail to the portions closer to the lake.

The Pope Canyon Trail begins at a pullout along Pope Canyon Road. Climb over the gate and immediately head downhill. At the bottom of the slope, a short use trail leads to a great vantage overlooking Pope Creek. Upstream, a large rocky peak towers above the canyon. Continuing on the trail, the path runs alongside the creek but stays about 50 to 60 feet above the water. The old road passes through open, grassy fields

Pope Creek.

dotted with oak trees. On the opposite side of Pope Creek, vegetation is dominated by thick chaparral and gray pine.

After 0.3 mile a section of the road is washed out, but the trail has beaten a clear path around the collapsed area. A short distance later the trail bends to the left, and the walls of the canyon steepen noticeably. Serpentine rock is visible on the walls and scattered around the roadbed. Chaparral, able to withstand the intense summer heat and hearty enough to grow in the poor serpentine soil, begins to dominate the areas beside the Pope Canyon Trail. About 0.6 mile from the beginning of the hike, the trail passes a large rock outcropping that juts into the path of Pope Creek. Another 0.1 mile leads to a short side trail that descends to the creek.

The trail continues a little farther and makes a broad turn to the east. From here the wide, old road begins to lose elevation. As the path heads downhill, the canyon widens and the trees pull back, revealing a broad grassy area. Pope Creek is stilled at this point when Lake Berryessa is full. As the trail continues its descent, it passes through some fences. These only indicate the passage of land oversight from the Bureau of Land Management to the Bureau of Reclamation. At the bottom of the long slope, the valley broadens significantly. The trail proceeds through high grass and scattered oaks until it disappears beneath the high water of Lake Berryessa. If the lake's water is low, the old roadbed appears to be obliterated. In either case, it is a nice spot from which to enjoy the water and the views. To return to the trailhead, retrace your steps.

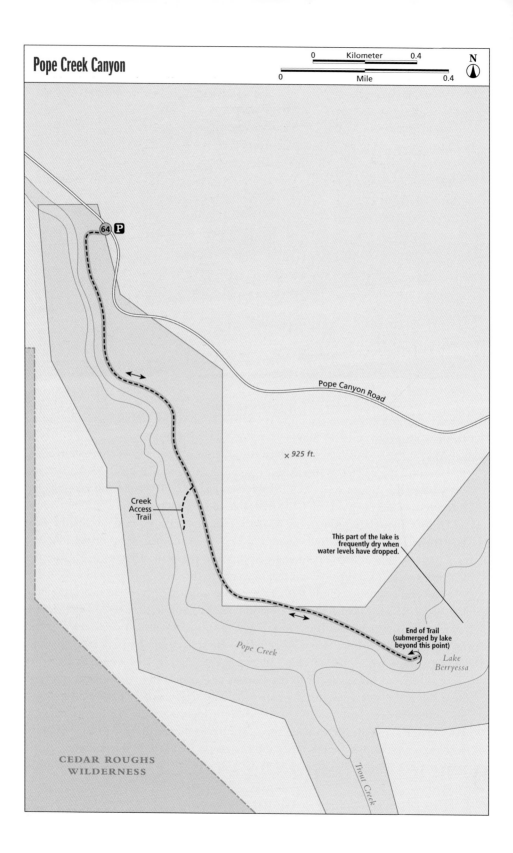

Pope Creek Canyon

0   Kilometer   0.4

0   Mile   0.4

N

64 P

Pope Canyon Road

× 925 ft.

Creek
Access
Trail

This part of the lake is
frequently dry when
water levels have dropped.

End of Trail
(submerged by lake
beyond this point)

Pope Creek

Lake
Berryessa

Trout Creek

CEDAR ROUGHS
WILDERNESS

Miles and Directions

0.0   Climb over the gate at the trailhead and walk down the hill. When the trail levels off, walk to the edge of the canyon for a nice view upstream.

0.3   A narrow trail skirts the edge of a washed-out section of the old road.

0.6   Look for a large, rocky cliff that drops away from the trail down to the creek.

0.7   A trail branches off to the right and descends to the creek.

1.4   The trail is submerged beneath the waters of Lake Berryessa. Retrace your steps back to the trailhead.

65 Cedar Roughs Trail

Penetrating one of the most fascinating but inhospitable areas in the Wine Country, this hike explores Pope Creek, before climbing through remote country to an awesome overlook high above rustic Pope Valley.

Total Distance: 3.6 miles out and back
Hiking Time: About 3 hours
Difficulty: Strenuous
Elevation Gain: 750 feet
Season: All year
Canine Compatibility: Dogs are permitted
Fees: None

Trail Contact: Bureau of Land Management Ukiah Field Office, 2550 North State St., Ukiah, CA 95482; (707) 468-4000; www.blm.gov/ca/st/en/fo/ukiah.html
Other: Pope Creek can be impassable at times during winter and spring. If it is, do not attempt to cross it.

Finding the trailhead: *From Angwin:* Beginning in central Angwin near Pacific Union College, drive north on Howell Mountain Road for 4.1 miles. Merge onto Chiles Valley Road and continue for 0.8 mile. Turn left on Pope Valley Cross Road and proceed for 1.0 mile. Turn left onto Pope Canyon Road and go 6.4 miles. Turn right into the unsigned pullout next to a white gate. GPS: N38°37.56217'/W122°19.50017'

From the south end of Lake Berryessa: Starting at the intersection of CA 128 and Berryessa Knoxville Road, drive north on the Berryessa Knoxville Road for 13 miles, then turn left onto Pope Canyon Road. Drive 2.4 miles and turn left into the unsigned pullout next to a white gate.

The Hike

Forming the divide between rustic Pope Valley and Lake Berryessa, the Cedar Roughs are a rugged and remote cluster of hills in eastern Napa County. The name is derived from the presence of the Sargent cypress, a species of tree that is endemic to California. Early pioneers in the area misidentified it as a cedar, which gave the area its name. It certainly is rough.

In addition to the namesake tree, the hills are covered in a nearly impenetrable chaparral thicket. The dense brush discouraged exploration or attempts to utilize the land. Efforts were further deterred by the composition of the hills, which are largely serpentine. This inhospitable mineral creates harsh living conditions, and only the heartiest of plants can survive in this environment. However, what may be deemed useless can still have value. The forsaken nature of the land ultimately led to its designation as the Cedar Roughs Wilderness, the only federal wilderness area in the Wine Country. Set aside as a wild preserve forever, the land retains a primeval beauty despite its severe nature.

Like the land it travels, the Cedar Roughs Trail may be one of the least known and used trails in the Wine Country. It is a surprisingly well-constructed trail. Although most of the Cedar Roughs remains inaccessible to hikers because of the seemingly

Lake Berryessa highlights the scene on the Cedar Roughs Trail.

impassable brush, the Cedar Roughs Trail is a rare opportunity to experience the interior of a very uninviting landscape; however, "uninviting" does not mean it is not scenic. There is a stark, forlorn beauty to the landscape that is enhanced by some unique and spectacular vistas.

The hike begins at an anonymous pullout on Pope Canyon Road. A yellow and brown gate marks the beginning of a trail. A tattered sticker with a hiking symbol on the gate indicates that this is, indeed, a trail. Though this was initially an old dirt road, the trail descends steeply down the hillside toward Pope Creek. At the bottom of the hill, the trail splits. Going left provides some access to the creek. Stay to the right and follow the path upstream. After a few hundred yards, the path follows a ledge cut into a serpentine cliff and then immediately descends a pair of switchbacks. Beyond the switchbacks the trail weaves through some rocks at the base of the cliffs. Look for cairns and a narrow path dropping down to the creek by some large boulders. This is the route of the Cedar Roughs Trail. An obvious but unofficial trail continues upstream but quickly becomes entangled in overgrowth. If hiking upstream beyond the switchbacks and you come upon trees downed on the trail, backtrack to the rocky area and look for the narrow footpath leading down toward the creek.

Once on this path, it is necessary to cross Pope Creek. There are no bridges, so if the water level is high, turn back rather than attempt an ill-advised crossing. When water levels are appropriate, cross the narrow channel to the grassy island and follow the path through the vegetation, crossing more small channels amid the trees. An old, thick iron frame eases one of the crossings. On the other side of the island, the route

A spectacular morning view of Pope Valley from the end of the Cedar Roughs Trail.

crosses a wide, rocky channel of Pope Creek, where rocks may help in keeping shoes dry when the water level is low.

On the far side of the creek, a narrow sign indicates where the trail resumes. Climb to the left and begin hiking an old roadbed. To the left, look for a collapsed building undergoing reclamation by the forest. The old road leaves the forest and skirts a meadow before making a sharp left onto another old roadbed about 0.55 mile from the trailhead. Continue climbing for 0.3 mile before the trail makes a hairpin turn. Another 0.1 mile leads to a pair of short switchbacks. Small serpentine outcroppings abound along the trail, and the chaparral is foreboding. However, the trail soon leaves the brushy thicket and enters a large grassy area with bands of oak trees along its perimeter. Follow the path through the clearing. It then passes between two small hills before making a sharp turn to the right, reentering the chaparral once again. A short climb leads to a sign marking the boundary of the Cedar Roughs Wilderness.

As the trail enters the wilderness, it becomes a little less distinct but is now marked by a series of cairns. The route is easy to follow as it winds through the brush. A short distance from the wilderness boundary rests a large cluster of rocks from which there is a good view of the central portion of Lake Berryessa to the east. The far side of Pope Creek Canyon looms to the north. From here the trail climbs an easy grade through the Cedar Roughs for 0.6 mile. The trail ends at the top of the hill to another view of Lake Berryessa as well as a surprising but incredibly lovely view of bucolic Pope Valley. Until this point there has been little indication that the vineyard-filled valley was so close, but from this vantage point the sea of grapevines is a beautiful

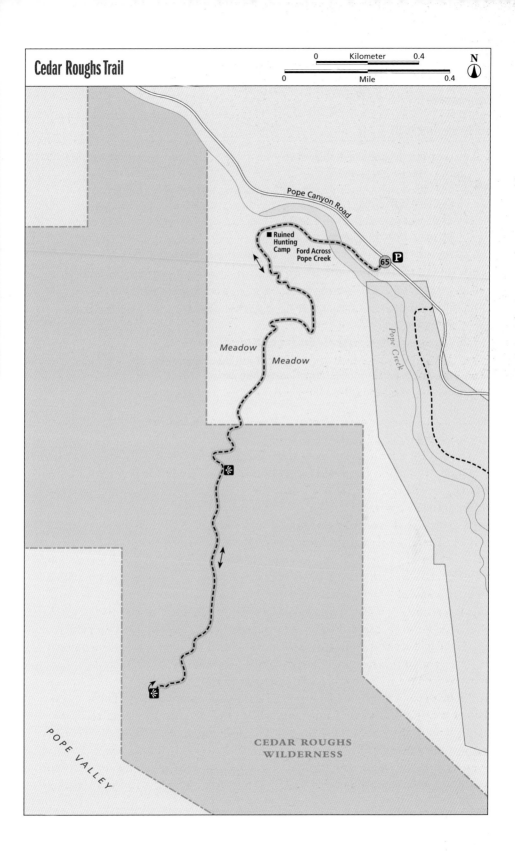

Cedar Roughs Trail

0   Kilometer   0.4

0   Mile   0.4

N

Pope Canyon Road

■ Ruined
Hunting
Camp

Ford Across
Pope Creek

65 P

Pope Creek

Meadow

Meadow

POPE VALLEY

CEDAR ROUGHS
WILDERNESS

revelation. The massive bulk of Mount Saint Helena crowns the hills behind Pope Valley, adding a sense of scale and depth to the wonderful scene. Return to the trailhead by retracing your steps.

Miles and Directions

0.0 Climb over the gate and descend steeply down the hill. When the trail levels off, turn right and follow the trail upstream.

0.2 After descending a couple of short switchbacks, cross the creek near a cluster of large boulders. Here a path of sorts crosses grassy areas in the middle of the creek, but it is rough and overgrown. Look for a large iron frame put in place to help cross. Once across the creek, the trail begins to climb to the right.

0.4 The trail intersects an old road. Turn left and follow the old road uphill.

0.7 After climbing through thick brush, the trail makes a hairpin turn and continues climbing.

0.85 After a couple of short switchbacks, the trail enters a broad, grassy valley.

1.1 On the far side of the valley, the path begins to climb again and enters the Cedar Roughs Wilderness area.

1.25 At a cluster of rocks beside the trail is a good view of Lake Berryessa.

1.8 Arrive at the end of the trail atop a high knoll with a spectacular view of Pope Valley and Lake Berryessa. Retrace your steps back to the trailhead.

66 Zim Zim Falls

The hike to Zim Zim Falls is a beautiful journey through lonely country. The trail follows Zim Zim Creek most of the way to the falls and crosses expansive meadows surrounded by oak forests and large swaths of chaparral. The waterfall is one of the highest and prettiest in the Wine Country.

Total Distance: 6.5 miles out and back
Hiking Time: About 4 hours
Difficulty: Moderate
Elevation Gain: 470 feet
Season: All year
Canine Compatibility: Dogs are permitted
Fees: None

Trail Contact: California Department of Fish and Game, Bay Delta Region Napa Office; (707) 944-5500; www.wildlife.ca.gov/Lands/Places-to-Visit/Knoxville-WA
Other: Zim Zim Creek can be impassable at times during winter and spring. If it is, do not attempt to cross it.

Finding the trailhead: *From Angwin:* Beginning in central Angwin near Pacific Union College, drive north on Howell Mountain Road for 4.1 miles. Merge onto Chiles Valley Road and continue for 0.8 mile. Turn left on Pope Valley Cross Road and proceed for 1.0 mile. Turn left onto Pope Canyon Road and go 8.4 miles. Turn left on Berryessa Knoxville Road and drive north 1.1 miles to the bridge over Putah Creek. From the bridge, continue driving on Berryessa Knoxville Road for 9.9 miles. The road rounds the north end of Lake Berryessa and goes north along Eticuera Creek. Cross over the creek four times and park in the pullout at mile marker 24, just before the fifth crossing of the creek. A green gate is across the street from the parking area. GPS: N38°45.12083'/W122°17.03450'

From the south end of Lake Berryessa: Starting at the intersection of CA 128 and Berryessa Knoxville Road, drive north on the Berryessa Knoxville Road for 14.1 miles to the bridge over Putah Creek (the second bridge as you drive north). From the bridge, continue driving on Berryessa Knoxville Road for 9.9 miles. The road rounds the north end of Lake Berryessa and goes north along Eticuera Creek. Cross over the creek four times and then park in the pullout at mile marker 24, just before the fifth crossing of the creek. A green gate is across the street from the parking area.

The Hike

Zim Zim Creek flows through the 33,992-acre Knoxville Wildlife Area, a part of Napa County's remote northern backcountry. Although this area is semiarid from the lack of significant rainfall, it is remarkably lush. Majestic oak trees populate the hillsides and valley floors and are interspersed with gray pine and large swaths of chaparral. In some areas, poor soil with a high concentration of serpentine has resulted in very sparse plant communities. Nonetheless, throughout this area flow a few large creeks, among the most significant of which is Eticuera Creek. This creek is among the larger contributors to Lake Berryessa. Zim Zim Creek is, in turn, one of the largest tributaries of Eticuera

Zim Zim Falls.

Creek. Cutting through the rugged hills of the Knoxville region, Zim Zim Creek is a refreshing oasis in dry country. It is crowned by the impressive plunge of Zim Zim Falls.

To begin the hike, cross over the Berryessa Knoxville Road from the parking area. Pass the green gate and follow the trail, which was once an old road, along the banks of Eticuera Creek for a little over 100 yards. The creek soon veers to the north while the trail maintains a northwesterly trajectory through a grassy field before arriving at the bank of Zim Zim Creek and the first of many crossings. At the creek, look eastward to see the rugged cliffs of the Blue Ridge, the main crest of the divide between this area and California's great Central Valley. The region almost has the appearance of the rusty cliffs of Arizona's Salt River region. Hop across the rocks to the far side of the creek and enter a narrow canyon, which soon opens into a broad grassy valley dotted with large, beautiful oak trees. After about 0.5 mile, the trail crosses over Zim Zim Creek for the second time and then runs parallel to the creek for a short distance before passing some old structures, remnants of an old hunting camp.

Past the camp, the path proceeds alongside the creek for another 0.25 mile before arriving at the third creek crossing. Views toward the end of the canyon begin to improve, and the rugged, brush-choked slopes give a sense of just how ragged these mountains are. Only 0.2 mile farther and you cross Zim Zim Creek yet again. The trail continues to follow the creek through the thick grass that covers the valley floor. Occasional oaks provide some shade as the level path penetrates farther up the canyon. After continuing for 0.5 mile, the old road crosses the creek again, followed by another crossing only 100 yards later. A short distance later, the trail comes close to the edge of the creek where it pours over a small, wide waterfall. The short precipice

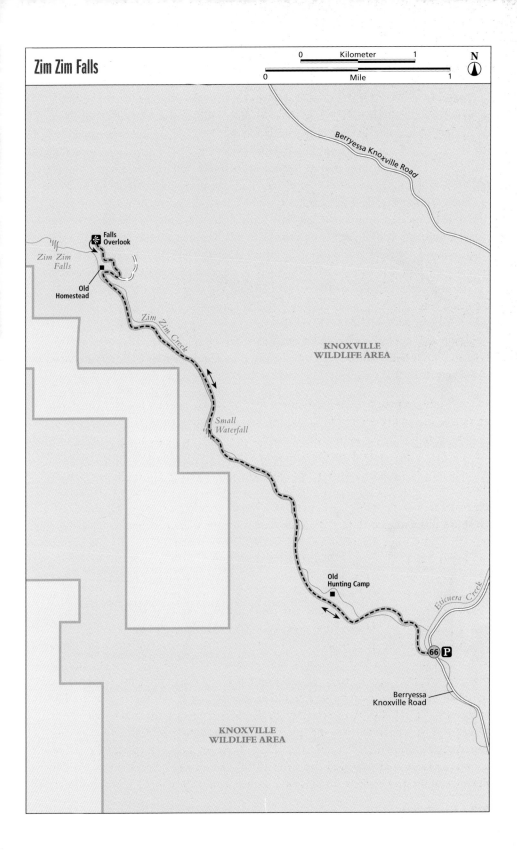

Zim Zim Falls

0   Kilometer   1

0   Mile   1

N

Berryessa Knoxville Road

Falls
Overlook

*Zim Zim
Falls*

Old
Homestead

Zim Zim Creek

KNOXVILLE
WILDLIFE AREA

*Small
Waterfall*

Old
Hunting Camp

Eticuera Creek

66 P

Berryessa
Knoxville Road

KNOXVILLE
WILDLIFE AREA

is composed of interesting rock of a variety of aggregates cemented together. This is the nicest place to stop and take a break on the entire trail up the canyon.

Over the course of the next mile, the canyon narrows considerably. Interestingly, there is a distinct difference between the two sides of the canyon. The left-hand side is dominated by hopelessly dense chaparral, while the right side, on the opposite side of the creek, is more inviting, consisting of grassy slopes and oaks. The route crosses Zim Zim Creek two more times before arriving at the ninth and final crossing, 2.9 miles from the trailhead. On the far side of the creek are the remnants of an old homestead.

Here a fork is marked by a reddish boulder that seems out of place compared to the other rocks. Going to the left only leads a short distance up the creek before the trail dissipates and the canyon narrows too much to make exploration worth the effort. Instead, go right at the fork. The path begins to climb in earnest for the first time on the hike. Though the route is obvious and easy to follow, be sure to watch for the arrows carved into the oak trees pointing the way up to the Zim Zim Falls overlook. After climbing a short distance, the trail arrives at another fork. Go left here, which is again indicated by marks on the trees.

As the trail continues to climb, it emerges from the tree cover and crosses a chaparral area. Press on for another 0.2 mile before Zim Zim Falls comes clearly into view. It is a surprising and excellent vista. Backed by a distant peak, the brushy slopes are highlighted by a large, craggy cliff. Zim Zim Falls plunges over the cliff, pouring out of a narrow notch in the cliff. A few more large cascades near the bottom of the falls add a little interest to the spectacle. Around 100 feet high, the falls seems out of place in the semiarid landscape. It is a fitting climax to a scenic hike. The trail continues to climb beyond this vantage point and follows the creek farther upstream beyond the falls. Dedicated hikers can continue for a couple more miles, but the best scenery now lies on the return trip back to the trailhead.

Miles and Directions

0.0 Cross over Berryessa Knoxville Road and go through the green gate to begin the hike. The first section of the trail follows Eticuera Creek. The path soon veers away and approaches Zim Zim Creek.

0.2 Cross over Zim Zim Creek and pass through a short, narrow canyon. Several more creek crossings follow.

0.75 Pass the remnants of an old hunting camp.

1.9 Zim Zim Creek flows through a rocky channel and then plunges over a lip of rock, falling a few feet.

2.9 Cross Zim Zim Creek for the ninth and final time. At a fork on the opposite side of the creek, stay to the right and begin climbing the side of the canyon.

3.0 At another fork, make a hairpin turn to the left and continue climbing.

3.25 Arrive at a great vantage point overlooking Zim Zim Falls. The trail continues beyond this point, but this is a good place to enjoy the view and then turn around and retrace your steps back to the trailhead.

67 Long Canyon

Long Canyon may possibly be the loneliest trail in the Wine Country; it certainly is one of the most isolated. The hike first follows Eticuera Creek toward its headwaters in Long Canyon. The rugged Blue Ridge looms ominously above the trail while it climbs. Near the top of a side canyon, the route loops back down toward the main trail while providing awesome views of the Blue Ridge cliffs stretching off to the south.

Total Distance: 4.0-mile lollipop
Hiking Time: About 3 hours
Difficulty: Moderate
Elevation Gain: 550 feet
Season: All year
Canine Compatibility: Dogs are permitted

Fees: None
Trail Contact: California Department of Fish and Game, Bay Delta Region Napa Office; (707) 944-5500; www.wildlife.ca.gov/Lands/Places-to-Visit/Knoxville-WA

Finding the trailhead: *From Angwin:* Beginning in central Angwin near Pacific Union College, drive north on Howell Mountain Road for 4.1 miles. Merge onto Chiles Valley Road and continue for 0.8 mile. Turn left on Pope Valley Cross Road and proceed for 1.0 mile. Turn left onto Pope Canyon Road and go 8.4 miles. Turn left on Berryessa Knoxville Road and drive north 1.1 miles to the bridge over Putah Creek. From the bridge, continue driving on Berryessa Knoxville Road for 14.2 miles. The road rounds the north end of Lake Berryessa and goes north along Eticuera Creek. Park in a large pullout next to a corral. GPS: N38°47.76700'/W122°18.16300'
From the south end of Lake Berryessa: Starting at the intersection of CA 128 and Berryessa Knoxville Road, drive north on the Berryessa Knoxville Road for 14.1 miles to the bridge over Putah Creek (the second bridge as you drive north). From the bridge, continue driving on Berryessa Knoxville Road for 14.2 miles. The road rounds the north end of Lake Berryessa and goes north along Eticuera Creek. Park in a large pullout next to a corral.

The Hike

The Long Canyon Trail is one of the most remote trails in Napa County. Seemingly lost in the wild mountains of the Knoxville Wildlife Area, Long Canyon has excellent scenery and the opportunity for deep solitude. The wildlife area is a 33,992-acre natural preserve north of Lake Berryessa that contains a seemingly endless collection of valleys and ridges. The heart of the wildlife area is bisected by Eticuera Creek, one of the largest creeks that feed into Lake Berryessa.

Beginning near the confluence of the Knoxville and Eticuera Creeks, the Long Canyon Trail climbs through the eponymously named canyon. The highlight of the trail is the awesome views of the Blue Ridge, a long, craggy crest that forms the North Coast Range's eastern bulwark against the Central Valley. Rather than simply ascending the Long Canyon and returning along the same route, the Long Canyon

Long Canyon passes beneath the rugged Blue Ridge.

Trail has a great loop at the end that climbs through seldom-traveled canyons and yields awesome views to the south.

The Long Canyon trailhead is next to a large corral. A well-worn trail leads through a gate and past the corral. Walk through the fenced area for a couple hundred yards before leaving the corral behind. The trail leads north through Long Canyon, alternating between grassy meadows and cool oak forest. The remains of ranch equipment are scattered throughout the area. Eticuera Creek runs parallel to the trail, although they are not always next to each other.

Roughly 0.4 mile from the trailhead, the path begins to arc to the east. Another 0.15 mile later the trail crosses the creek for the first time. A second crossing comes 0.1 mile later. The path heads through the alternating pattern of oak forest and grassy meadows for another 0.4 mile, arriving at the unsigned trail junction 1 mile from the beginning of the hike. The junction is not immediately obvious because the trail coming down the side canyon to the north is not as wide as the main path. However, this junction marks the end of the loop that forms the second half of the hike. Continue straight on the main trail, maintaining a course alongside Eticuera Creek.

Almost immediately after the junction, the trail turns to the north, following the topography of Long Canyon. It soon merges onto an old ranch road. As the route begins to climb in earnest, views of the Blue Ridge to the east improve. The tall wall, topped by sheer cliffs, is a dramatic sight. Beyond this rampart lies the Capay Valley, a finger of California's vast Central Valley. This isolated canyon seems far removed from the great agricultural heartland, even though they are less than 4.5 miles apart.

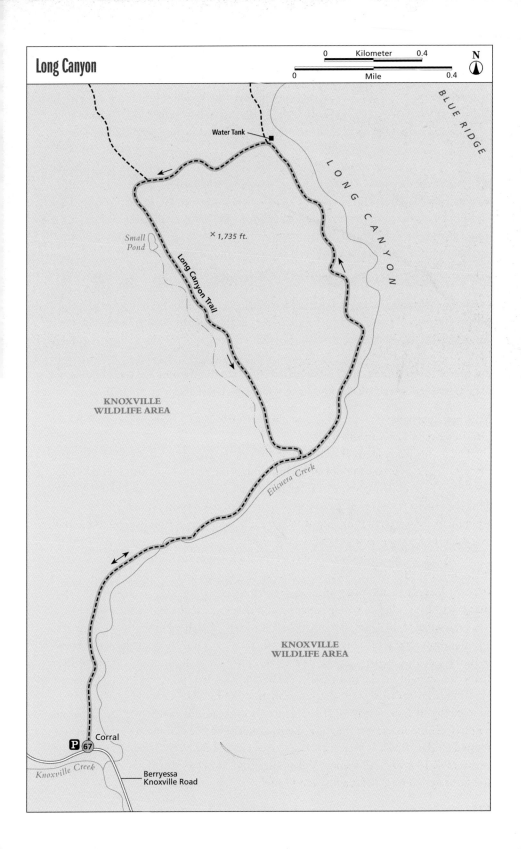

Long Canyon

Kilometer
0 0.4

Mile
0 0.4

N

BLUE RIDGE

Water Tank

LONG CANYON

× 1,735 ft.

Small
Pond

Long Canyon Trail

KNOXVILLE
WILDLIFE AREA

Eticuera Creek

KNOXVILLE
WILDLIFE AREA

Corral

P 67

Knoxville Creek

Berryessa
Knoxville Road

The old roadbed climbs to the north, gaining elevation as it ascends the side of Eticuera Creek. The views of the Blue Ridge improve as the trail weaves in and out of small drainages on the side of the canyon. Eventually, after climbing for 0.8 mile, the trail enters a grassy clearing with a large water tank at its north end. The trail splits by the water tank. Stay to the left, ascending a side canyon and leaving Long Canyon behind.

The grade is moderate during the passage through the side canyon, and it finally tops out at another large clearing tucked away in a small valley, about 0.4 mile since leaving Long Canyon. This valley is the highest point on the Long Canyon Trail. Unfortunately the path becomes less apparent in the valley's tall grass. Although the most obvious trail cuts through the center of the meadow, heading to the northwest, the return route climbs a low saddle at the south end of the valley.

Once out of the small valley, the track makes a steady descent through a lovely, grassy canyon. As the trail passes a small pond, the views to the south open up to reveal a spectacular vista overlooking the cliffs of the Blue Ridge as it marches south toward Berryessa Peak. Though there are trees in the area, the trail is out in the open amid grassy fields. The side canyon is much smaller and narrower than expansive Long Canyon, and the grand views from the more intimate setting give this part of the hike a special allure. It all lasts for 0.8 mile, at which point the path rejoins the main trail. Turn to the right and retrace your steps 1 mile back to the trailhead.

Miles and Directions

0.0 The hike begins next to an old corral. Slip through the gap in the fence and follow the trail into the canyon.

0.55 Cross over Eticuera Creek. Continue hiking only a short distance before crossing back over the creek.

1.0 Stay right at a fork in the trail. To the left is the return leg of the loop. Beyond the fork the trail follows the creek a little farther before climbing higher into Long Canyon.

1.85 Next to an old water tank in a clearing, go left at a fork and start climbing an old road through a side canyon.

2.25 Arrive at a fork in a small valley. Turn left and climb over a low rise and then continue down another side canyon. The views to the south improve as you descend.

2.4 Pass a small pond.

3.1 The trail reaches the junction with the main trail, completing the loop. Turn right and return to the trailhead.

4.0 Arrive back at the trailhead.

Hike Index

About the Author

A native of Sonoma County in California's Wine Country, Christopher "Bubba" Suess grew up hiking the trails on his home turf as well as those in the famed Sierra Nevada. His first backpacking trip at age five sparked a love affair with granite and rushing water. Deeply influenced by his parents to appreciate the outdoors and by his older brother to always strive and persevere, Bubba was further moved to value the conservation of wilderness during his time in the Boy Scouts. A four-year sojourn in Texas for graduate school forced Bubba to find beauty in more subtle places and areas that are generally overlooked. Now a resident of Mount Shasta in far northern California, he loves living a rural life, centered around time spent with his wife, Harmony, and three children.

Your next adventure begins here.

falcon.com

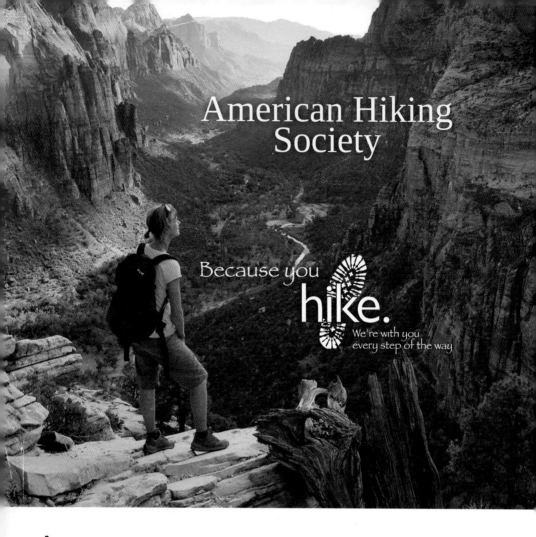

American Hiking Society

Because you hike.
We're with you every step of the way

As a national voice for hikers, **American Hiking Society** works every day:

- Building and maintaining hiking trails
- Educating and supporting hikers by providing information and resources
- Supporting hiking and trail organizations nationwide
- Speaking for hikers in the halls of Congress and with federal land managers

Whether you're a casual hiker or a seasoned backpacker, become a member of American Hiking Society and join the national hiking community! You'll enjoy great member benefits and help preserve the nation's hiking trails, so tomorrow's hike is even better than today's. We invite you to join us now!

American Hiking Society